Praise for *The Glory of Giving Everything*

The Glory of Giving Everything closely tracks Swift's art and Swiftie culture by drawing us into a deep, multilayered economic environment. Haryanto is a longtime Swiftie who later grew into her economic expertise, as she notes, and her exceptional grasp of details and arcs of meaning within this environment gives her a unique perspective. This book delivers on that promise by using economic concepts and examples to illuminate nuanced, complex patterns of action by Swift and her fans, providing a distinctive analysis of Swift's strategies and their impact. While the book is diligently researched, its true hallmark is that Haryanto commands her material with the overwhelming authority of someone for whom the passion comes from within.

—Keith Nainby, PhD
California State University, Stanislaus
Author of Examining Blank Spaces and the Taylor Swift
Phenomenon: An Investigation of Contingent Identities

With *The Glory of Giving Everything* Crystal Haryanto has procured a relevant and well-researched text that explores the layers of Taylor Swift's career, both as a songwriter and as a marketing phenomenon. As Haryanto points out throughout the manuscript, Swift has continued to build her brand as a relevant, fan-driven artist who has created a niche that many will try to replicate. Haryanto's examination of Swift and her fandom is something that only a true Swiftie could explore, and explore it she does, to a fascinating and educational degree.

—Adrienne Trier-Bieniek, PhD
Editor of In the Swiftie Era

This book is a revelation. With sharp insight and compelling analysis, it offers a rare step-by-step blueprint of the business model every brand aspires to—one that few have approached and only one has truly perfected. Eye-opening, thought-provoking, and profoundly relevant, this is an essential read for business leaders, creatives, and Swifties alike.

—Holly Tolino
Founder/CEO of Sparkx Fly

The Glory of Giving Everything is a stunningly ambitious project for such a young author. Looking at the entirety of Taylor Swift's output and the vast array of Swift's multimedia practices around her music, Haryanto embarks on a survey of Swift's empire while delivering comparative lessons in business, marketing, and economics along the way. Her insider position as a fan will be appreciated by other fans who will find the writing relatable and by scholars who will benefit from her articulate testimonies. They are often clever but never forget to be kind—Haryanto's trenchant analyses of Swift's business model and branding remain sensitive to her humanity and individuality. With a thorough mastery of every layered reference and context of Swift's history, she invites readers to return to Swift's music again and again with a new understanding of its significance.

—Eric Smialek, PhD

Marie Skłodowska-Curie Actions (MSCA) Postdoctoral Fellow,
University of Huddersfield
Co-founder, European Taylor Swift Research Network

The Glory of Giving Everything

The Glory of Giving Everything

The Taylor Swift Business Model

Crystal Haryanto

WILEY

Copyright © 2025 by John Wiley & Sons, Inc. All rights reserved, including rights for text and data mining and training of artificial intelligence technologies or similar technologies.

Published by John Wiley & Sons, Inc., Hoboken, New Jersey.
Published simultaneously in Canada.

No part of this publication may be reproduced, stored in a retrieval system, or transmitted in any form or by any means, electronic, mechanical, photocopying, recording, scanning, or otherwise, except as permitted under Section 107 or 108 of the 1976 United States Copyright Act, without either the prior written permission of the Publisher, or authorization through payment of the appropriate per-copy fee to the Copyright Clearance Center, Inc., 222 Rosewood Drive, Danvers, MA 01923, (978) 750-8400, fax (978) 750-4470, or on the web at www.copyright.com. Requests to the Publisher for permission should be addressed to the Permissions Department, John Wiley & Sons, Inc., 111 River Street, Hoboken, NJ 07030, (201) 748-6011, fax (201) 748-6008, or online at http://www.wiley.com/go/permission.

The manufacturer's authorized representative according to the EU General Product Safety Regulation is Wiley-VCH GmbH, Boschstr. 12, 69469 Weinheim, Germany, e-mail: Product_Safety@wiley.com.

Trademarks: Wiley and the Wiley logo are trademarks or registered trademarks of John Wiley & Sons, Inc. and/or its affiliates in the United States and other countries and may not be used without written permission. All other trademarks are the property of their respective owners. John Wiley & Sons, Inc. is not associated with any product or vendor mentioned in this book.

Limit of Liability/Disclaimer of Warranty: While the publisher and author have used their best efforts in preparing this book, they make no representations or warranties with respect to the accuracy or completeness of the contents of this book and specifically disclaim any implied warranties of merchantability or fitness for a particular purpose. No warranty may be created or extended by sales representatives or written sales materials. The advice and strategies contained herein may not be suitable for your situation. You should consult with a professional where appropriate. Further, readers should be aware that websites listed in this work may have changed or disappeared between when this work was written and when it is read. Neither the publisher nor authors shall be liable for any loss of profit or any other commercial damages, including but not limited to special, incidental, consequential, or other damages.

For general information on our other products and services or for technical support, please contact our Customer Care Department within the United States at (800) 762-2974, outside the United States at (317) 572-3993 or fax (317) 572-4002.

Wiley also publishes its books in a variety of electronic formats. Some content that appears in print may not be available in electronic formats. For more information about Wiley products, visit our web site at www.wiley.com.

Library of Congress Cataloging-in-Publication Data is Available:

ISBN 9781394331444 (Cloth)
ISBN 9781394331451 (ePub)
ISBN 9781394331468 (ePDF)

Cover Design: Paul McCarthy
Cover Art: © Getty Images | Noam Galai / Stringer

SKY10106121_052225

For Comet, my English Cream Golden Retriever, who made peace with shorter walks during the writing of this book while still faithfully doing his job at UC Berkeley's Paws for Mental Health. He is equally overjoyed with its publication.

Epigraph

1. This manuscript was written around the time of the last leg of the Eras Tour. At the time of completion, *The Tortured Poets Department* was Taylor Swift's latest album. *Taylor Swift (Taylor's Version)* and *Reputation (Taylor's Version)* were neither announced nor released.

2. The albums *folklore* and *evermore* are stylized as such in the text. The albums *Red*, *Reputation*, and *The Tortured Poets Department* are stylized as such in the text, although they may be stylized as *RED*, *reputation*, and *THE TORTURED POETS DEPARTMENT* in the world outside of this text.

3. Different editions of an album are not distinguished unless pertinent to the analysis. For our purposes, songs from *Speak Now*, *Speak Now (Deluxe Edition)*, and *Speak Now (Taylor's Version)* are considered part of the album *Speak Now*.

4. Songs "From The Vault" that appear on re-recorded editions are not distinguished from original edition songs unless pertinent to the analysis. For our purposes, "Slut! (Taylor's Version) [From The Vault]" is simply called "Slut!" and considered part of the album *1989*.

5. Taylor Swift's personal life is discussed with respect and to the extent that it is pertinent to the analysis.

Contents

Epigraph		*ix*
List of Exhibits		*xiii*
Foreword		*xv*
Prologue		*xix*

Chapter 1	A Brand of Adaptable Authenticity	1
Chapter 2	Carving Out a Niche	11
Chapter 3	What Does an Economist Know About Songwriting?	29
Chapter 4	The Layered Musical Universe	47
Chapter 5	Fans: Consumer and Stakeholder	57
Chapter 6	Friends: Candid and Strategic	83
Chapter 7	Reaching Your Billionaire Era	95
Chapter 8	Impact, Implicated	113
Chapter 9	For the Critics	125
Chapter 10	The Evolution of Miss Americana	143

Epilogue	*155*
Endnotes	*163*
Acknowledgments	*203*
Index	*205*

List of Exhibits

Exhibit 2.1—Paparazzi Photos Taken of Taylor
Swift, 2007–2023 — 19

Exhibit 2.2—Songs from *Fearless* on the Billboard Hot 100 — 24

Exhibit 3.1—Song Structures Guide — 34

Exhibit 3.2—Song Structures by Album — 39

Exhibit 3.3—"My Boy Only Breaks His Favorite Toys" — 45

Exhibit 5.1—Musical Releases Over the Years — 63

Exhibit 7.1—Taylor Swift's Wealth Breakdown as
of October 2023 — 96

Exhibit 7.2—Multiplier Effect — 109

Foreword

As I sit down to write this, I can't help but think fondly of all the times Crystal has supported me in my publications. It's a full-circle moment that I get to introduce her debut full-length publication.

Of course, I have written her letters of recommendation, as any good professor does. Of course, I have had conversations with her about her professional paths, as any good mentor does. Of course, I have applauded her crossing the finish line on her bike, as any good friend does. But in this moment, Crystal has given me a "first" at a time in my career where there tend to be more "lasts"—a feat above that of any good student. I carry the honor of being the first words you read upon opening the first economics book about Taylor Swift.

I'd like to say that Crystal learned to be a trailblazer from me. The only thing I did, though, was present her with opportunities to excel in. After several months of working with me at the Nicholas C. Petris Research Center, a health economics and policy institute I founded in 1999, I entrusted her to be a panelist alongside industry leaders for UC Berkeley's "Health Policy in the Age of COVID-19" event. Additionally, Crystal was directly involved in a number of my high-profile projects. One has been presented to the Attorney General of California, while another has been discussed with the legislators and stakeholders at the State Capitol. She witnessed both of these unfold. In other words, Crystal is no stranger to the room where trailblazing happens.

xvi

Foreword

Between research projects, I would find myself looking forward to hearing her life stories, from her work at the Federal Reserve Board to her cycling trip across Zambia as part of her philanthropic endeavors. As you can imagine, Crystal's graduation was bittersweet to me. On one hand, it meant no longer having her as an integral part of my research center. On the other hand, I knew that there were communities out there waiting to welcome her as an integral part of their worlds. With a highly motivated attitude and ability to solve complex problems, I knew she would thrive in her next chapter at an economic consulting firm.

I should have known that was not all she would be doing.

When she told me that she'd be writing this book, I was truly excited that her efforts were directed toward a field that I had dedicated my entire career to. My 2008 book, *Is There a Doctor in the House? Market Signals and Tomorrow's Supply of Doctors*, used economics to shed light on the healthcare system and workforce. My 2014 book, *The ADHD Explosion: Myths, Medication, Money, and Today's Push for Performance*, used economics to shed light on psychology and mental illness. Now, Crystal is applying the economic tools she has gleaned both theoretically and practically to the emerging field of celebrity studies. Once again, she has found herself doing her best work at the most relevant place at the most relevant time.

The book in your hands is a one-of-a-kind symbol of the next generation in our discipline. Crystal offers a novel perspective of how artistic success can be subject to the underlying principles of economics. After having been immersed in rigorous and academic research methods, she's making economics, business, and policy relatable to readers. I envision that this original and critical work will appeal to readers across and beyond these areas. And as the only young female among the authors currently putting out titles on Taylor Swift and one of the few published young females in our discipline, I hope they will find inspiration in Crystal's voice. She has the unique authority to deeply discuss the value of the artist's empathy and vulnerability through an interdisciplinary lens.

Foreword   xvii

The most admirable part is that for Crystal, this isn't work. It's an intellectual playground. She isn't just in the room where it happens; she's the driver of a movement. I can say with confidence that one of the joys of being an educator is watching a protégé absorb what you've given them and make it undeniably and completely their own.

Yours,
Dr. Richard M. Scheffler
PhD, Economics
Distinguished Professor Emeritus of
Health Economics and Public Policy in the
Graduate School of Public Health and Goldman School
of Public Policy, University of California, Berkeley
Director, The Nicholas C. Petris Center

Prologue

My name is Crystal, and I was born in 2002—13 years after Taylor Swift at 3:13 p.m. on a Saturday.

If that sentence was meaningful to you, you've already been exposed to the grip of the multifaceted Swift experience. Whether you're a 2014 or 2024 fan, your brain instantly associated it with the live component of the most awarded pop album of all time, *1989*, which has been revived in the opening compilation of the Eras Tour.[1] You nodded to yourself, perhaps approving of the succinct manner I simultaneously referenced a culturally significant record and made your personal acquaintance. Perhaps you could connect this dichotomy, on a primal level, to how Swift herself balances universality and specificity.

If the first sentence left you thinking I could use a crash course on writing hooks, you would be correct, but not in the way that you believed you were. You didn't know (or more importantly, didn't know why people cared) that Swift was born on the 13th of December. You were blissfully unaware that she turned 13 on Friday the 13th; that her first album, *Taylor Swift*, was certified gold by the Recording Industry Association of America in 13 weeks; that her first #1 Hot Country Songs hit, "Our Song," had a 13-second introduction; that the first time she performed at the Country Music Awards, the producer told her that she'd be on in 13 seconds; that her latest album, *The Tortured Poets Department*, spent 13 nonconsecutive weeks at #1 on the Billboard 200…need I go on?[2] Because your limited understanding prevented you from marveling at my additional 13-synchronicities, you've underestimated my hook. I've now arrived at the punchline of this paragraph: I would be the first to sign up for a crash course in songwriting hooks, but I've been adequately versed in prose hooks. Perhaps you could connect this double meaning, on a primal level, to how Swift herself fluently moves through creative writing.

This book is for both of you. These pages are for the curious listener and the diehard devotee of any age. These words are for the ambitious start-up creator and the serious business owner of any age.

My goal is to make entrepreneurial techniques accessible through a globally renowned phenomenon, all the while developing a holistic appreciation of Swift by interweaving other disciplines, including economics, psychology, and policy. Due to Swift's stellar songwriting capacity, her career as a masterclass in branding and marketing is overlooked and understudied. I hope to bridge a gap between a subject superficially reserved for corporate traditions and a celebrity superficially reserved for feminine customs. Swift, as arguably the most relevant figure in contemporary pop culture, has pushed boundaries on all of these fronts.

Recently and ever increasingly, many respectable Swift scholars have turned to analyzing such boundaries through the lens of their chosen specialty, after spending valuable years researching, producing, and contributing to that field. For me, while my own doctorate degree lies in the future, an equivalent amount of time and labor have gone into being a lifelong fan of Swift—living the songs line by line, going to the concerts, and founding a course entitled "Artistry, Policy, & Entrepreneurship: Taylor's Version" at my alma mater, the University of California, Berkeley. In contrast to my notable fellow Swift academics, I was a Swiftie first, and my economics training rose to the occasion. When I was asked to spearhead this project, I knew that this fell in line with the boundaries I aspire to push every day, sculpting my place as both a woman in STEM and a young Swift educator. I wouldn't have it any other way.

If you also wouldn't have it any other way, I invite you to take my hand and join me on the first-of-its-kind journey through Taylor Swift's enterprise in and out of the spotlight.

1 | A Brand of Adaptable Authenticity

Six days before the release of the original version of *1989*, the highest charting song in Canada wasn't "Welcome To New York" (#2 on the Canadian iTunes chart), "Shake It Off" (#3), or "Out of the Woods" (#8), which were all out on iTunes in advance of the album drop. The coveted #1 spot was held by a cryptically titled "Track 3" that was in actuality eight seconds of white noise.[1] In multitudes, music listeners discernibly gravitated toward the mystery song, despite their only given information being who the singer was.

The success of the accidental release of static was no accident. It was the product of a homegrown, perfected-over-the-years recipe for the brand of Taylor Swift. Fundamentally, Swift had long established herself as a potent songwriter. Singing was almost secondary to her, her voice simply a medium of conveying her words.[2] Reflecting on the future in an interview with BBC Radio 1, she questioned whether she'd still be performing by the time she'd be 34 years old. Nevertheless, she emphasized her desire to still be writing songs, commenting that she'd even enjoy doing it for other artists.[3] Much like the narrator of "Love Story," little did Swift know…that not only would she be on a stage at the age of 34, but she'd be on the stage of the most historic tour of her time, singing songs she'd released up until that year.

2   The Glory of Giving Everything

Beyond simply calling for songwriting, the recipe's secret ingredients were artistic adaptability and audacious authenticity. The indispensable step was carefully mixing in the right amounts of each. It was evident that Swift had developed her trademark in vulnerable storytelling; what solidified her longevity was that Swift had derived her value in versatile storytelling. These double features have made up the forefront of many of Swift's creative decisions, and they have never been quite as exemplified as when she was on the cusp of a genre switch. Returning to the metrics of pop music, a commercially successful song would typically be paraded on the radio and in live appearances as each listener did their part to hoist it up the charts. In the case of our dear "Track 3" on *1989*, there were enough people who purchased the $1.29 track all at once to push it to #1, before the word could spread that it was an unintentional bait-and-switch.

This was Swift's brand working for her, in a show of power that every business-minded entity aspires to master. A well-positioned brand is key for a business to acquire and sustain customers, level up with competitors, and eventually market itself as it becomes widely and credibly recognizable. Membership-based warehouse retailer Costco understands this, keeping its famous hot dog priced at $1.50 in spite of inflation dictating that it would now be worth $4.40 (as of 2024).[4] That lost monetary value is made up for by loyal Costco patrons for whom grabbing a hot dog is a nostalgic tradition. Assuredly, customers spend more time at Costco than at competitors Walmart and Target.[5] On a more regional scale, before Boichik Bagels opened its flagship brick-and-mortar bakery in Berkeley, California, founder Emily Winston debuted her bagels at the 2017 Eat Real Festival in neighboring Oakland. When she started selling them from her home, she attracted a long line even before doors opened and ended up sold out in 12 minutes.[6] Winston's brand of fresh West Coast takes on New York–style bagels earned her hundreds of mailing list customers, who turned into in-person customers waiting in line at Boichik Bagels locations around the Bay Area. And in the 20 years following its launch in 2003, Tesla maintained an anti-advertising campaign, instead opting to focus on its brand of innovation and sustainability, with sales being substantially spurred by media coverage.[7]

Here's when Tesla and Taylor Swift diverge. In 2023, Tesla began to dip its toes in advertising due to lessened demand. On the other hand, in 2024, *The Tortured Poets Department*, Swift's new album, became the most presaved album on Spotify leading up to its release.[8] Where Tesla needed to combat claims that the company was not practical nor accessible to a large customer base, Swift was continuing to connect with her fan base. The fan base that once, knowing they'd receive a wonderfully blended dosage of comfort and change, made an eight-second nonsong the most purchased item on iTunes in Canada was still with her 10 years later and counting.

Essential to Swift's brand is consistency. Everyone is familiar with a plummeting sense of quality in certain product lines over time.[9] Yet, Swift's proficient exercise of quality control has helped prevent her from falling into the trap of one-hit-wonder stardom. As a country artist, Swift boldly detailed her personal life through music. During the making of *Red*, co-writing sessions would begin with "girl talk."[10] In fact, its lead single, "We Are Never Ever Getting Back Together," was written after an unexpected run-in at the studio with a former flame's friend. Swift felt heated and went on chatting about the incident with collaborators Max Martin and Karl Johan Schuster (known professionally as Shellback). Then and there, with her guitar and her girl talk, she scored her first #1 hit on the Billboard Hot 100.[11]

From a young age, her preferred form of rebellion was performing a song about a specific person who was in the audience—for instance, singing self-penned "I'd Lie" about a crush on a classmate at her high school talent show.[12] In a high school setting, the identity of the song's subject was likely to be unmistakable, with lyrics dishing out information on the crush's family, birthday, and personality. While Swift's eponymous debut album left out "I'd Lie," its second single, "Teardrops On My Guitar,"[13] elevated the technique by directly naming the subject of the song. Referencing Drew, presumably another (or the same?) high school crush, was a deliberate choice, as the original demo lyrics had the song's mentions of "Drew" replaced with "you."[14] This decision set the scene for a future of weaving in names to mark people in Swift's life: from her English class best friend, Abigail Anderson, in *Fearless*'s "Fifteen," to her maternal grandmother, Marjorie Finlay, in *evermore*'s "marjorie"; from the passing infatuation with Stephen Barker Liles in *Fearless*'s "Hey Stephen" to the lasting wounds from John Mayer in *Speak Now*'s "Dear John"; from the historic inspiration she found in Robert F. Kennedy in *Red*'s "Starlight" to the generational predecessor she found in Rebekah Harkness in *folklore*'s "the last great american dynasty."[15]

4   The Glory of Giving Everything

Nonetheless, it'd be incomplete to relegate Swift's discography to who the songs are about. More importantly, Swift's songs capture indelible experiences and the fleeting sentiments attached to them. The narrator of the crown jewel of *Speak Now*, "Enchanted," promises the addressee that she will "forever" reminisce on the possibilities of their serendipitous encounter. Perhaps the most quintessential instance from her time in the country genre is "All Too Well," a raw portrait of finding oneself stuck in a series of recurring moments, namely, a collection of memories that was no longer being added to. Lesser known is the related *Red* deluxe track "The Moment I Knew," which depicts the humiliation Swift went through at her twenty-first birthday celebration. Making up for that was what Swift had dubbed her favorite birthday, preserved in the *Red* favorite "22," a mini power play of its own that lends significance to a typically nonmilestone age.[16] Through her writing, Swift tackles the crux of the human condition—that although emotions are temporary, we act as if they are permanent.[17] It's no surprise that to Swift, music is the "closest sensation we have to traveling in time."[18]

Swift has kept that core component with her, ensuring that the quality of her work remained constant no matter how she bent. So when she transitioned to pop, while her fan base exploded,[19] she did not alienate her country fans. On the Reputation Stadium Tour in 2018, Swift performed an acoustic version of "Dancing With Our Hands Tied," which appears on the *Reputation* album with a quick-paced, drum-laced beat. In the song's introductory speech, she outlined her priorities in songwriting: the lyrics, the feeling, and the melody, and letting those shine, irrespective of the production.[20]

Balancing the pressure to be a well-liked pop hitmaker and the responsibility to stay true to her songwriting philosophy raised the stakes, only for her to conquer them. Eloquently and impressively, Swift brought a natural feature of the country genre—stories—to her next phase. In an essay published in *ELLE* in 2019, Swift discussed the necessity to abandon generic pop writing for the purpose of creating timeless songs.[21] She addressed her instinct of making pop unconventionally confessional: "I want to remember the colour of the sweater, the temperature of the air, the creak of the floorboards, the time on the clock when your heart was stolen or shattered or healed or claimed forever. The fun challenge of writing a pop song is squeezing those evocative details into the catchiest melodic cadence [and] sprinkling personal mementos and shreds of reality into a genre of music

A Brand of Adaptable Authenticity

that is universally known for being, well, universal…[M]usic lovers want some biographical glimpse into the world of our narrator, a hole in the emotional walls people put up around themselves to survive."

Speaking of survival, the next wave of Swift's reach consisted of the mass of quarantine Swifties. In early 2020, full-fledged into the charming pastels of seventh studio record *Lover*, Swift intended to put out "Cruel Summer" as a single and embark on a festival tour called Lover Fest.[22] Then, the COVID-19 pandemic hit, canceling everyone's plans (sadly, not just in case someone would call, à la the narrator of "august"). As the world locked down into a legitimately cruel period of time, Swift knew that a summer 2020 "Cruel Summer" single would not only be untimely but insensitive. Instead, she turned inward, seemingly taking her foot off the gas pedal of stardom. She immersed herself in books and movies until her calling to create poured out of her.[23] On the verge of another major genre switch, Swift remembered to mix her secret ingredients. She leaned into her ability to be surprising for the rollout (or rather, the lack of a rollout) of her isolation project, *folklore*, and retained her signature rawness on the project itself.

Unpredictability, after all, is the younger sister of reinvention. She had already positioned herself as someone who could strategically reinvent, and the global pandemic's uncertainty offered her the opportunity to do so unpredictably. With no lead-in singles, music videos, or warning signs, Swift announced *folklore* via social media on July 23, 2020. Swift released *folklore* less than 24 hours later on July 24, 2020. From the same playbook, she surprise-dropped her first-ever sister album, *evermore*, a mere six months later on December 11, 2020. The unifying element across these sister rollouts was Swift's empathy. In the *folklore* announcement, Swift opened up about her pattern of overthinking promotional timelines and how she was able to let go of that.[24] As a nonartistic example, in 2011, outdoor gear company Patagonia ran a controversial "Don't Buy This Jacket" Black Friday ad in an effort to reduce consumption. Although it seemed counterintuitive, the campaign aligned with the environmental values of founder Yvon Chouinard. Consumers connected to the authenticity of Chouinard and consequently of the brand, and Patagonia's revenues grew by 30 percent in the next year.[25] Meanwhile, Swift's *evermore* announcement framed the album as a birthday present to fans—even though it was her birthday, and a special birthday at that (she was turning 31, her self-proclaimed lucky number backwards).[26]

The Glory of Giving Everything

This embodied inclusivity. Pennsylvania-based department store Boscov's employed a similar strategy by engaging in giveaways worth over $20,000 for its 110th anniversary in 2024.[27] While Boscov's post-giveaway metrics are to be determined, the retail chain has thrived for a century, accumulating $1.2 billion in sales and opening a 50th location by 2023.[28]

Such empathy was woven through the intimate tales of not-country, not-pop, but indie *folklore* and *evermore*. They boasted the skills of the same songwriter, freshly wrapped in alternative hues, in a time where people needed a voice more than ever. Swift spun stories rooted in both fiction and truth, providing a heightened sense of her usual relatability to fans and yet-to-be-fans. She drew parallels between her paternal grandfather's involvement at the Battle of Guadalcanal in World War II and the healthcare workers' daily battles during COVID-19 in the tribute that is "epiphany."[29] Comparably, *evermore*'s title track called back to 2016, fusing her personal difficulties that year with the broader societal event of the election.[30] In "peace," she shared her struggle with paparazzi and the ensuing consequences on her relationships. Co-writer Aaron Dessner attributed the song to his own struggle with depression and the ensuing relational consequences,[31] epitomizing the myriad of ways listeners interpret Swift's lyrics and apply them to their own lives.

For an artist who overcomes writer's block by being inspired from living her life,[32] this is more than an individual dream come true. This is what breathes collective meaning into every one of Swift's songs. Because she finds new ways to tell classic human stories, fans can find pieces of themselves in the crevices of her vulnerable, versatile discography. It's an unwavering gift she passes along, since she, too, seeks personal enlightenment in this manner. The star-crossed lovers of William Shakespeare's *Romeo and Juliet* weren't only characters that she thought deserved a better fate; they were characters that she understood after her own family and friends disapproved of a romantic prospect.[33] With "Love Story," the result of 20 minutes alone in her teenage bedroom, she inserted herself in the writing that came before her. As an adult facing backlash for virtually the same thing, she turned to another fable, albeit more subtly. Swift might have dressed up as Ariel at her childhood-hero-themed party to ring in the 2019 New Year, but the titular reference to Disney's animated film *The Little Mermaid* (which came out in 1989!) in "But Daddy I Love Him" five years later makes it clear: great stories beget great introspection, and vice versa, in a glorious endless cycle.[34] Swift related to classic protagonists, and she emerged as a verbose modern protagonist. Because of her authenticity and adaptability, fans of any and all backgrounds can insert themselves in the writing that comes before them on a Taylor Swift song or album.

The most interesting thematic concept that has prevailed throughout Swift's career just might be her complex relationship with fame. Situated against the backdrop of the music industry, these tracks merit a category all on their own, and tracing them offers a comprehensive look at Swift's genre evolution.[35] All three genres—country, pop, and alternative/indie folk— reflect on Swift's existence within a wider context: written at 13, country's "A Place In This World" explores a desire to sculpt a musical legacy for herself; written right after Lover Fest was canceled, indie's "mirrorball" grapples with the duty of maintaining that musical legacy; written on society's bitter treatment of creative minds, pop's "Who's Afraid of Little Old Me?" displays the ramifications of excelling in that musical legacy. All three genres delve into Swift's observations and resulting fears of the path she'd chosen: pop's "Clara Bow" and country's "Nothing New" comment on the transience of working in entertainment as a female; indie's "the lakes" fantasizes about escaping societal constructs; country's "The Lucky One" pays homage to unspecified musical heroes who underwent both experiences. But the flip side of terror is wonder, and Swift has taken care to memorialize those feelings as well. Through the story of Rebekah Harkness, the previous owner of Swift's Rhode Island home, she celebrates her own defiance in indie's "the last great american dynasty." Country's "Change" and "Long Live" illustrate the triumphs of everyone on her side, from the recording team to the stage crew to the fans. The journey to success culminates in pop's "You're On Your Own, Kid," a coming-of-age narrative reminding us that the lesson of loss is to embrace more, not less. The essence of this collection is that it more closely follows Swift's evolving perspective with respect to her industry trajectory, rather than depend on her current identified genre. These songs encapsulate Swift's earnestness and humility, which underscore her success.

Swift's adaptable authenticity not only has granted her a committed fan base, but has also made her the first person to win Album of the Year at the Grammy Awards four times.[36] The winning records of *Fearless* (country), *1989* (pop), *folklore* (alternative), and *Midnights* (pop) spanned the 2000s, 2010s, and 2020s. (Don't worry, this *1989* had the produced-to-perfection tune "Style" as its Track 3, not a cut of white noise.) Notably, each of these

The Glory of Giving Everything

wins were culturally distinct. To this day, if a person knew only one Taylor Swift song, it would undoubtedly be *Fearless*'s "Love Story" or "You Belong With Me." If that person actually knew two Taylor Swift songs, it would undoubtedly be *Fearless*'s "Love Story" and *1989*'s "Shake It Off." Accompanied by nostalgia, *Fearless* catapulted Swift to the beginnings of mainstream prestige; accompanied by novelty, *1989* secured her spot there while launching her to the beginnings of industry advocacy.[37] Accompanied by imagination, *folklore* was the soundtrack to the world's musings of stillness during quarantine; accompanied by contemplation, *Midnights* was the score to the record-smashing Eras Tour that had taken over the world. Without a consistently strong brand, these achievements would not have been possible.

Swift, however, is careful to curate that brand and disassociate herself from corporate language. "The bigger your career gets, the more you struggle with the idea that a lot of people see you the same way they see an iPhone or a Starbucks," Swift told *Variety* in early 2020.[38] "They've been inundated with your name in the media, and you become a brand. That's inevitable for me, but I do think that it's really necessary to feel like I can still communicate with people. And as a songwriter, it's really important to still feel human and process things in a human way." She must reconcile a personal aversion to becoming a brand with the requisite of becoming a brand in order to do what she loves for as long as she can. The solution is clear: build a brand revolving around communication and humanity. And by finding the equilibrium between fulfilling her creative needs and meeting the demands of an ever-changing industry, she is unprecedentedly adept at it.

Whether it originates from our personalities, beliefs, or experiences, we all have an innate brand. Your brand is what your friends unconsciously consider when introducing you to potential suitors, what your family unconsciously assesses when choosing the perfect gift for you, and what your managers unconsciously evaluate when assigning you specific projects. If your goal is to establish a profitable entity, mindfully expanding upon that brand would bring you closer. Swift certainly knew this, setting up a brand of adaptable authenticity as her North Star in creating music. In the songwriter's own words from 2010: "I think it's important that you know that I will never change. But I'll never stay the same either. Must be a Sagittarius thing."[39]

Next Chapter

2

Carving Out a Niche

When Swift invoked the symbol of the Sagittarius on *Lover*'s "The Archer," she mused that she'd been both the archer and the prey. The brilliance of Swift isn't only that she has a breadth of perspectives. It's that she precisely times and executes the portrayal of each role, which takes guts, creativity, and strong business instincts to do flawlessly. Indeed, the attributes that we've seen make Swift a successful songwriter are the same ones that make her a savvy businesswoman. The details she lends to her anecdotes complement the intricacy with which she lays out clues for her fans (more on this in Chapter 5). The honesty she spills in her lyrics pairs with the endearment she uses to grow her network in good faith (more on this in Chapter 6). The sensitivity she treats her characters with is matched by the intuition she acts upon in defending her vision at critical moments (more on this in—you're in luck—Chapter 2!). Her artistry and entrepreneurship are powerfully linked.

Swift's drive to stay relevant, punctuated by her aptitude to remain true to her values, has allowed her to carve out a niche in the music industry. A niche is defined[1] as:

1. a place, employment, status, or activity for which a person or thing is best fitted
2. a specialized market or distinct segment of the market

12 The Glory of Giving Everything

Named after musician James Taylor and born to the daughter of an opera singer, Swift has described music as vital to her happiness and expressed gratitude that it doubled as her long-term career path.[2] If we consider music to be Swift's calling, she slides in seamlessly with definition #1. Definition #2, however, is a little trickier. Niche markets can be contextualized by a number of factors, including price (think high-end fashion), demographics (think college preparatory services), and geography (think rural supply stores). All start-up founders believe they have a million-dollar idea; identifying a niche and taking the initiative to provide value for it is a concrete way of actualizing that idea. Exotic Nutrition, for example, operates in a distinct submarket of the pet owner market. This pet supply store sells products for reptiles, birds, monkeys, and rodents, not dogs or cats.[3] Within the beauty market, Lush caters to ethical and conscious consumers, ensuring that its cosmetics products are fresh, sustainable, and free from preservatives, packaging, and animal testing. Lush sources its salt from the marshes in Portugal, which both contributes to a natural product for humans and protects the habitat for migrating birds.[4] In San Francisco, and in spawned specialty stores at tourist destinations, Lefty's produces a line of stationery items designed for left-handed folks, who make up 10–12 percent of the population.[5] These have all seen a version of success: Exotic Nutrition was picked up by big names Walmart and Chewy, Lush was able to spend roughly $8 million to expand its presence across Europe, and Lefty's garnered the attention of the press as well as individualized appreciation.[6]

For Swift, her early success stemmed from expanding the younger demographic in the market for country music. Growing up a country fan, she realized that everything playing on country radio was about settling down to have a family, which she couldn't identify with.[7] When she would attend Country Radio Seminar, an annual educational event congregating business pioneers across the fields of radio and music, she would hear talk of needing to appeal to a younger cohort.[8] At 11, she convinced her family to visit Nashville for spring break and ran in and out of doors on Music Row, dropping off her demo CD. The CD featured two original songs—"Am I Ready For Love" and "Can I Go With You" (the latter co-written by Swift)—and four covers—"There's Your Trouble" by The Chicks (The Dixie Chicks at the time), "One Way Ticket (Because I Can)" by LeAnn Rimes, "Here You Come Again" by Dolly Parton, and "Hopelessly Devoted To You" by Olivia Newton-John.[9] At 12, she started playing guitar seriously

Carving Out a Niche   13

and wrote her first song, "Lucky You," about a girl named Lucky who forges her own path in life. At 13, she turned the head of RCA Records, a subsidiary of Sony Music Entertainment, and fully relocated to Nashville.

The catch, though, was that the label's offer was a development deal. Under the deal's terms, RCA Records would give teenage Swift time and money to record with no commitment on their end to support an album release (Swift likened it to a guy who wanted to date but not be a boyfriend). Optimistically, Swift wrote new material every week. In response, RCA Records always decided that it was getting better but that they still wanted to keep her in development until she was 18. With no record deal on the horizon, she did the unthinkable: she walked away.[10] She left Nashville's biggest record label, the one who had launched the careers of Kelly Clarkson and Christina Aguilera, because of a misalignment in priorities. She knew that her writing distinguished herself from other female singer wannabes. She also knew that RCA Records didn't see the value of her recording her own music, so there was no point in staying. Fourteen years old now, Swift already felt pressured for time. Having written a handful of songs, she was anxious to "capture these years of [her] life on an album while they still represented what [she] was going through."[11]

Her next move was performing her diaristic songs at arguably the most iconic venue in Nashville, the Bluebird Cafe (Faith Hill, one of Swift's role models, was discovered here). At the end of her show, she was approached by a man named Scott Borchetta. Borchetta made his interest clear that he wanted Swift to record her own music with him. The catch here, though, was that he didn't have a record label yet. As is what happens when you find the right partner (in business, romance, or life), this catch wasn't a hindrance for Swift—in fact, it was a value-add. With a mutual sense of faith in each other's dreams, creating something from scratch was exciting, not intimidating. She felt that it was adventurous to be the first person on an up-and-coming label. When *Entertainment Weekly* inquired about her firm decision to leave RCA Records, she said, "I needed my own direction and the kind of attention that a little label will give you...I wanted a record label that needed me, that absolutely was counting on me to succeed. I love that pressure."[12] Taking the risk paid off. Big Machine Records was founded soon afterward, and Swift's debut album, *Taylor Swift*, came out on October 24, 2006. *Taylor Swift* sold 39,000 copies in its first week and subsequently enjoyed a steady rise.[13]

14 The Glory of Giving Everything

What RCA Records failed to be a part of was the bigger discussion in Nashville about country music. At the time, country radio listeners had consisted largely of older women who mostly tuned in for male singers. Generally, country radio listeners had long been leaning toward age 35 and over, and Music Row had been trying to lower the median age for at least a couple decades. Swift's relatable writing and young sound attracted a wholly new audience to country music, thus finally accomplishing Music Row's objective. Girls who had never before been subject to the world of country music were telling Swift that they were "obsessed" ever since *Taylor Swift* and sophomore record *Fearless* entered the conversation.[14] On a smaller scale, Swift would go on to reinvigorate two more niche markets: personability within pop music and popularity within alternative music. Recalling Swift's *ELLE* essay, she cited Drake's "In My Feelings" (2018), The Chainsmokers' "Closer (feat. Halsey)" (2017), and Camila Cabello's "Havana (feat. Young Thug)" (2018) as outstanding examples of personally detailed, as opposed to generic, pop. Upon seeing the piece, The Chainsmokers shared that Swift's songs had inspired their own.[15] While the others might not have been directly influenced by Swift, these were products of a dynamic contemporary pop scene that had been stamped by Swift's own pop breakthrough in 2014. In a healthy cycle, besides the *ELLE* shoutouts, Swift furthered these artists' output the same year that essay went to print. On the opening track of 2019's *Lover*, "I Forgot That You Existed," Swift called herself "in [her] feelings more than Drake." During her Artist of the Decade performance at the 2019 American Music Awards, Halsey (real name Ashley Frangipane) and Camila Cabello joined her on stage for "Shake It Off." The appearances were on the heels of Cabello supporting the Reputation Stadium Tour as an opener and Swift complimenting Frangipane's "fierce" and "vocal" creative prowess while promoting *Lover*.[16] Swift's hiatus from pop the next year did not end up including a break from fame, and 2020's *folklore* and *evermore* sped up the shift toward making indie music mainstream.[17]

Swift's astute awareness of her presence has guided her to make both sensible and sincere choices. At the height of her self-titled era, she commented that the craziest thing she anticipated doing when she turned 18 would be casting a vote. Escapism and stress relief came in the form of songwriting, not alternate substances. To *Entertainment Weekly*, she explained,

"Yesterday, I did five hours of radio remotes, which is where you walk around to all the different radio stations and you're interviewed by everybody. And I honestly love that...I've just never been into going to parties as much as I've been into [furthering my career]. I guess I got used to having to make that choice when I was little...between being popular or not messing my life up. [M]aking that choice has kind of made a permanent mark on me to be responsible. Also, when you put out a single, whether you like it or not, you're a role model..."[18] Around the time of the Fearless Tour, NBC and *The Telegraph* broached the subject again. Nineteen-year-old Swift reaffirmed her stance that teenage boldness was defined by standing up for herself in the recording studio and with record labels: "I have always felt a little strange about it being so unique that I'm not a train wreck. Like, this weird fluke that I'm not—partying all the time and, you know, drunk in this interview."[19] She embraced this at the Country Music Television (CMT) Music Awards in 2009, in a moment of parody that wasn't just silliness. Dueting with rapper T-Pain in a parking garage, Swift assumed the nickname T-Swizzle and donned a baseball cap, cargo pants, and gold jewelry. The short track, "Thug Story," was rhythmically rap and lyrically girl-next-door. Swift rapped about the "gangster" lifestyle of living with her parents, baking cookies, and knitting sweaters. In a humorous conclusion, Swift's voice was bleeped out, followed by her insisting that she was not even swearing. She took the main stage for two performances, joining Def Leppard for the classic "Pour Some Sugar On Me" and singing her own hit "You Belong With Me." That night, "Love Story" won Video of the Year and Female Video of the Year.[20] But the song's "Thug Story" spinoff has remained memorable,[21] showing that in addition to her writing, her image had become something that set her apart. "The bigger pitfall," she told *Vogue's* Jonathan Van Meter in 2012, "is losing your self-awareness. The stakes are really high if you mess up, if you slack off and don't make a good record, if you make mistakes based on the idea that you are larger than life and you can just coast."[22]

Like all of us, Swift eventually grew up, accumulating experiences that would lead her to explore more adult themes. Unlike all of us, Swift grew up in the limelight. Even though no hard rules prevented her from doing what she pleased when she pleased, her cognizance of her image reflected the kind of maturity that let her flourish as a multifaceted artist. In writing

The Glory of Giving Everything

her fourth studio album, *Red*, Swift drafted lyrics that incorporated flippant curse words and melancholic drinking. She admits that she's had "too much to drink tonight" in "Nothing New," says "sh★t" in "I Bet You Think About Me," and drops the F-bomb in the 10-minute version of "All Too Well" ("f★ck the patriarchy" was a phrase on a physical object and not technically spoken by the song's narrator, but it is part of the lyrics nonetheless). Interestingly, none of these tracks made the cut on the final version of 2012's *Red* ("All Too Well" did, of course, but the swear portion was removed). She had written them to express her feelings but intentionally kept them off the record to preserve her good girl country persona. The public was given the whole story with 2021's *Red (Taylor's Version)*, the second "Taylor's Version" album of the re-recording project she was undertaking to gain ownership of her music. Each re-recording, accompanied by vault tracks that were written for an album but not included, offers us a case study into strategy. The racy *Speak Now (Taylor's Version)* vault song "I Can See You," as another instance, was deemed unfit for the then-20-year-old's third album that was almost christened *Enchanted*.[23] Take the *1989 (Taylor's Version)* vault track "Is It Over Now?," in which Swift details how a chaotic, passionate fling makes her want to "jump[] off of very tall somethings." The reference to taking one's life, although hyperbolic, did not appear on the original album, perhaps out of caution. A potential misinterpretation of such a lyric would not have been worth betting on at the time when so much about Swift's style change was jarring. On reinvention, Swift elaborated to Billboard in 2012, "You want to provide your fans with something exciting, but you don't want them to be listening to the album going, 'I don't recognize her.' So it's somewhere in the middle. You have to find a balance."[24] Earlier that year, Van Meter observed her "deeply ingrained sense of appropriateness," reporting that she "may be edgier than her image suggests, but…[s]he also knows her audience—and knows that they aren't ready for her to grow up quite yet."

That isn't to say that there wouldn't be a time and place for the explicit topics. Quite the opposite is true. The protection of her image wasn't only to ensure smoothness at those times, but also to introduce such themes when they're ready to emerge. References to self-destruction sneak their way onto *folklore*, where the narrators of "this is me trying" and "hoax" find themselves tempted by the edge of a precipice. Here, hopeless protagonists

Carving Out a Niche   17

appropriately meet the desperation of quarantine, instead of the eclectic 2010s pop party. Swift's hyperbolic lyrics are on display in 2024's *The Tortured Poets Department*, an artistic endeavor centered around fatalism.[25] In the title track, the entangled lovers overtly discuss killing themselves if the relationship were to end. In "But Daddy I Love Him," Swift claims she would "rather burn [her] whole life down" than accept unsolicited complaints, and "Guilty as Sin?" watches her consider "throwing [her] life to the wolves." Thematically, the concept fit in much more closely on *The Tortured Poets Department* than it would have on bright-eyed *1989*. As for post-21 activities, Swift debuted numerous alcoholic and sensual references as well as the word "sh★t" on 2017's *Reputation*, at a time when her entire image needed a revamp.

In the period after her *1989* peak and before her *Reputation* comeback, Swift's public fall from grace was palpable. The genesis of the unraveling was the volatile relationship between Swift and rapper Kanye West, whom she met at the Music Television Video Music Awards (MTV VMAs) in 2009. Swift had won Best Female Video for "You Belong With Me" over fellow nominees Beyoncé ("Single Ladies [Put a Ring on It]"), Katy Perry ("Hot n Cold"), Kelly Clarkson ("My Life Would Suck Without You"), Lady Gaga ("Poker Face"), and P!nk ("So What").[26] Infamously, West interrupted Swift's acceptance speech by grabbing the microphone from her and praising Beyoncé's video instead (later in the night, when "Single Ladies [Put a Ring on It]" won Video of the Year, Beyoncé invited Swift to the stage). Although West and Swift were eventually able to come to a place of mutual respect, it blew up in 2016 with the song "Famous." In that song, West declares that sex was on the table for him and Swift because he "made that b★tch famous." When Swift was put off by it, West claimed that the lyrics had her approval via a phone conversation. His then-wife, Kim Kardashian (West and Kardashian divorced in 2022), had recorded the aforementioned call without Swift's knowledge. To attest to West's claims, she posted an edited 3-minute version of it on Snapchat and essentially called Swift two-faced in an interview.[27] It wasn't until four years later that the whole 25-minute conversation leaked. Then, it became clear that the lyric Swift was agreeing to was the "tongue-in-cheek" line of the possibility of sex between the artists. When West brought up the line about making her famous, Swift sounded uneasy but agreed that West should have the

18   The Glory of Giving Everything

freedom to share his perspective, which is that he didn't know Swift prior to their first encounter. The only instance in the entire phone call that had the word "b★tch" was from Swift's mouth—when she expressed relief that the song was not mean to her, specifically using "b★tch" in her example of a mean lyric.[28] However, no one knew this back in 2016, and the public was quick to side with West and Kardashian.

Piling on the train was the debacle surrounding another 2016 hit. Calvin Harris (real name Adam Wiles) and Rihanna's "This Is What You Came For" was written by Wiles and an anonymous co-writer, Nils Sjöberg. Shortly after Wiles and Swift's breakup, TMZ divulged that Swift was behind the pseudonym. At the same time, Swift was moving on romantically with actor Tom Hiddleston. Wiles, who Swift dated for 15 months, retaliated to the leak on Twitter. In a series of since-deleted posts, Wiles contended that Swift was purposefully attacking him and implored her to focus on Hiddleston.[29] For a controversy-hungry public, the dissolution of Swift's longest relationship so far was fresh meat. Even though Wiles acknowledged the fault in his rant a few months later, the swirl of the media storm was already too convoluted to stop.

On National Snake Day in July 2016, Kardashian implied that the holiday was pointed toward Swift.[30] Snake emojis flooded Swift's Instagram comments section. And with #TaylorSwiftIsOverParty trending at #1 on Twitter globally, condemnation forced Swift to stay out of the public eye. "I just wanted to disappear," a shaky-voiced Swift shared in her *Miss Americana* documentary. "Nobody physically saw me for a year, and that was what I thought they wanted." Exhibit 2.1 shows the number of paparazzi photos taken of Swift from 2007 to 2023, along with tags of significant events.[31] Her two most photographed years were 2014 (18,242) and 2015 (7,578), which denoted the career pinnacle of the *1989* album and the 1989 World Tour. The two lowest years were 2007 (18), which was after her debut but before the treasured hits of *Fearless*, and 2020 (28), which was when the world was in lockdown. With only 44 photos taken, the year 2017 documented a difficult period in her life.

In August 2017, Swift marked the beginning of an unforeseen era. She reduced her website to a black page. She unfollowed everyone on social media and wiped her Facebook, Tumblr, and Instagram profiles clean. She then proceeded to post three captionless grainy videos each containing a

Carving Out a Niche 19

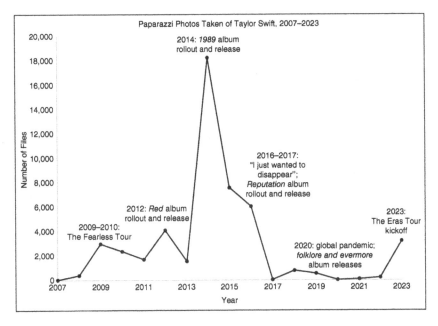

Exhibit 2.1 Paparazzi Photos Taken of Taylor Swift, 2007–2023

part of a snake. The full snake laid across her Instagram grid made an imminent announcement evident—her sixth studio album, *Reputation*, was slated to hit the anti-Swift world that November.[32] By incorporating the snake motif in the tone of *Reputation*, Swift skillfully redefined a symbol intended as hate to reclaim the narrative. Moreover, as the snake is the Chinese Zodiac of the year 1989, this connected to her previous era as well as responded to the backlash. She placed herself at the center of attention, and the snake drew in both those who adored and those who criticized her. The intense speculation she sparked with the cryptic social media behavior was confirmed with the release of the lead single, "Look What You Made Me Do." Its music video dethroned Psy (the South Korean personality behind "Gangnam Style") for the most YouTube streams in a 24-hour period with 43.2 million views.[33] The video featured stereotyped versions of Swift from her past, and no matter how the public perceived her, they couldn't look away. Unequivocally, Swift gave them something to look at. For the first time, she meaningfully carved out distinct personas as determined by her eras. There was now an "old Taylor"—proclaimed dead not by West, Kardashian, or the general public, but by the new Swift herself. In this

20   The Glory of Giving Everything

fashion, Swift strategically, and one might argue necessarily, acquired the control she had lost. As everyone held their breaths for the album drop, Swift delivered. Her first official swear word was formidable: "If a man talks sh*t, then I owe him nothing." With a singular line, she addressed the scandal, something she wouldn't have been able to pull off if she had kept the word on *Red* in a musical send-off to an ex. Similarly, her first mature mentions of sexual activity were distinguishable in that they were present on a record that was lyrically reflective of real love, instead of short-lived flings as in the cut *Speak Now* track and as in many other pop songs. If a public downfall was the body of *Reputation*, a private romance was its beating heart. Swimming in caverns of alcohol and intimacy, *Reputation* alerted the world that her rebirth wasn't just the result of internalized commentary, but also that it was a deeply personal shift.

In her resurgence, Swift channeled the marketing research of Northwestern University Kellogg School of Management Professor Emeritus Alice Tybout and Bucknell University Freeman College of Management Dean Michelle Roehm.[34] Tybout and Roehm's formula for crisis aversion is that there is no set formula: "[T]he most effective approaches are carefully calibrated to the characteristics of the brand, the nature of the event, and the company's degree of culpability." Such approaches would not only limit negative repercussions, but also give opportunities to strengthen the firm-customer alignment. Often, managers and customers' points of views are misconstrued to be more in line than they really are. In the wake of a crisis, business managers adopt an analytical evaluation framework due to their expertise, while customers assess the situation emotionally and defensively. Bridging this gap is key to mitigating harm. When the Swift entity suffered from the allegations surrounding the "Famous" lyrics, Swift needed time to heal. But she didn't let the rest of her livelihood disintegrate. She understood the mindset of the public, which consisted of both willing and unwilling consumers of the Swift entity. For the unwilling consumers, she knew that even if they pushed her into hiding, they remained ravenous for content. There was no better way to satiate their need than by owning the name they decided she was. The Reputation Stadium Tour opened with audio clips of critics slamming Swift, but the clincher was that Swift invited those journalists to the tour. They were seemingly happy to take part in her downfall, so they were given a prime seat to her triumphant return.

The tour's permanent guest of honor was a huge inflatable snake affectionately known as Karyn.[35] For the willing consumers, Swift likely believed that they would empathize with the mental toll the accusations had had on her. Nevertheless, her advanced sense of perception activated. She knew she'd signed up to be a role model when she put out her first single, and difficult times were when a role model was truly tested. So, she chose to show her fans courage in the form of a comeback, telling them that they, too, could transform adversity into empowerment. In sold-out shows, she spread the message that bullying could put its victims in a position of strength rather than defeat. Raking in $345.7 million, the 2018 Reputation Stadium Tour became the highest grossing tour in United States history at that point, beating out the 2005–2007 A Bigger Bang Tour put on by The Rolling Stones.[36]

Despite the leaps that *Reputation* made, it was not nominated for any of the major Grammy Awards categories: Album of the Year, Record of the Year, or Song of the Year (Record deals with artistry and production of a song, while Song recognizes songwriting). Upon hearing the news, Swift's reaction was simply that she "need[ed] to make a better record." *Reputation* did get one nomination for Best Pop Vocal Album but lost to Ariana Grande's *sweetener*.[37] Instead of questioning the credibility of the Recording Academy, she took responsibility for not meeting the metric. This is also the origin story behind the smash hit that was *1989*. Swift was confident that *Red* would be crowned Album of the Year at the 2014 Grammys, but the award went to Daft Punk's *Random Access Memories*. Later, she discussed the announcement as if it had happened in slow motion, the common starting letter of both records momentarily deceiving her into thinking she'd won. She turned the frustration into fuel and immediately began planning her next direction. At 4 a.m. the next day, she awoke knowing that it would be a pop project called *1989*. The homage to her birth year came out nine months later.[38]

"We don't make music so we can like win a lot of awards," Swift elucidated to Grammy Pro.[39] "But you have to take your cues from somewhere if you're going to continue to evolve." She continued by outlining the possible trajectories from losing: "For one, you can decide like, 'Ugh, they're wrong. They all voted wrong.' Second, you can be like, 'I'm gonna go up on the stage and take the mic from whoever did win it' [Kanye West style], or third, you can say, 'Maybe they're right. Maybe I did not make the record of my career. Maybe I need to fix the problem which was that I have not been making sonically cohesive albums. I need to really think about whether I'm listening to a scared record label and what that's doing to the art I'm making.'" She carried this line of thinking over what would become her next Album of the Year, two records after *Reputation*. She was apprehensive about getting her label's blessing for the surprise drop of *folklore*, but pitched it anyway because she believed in the album.[40] Her concerns turned out to be unfounded, as she was given the green light.

Swift's consistent motivation to find ways to be relevant demonstrates a pivotal business point. Pursuing dreams doesn't have to be inherently capitalistic, and people don't do it for the sole reason of being acknowledged. When Swift was bestowed with the Songwriter-Artist of the Decade honor at the Nashville Songwriter Awards in 2022, she confessed that she'd still be in this line of work if she hadn't gotten a single recognition for it.[41] Nevertheless, it's important to recognize stagnancy in order to grow. Children's toy Play-Doh started off as wallpaper cleaner in the early 1900s sold under Kutol Products, the largest manufacturer of its kind. By the 1950s, with improvements in gas, oil, and electricity, the cleaner was no longer in demand. Joseph McVicker, who was working to save Kutol Products, happened to have nursery school teacher Kay Zufall as a sister-in-law. Zufall tried out the (nontoxic) material on her students, and it was a hit at playtime. In 1956, the remade product of Play-Doh entered the market, selling over 3 billion cans to date.[42] More recently, in 2019, Mexican food chain Chipotle established "Chipotlanes," mobile order pickup windows, in response to customers' needs for convenience. Chipotle locations with "Chipotlanes" were found to bring in around 15 percent more sales than traditional Chipotle locations.[43] Both of these companies were already successful (as were *Red* and *Reputation*), but their visibility efforts unlocked a higher level. Whether your desired standard is sales, awards, or some type of personal fulfillment, acting correspondingly when it's time to change is worth the hard work. As with the dichotomy of being a brand, it's only when you welcome the commercial aspects of your career that you can focus on your passion for it.

On the flip side, hold on to your strengths. Lessons from the *Fearless* era begin with another phone call. This time, it's the more innocuous but still inconsiderate 27-second phone call Joe Jonas made to break up with Swift.

When the unexpected incident happened, Swift put pen to paper (or melody to feeling) for *Fearless's* last addition of "Forever & Always." As it was only a day before the final submission was due, Swift begged Borchetta to let her include it on the record.[44] Because she wrote about her personal life, she sensed that this piece would be the finishing touch on this album and, by definition, on this chapter of her life. Her determination got her what she wanted. She might have known the story of actress Kate Winslet from a decade earlier. To get the coveted role of Rose DeWitt Bukater in *Titanic*, she asked her agent for director James Cameron's personal cell, first calling him and later sending him roses signed, "From your Rose." She also tracked down co-star Leonardo DiCaprio while he was at the Cannes Film Festival to convince him to star alongside her as Jack Dawson. Cameron saw the fire in Winslet and knew she would match the spunk of Rose. For both women in entertainment, the persistence worked because it originated from a place of pure intent. After writing the song, Swift felt that "Forever & Always" was meant to be on *Fearless*. After reading the script, Winslet felt that she was meant to be Rose.[45]

Titanic went on to capture hearts worldwide and win 11 Oscars, including Best Picture.[46] To propel "Forever & Always" to a comparable status on its own scale, Swift put out *Fearless (Platinum Edition)*. With six new songs, the platinum edition came out on October 26, 2009, almost a year after *Fearless* did on November 11, 2008. One of the new songs was a reimagined acoustic version of none other than "Forever & Always," suitably dubbed "Forever & Always (Piano Version)." By repackaging what was proven to be working, Swift further capitalized on the career high she was riding. The platinum release made Swift the first artist in history to have five songs chart within the top 30 on the Billboard in one week. It also gave her nine songs on the Billboard Top 100 overall, the most that any female artist had had previously. The songs were "Jump Then Fall," "You Belong With Me," "Untouchable," "The Other Side of the Door," "Superstar," "Come In With the Rain," "Forever & Always," "Fifteen," and "Two Is Better Than One," where Swift is a featured artist.[47] (As of 2024, Swift still holds this record with 32 charted songs in a single week with 31 *The Tortured Poets Department* songs and Eras Tour bop "Cruel Summer." For all artists, Morgan Wallen holds the record with 36 charted songs in a single week. In 2009, the Beatles held this record with 14 entries in a single week.)

24   The Glory of Giving Everything

Exhibit 2.2 shows the chart positions of *Fearless* tracks, some whose success she built upon and some whose success was bumped with the platinum edition.[48] Rows with no asterisks contain songs from the original *Fearless*, rows with one asterisk contain songs from *Fearless (Platinum Edition)*, and the row with two asterisks is the song by Boys Like Girls featuring Swift. Prior to the drop of the platinum edition, eight songs from *Fearless* were basking in chart success, with "Love Story" and "You Belong With Me" climbing from #16 to #4 and #12 to #2, respectively. After the drop of the platinum edition, as shown in the lower half of the exhibit, another eight songs began to trend. Swift had effectively doubled her hits during this period. The piano version of "Forever & Always," while absent from the Hot 100, prompted the original "Forever & Always" to enter the chart within the Top 40. "Fifteen," a song from the original *Fearless*, debuted at #79 in 2008 but didn't peak until after the release of the platinum edition. "Two Is Better Than One," which was released on October 19, 2009, debuted at #92 but didn't stay on the Hot 100 the following week.[49] However, it was able to re-enter at #79 by the week after

Songs from *Fearless* on the Billboard Hot 100			
Song	Debut Position	Peak Position	Peak Date
Fearless	9	9	11/1/2008
You're Not Sorry	11	11	11/15/2008
White Horse	13	13	11/29/2008
Hey Stephen	94	94	11/29/2008
The Way I Loved You	72	72	11/29/2008
Breathe	87	87	11/29/2008
Love Story	16	4	1/17/2009
You Belong With Me	12	2	8/22/2009
Jump Then Fall*	10	10	11/14/2009
Forever & Always	34	34	11/14/2009
Untouchable*	19	19	11/14/2009
The Other Side of the Door*	23	23	11/14/2009
Superstar*	26	26	11/14/2009
Come In With the Rain*	30	30	11/14/2009
Fifteen	79	23	12/19/2009
Two Is Better Than One**	92	18	1/30/2010

Exhibit 2.2   Songs from *Fearless* on the Billboard Hot 100

that, or the week of November 2, 2009, which was shortly after *Fearless (Platinum Edition)* said hello to the world. These feats were all accomplished because Swift leveraged existing material, instead of scrambling to concoct something from scratch.

When it does come time to create from scratch, Swift is an expert at drawing inspiration. Consider the title track of *Speak Now*, her third studio album, whose inception comes from a friend. The friend was telling Swift about her high school sweetheart, who she always thought would find his way back to her, marrying someone else.[50] The bride-to-be supposedly was insufferable and isolated the groom-to-be from his friends and family. Swift jokingly asked if the friend would halt the wedding, and the conversation was so striking to Swift's brain that she soon dreamt of her own ex-boyfriend marrying another girl. She knew then that the story warranted its own song. (The friend, if you were wondering, was rumored to be Hayley Williams from rock band Paramore.) "Speak Now" (the song) delineates the cheeky arc of a narrator interrupting a church wedding and running away with the groom before it's too late.

Not only did the story become its own song, but it blossomed into a full-length body of work. Swift presented *Speak Now* (the album) as a "collection of confessions—things [she] wish[es] [she] had said when [she] was in the moment." In the album's liner notes, she revealed that these songs were "open letters…written with a specific person in mind, telling them what [she] meant to tell them in person" and listed a few prominent examples.[51] Swift cleverly turned a secondhand experience into an intact thematic concept that turned into a musical record. Furthermore, she had found a way to make wedding ceremonies relatable to her demographic of young girls. In the first year of her twenties when *Speak Now* was released, marriage wasn't on her mind, and neither was the traditional "speak now or forever hold your peace" uttered just before the couple ties the knot. By opening up that statement to all confessions, Swift put a refreshing spin on an age-old construct at a time when such constructs are idealized. On average, young women daydream about their wedding at the age of 19 and get married at the age of 28.[52] *Speak Now* appealed to the part of her demographic that simultaneously romanticized nuptial emotions and reflected on novel agency. In the prologue of *Speak Now (Taylor's Version)*, Swift credited

26 The Glory of Giving Everything

its special place to its unfiltered rawness, emotional potency, and "vast extremes."[53]

"Speak Now" (the song) wasn't the only corner of her catalog where her subconscious played a role. *1989*'s "All You Had To Do Was Stay" was conceived after another dream about an ex. In the dream, the ex showed up on her doorstep to get her back, and her response was a repetitive high-pitched "stay!" exclamation. Swift conceded that it was too unique not to try experimenting with, and the "stay!" ended up on the hook. *Reputation*'s "I Did Something Bad" paraded (besides the word "sh★t") a distinct production of a foreign and catchy sound in the post-chorus. Like the "stay!" interjection, the sound came to Swift in a weird dream, and she brought it to the studio intending for it to be replicated by an instrument. When an instrument wouldn't scratch the itch, Max Martin proposed recording Swift's voice making the sound and "pitch[ing] it down so that it sounds like an enchantress/dude." Like many of her other songs, Swift had written the track on piano; hence, it was this specific sound that signaled to her the creative and sonic vision of *Reputation*.[54]

In a similar vein, *Speak Now* (the album) wasn't the only corner of her catalog where a little bit of inspiration stimulated a lot of storytelling. "I think as a songwriter you need to have a completely wild imagination about what could be and what might have been," Swift postulated to the *Los Angeles Times* in 2008.[55] "Some of your most heartbreaking material is what could have been, and some of your most romantic material is what could be." Going back to *Fearless*, Swift had written the lovestruck title track while single, stating that it was about the best first date she hoped to have. The idea for "You Belong With Me" started when she overheard a friend on the phone with his girlfriend, who was yelling at him over something trivial. She ruminated on why he let her treat him that way and was moved to write the character of a girl who would appreciate him.[56] Indubitably, when Swift mines her personal life for details, she does so with care—she locates the gold, polishes it off, and molds it into a compelling song. As a business and as a human being, being alert for any source of inspiration that might come your way is a crucial element of growth.

It's this open-mindedness toward inspiration that has led Swift to cement herself as the artist who had a song for every stage of a listener's life. What's impressive, though, is the way she did this right off the bat. Her debut album had five singles: "Tim McGraw," "Teardrops On My Guitar," "Our Song," "Picture to Burn," and "Should've Said No." These encompassed a wide range of emotions. For those wistfully reminiscing on a fading past, "Tim McGraw" was there. For those longing for an impossible future, "Teardrops On My Guitar" was there. If you were giddy in love, you had "Our Song." Plotting payback? "Picture to Burn." Betrayed? "Should've Said No." The record itself channeled Swift's mastery of product variety. As we saw in Chapter 1, "A Place In This World" covered ambition; written after learning of a popular classmate's eating disorder, "Tied Together With A Smile" covered life's insecurities; written for the older couple next door in Nashville, "Mary's Song (Oh My My My)" covered lasting love.[57] Because her name and legacy was unknown, it was necessary for Swift to pick the singles that would showcase what she had to offer. While it's easy to understand that Swift has achieved variety over the course of an 11-album career, it's remarkable that she was able to execute this at the ripe age of 16 with one album and one genre. She didn't have, or need to have, a lot of experiences yet. Her imagination, romanticism, and ability to find inspiration allowed her to be fruitful in creation.

And she'd do it over and over and over again if she could—and she did. When entering a market like the country music scene, the goal would be to differentiate yourself within the competitive landscape. But perhaps the true measure of accomplishment is one step higher. By the time Swift was promoting *Speak Now*, her primary artistic concern was writing a better song than the last song she'd written.[58] Once you've carved that niche, the new goal would be to continuously improve your game, until the only person you're competing with is yourself.

3

What Does an Economist Know About Songwriting?

Long-running pop culture cornerstone *Saturday Night Live* (*SNL*) has had a plethora of celebrity hosts. For the majority of hosts, their opening monologue is written by SNL staff, who have more familiarity with the tone and the audience. Not for Swift. In "Monologue Song (La La La)," she played guitar and played on her likings, tendencies, and the word *monologue*. It was a savvy attestation to her skill set. First, she entered a format that was decades older than her and made it her own (like with the country genre). Writing her own monologue and playing her own instrument to support it wasn't typical of a host. Second, she used her voice to respond to current events in her world (as with *Reputation*). Mentioning her phone breakup with Joe Jonas, her sweet correspondence with *Twilight* actor Taylor Lautner, and her stage incident with Kanye West highlighted both a personability and an awareness. Third, she spun a throughline to build the song upon. The events were grounded by an assertion that she would not be commenting on them "in [her] monologue," underlined by the contradiction of her doing so. Cleverly, the West lyrics were infused as her "VMA monologue," the second word being a melodic twin to the other "monologue"s. She referred to the song as her "musical

30 The Glory of Giving Everything

monologue," then escalated it by calling it her "SNL monologue," and ended with a tense change that that "was [her] SNL monologue."

Although SNL staff had already drafted a script for Swift for her November 2009 appearance, it never surfaced because it never had to. She presented her monologue to the team, and co-head writer at the time Seth Meyers compared it to the rare occurrence of receiving a gift precisely aligned with your needs.[1] Fans would say this is an appropriate depiction of all of her songs. If her brand is being an adaptable and authentic songwriter, her main products are the songs themselves. The central themes and purposes of her body of work thrive only because of sharp songwriting. Competitive edge is fostered through prudent marketing strategies but arises from great products. Like a perfect gift, Swift tailors (no pun intended) each of her products to match the message it is sending. In every song, the subject matter and the presentation of the subject matter are harmonious. Through literary, sonic, and structural devices, Swift lengthens the shelf life of her individual songs and strengthens their value to consumers. Shelf life is defined as[2]:

1. the period of time during which a material may be stored and remain suitable for use
2. *(broadly)* the period of time during which something lasts or remains popular

Commonly used for physical products stamped with an expiration date, ordinary people often think of shelf life while grocery shopping or meal prepping.[3] Sealed cheddar cheese, for example, has a shelf life of six months in the refrigerator or freezer, and unsealed cheddar cheese has a shelf life of three to four weeks. Hand sanitizer has a shelf life of three years. Lithium batteries have a shelf life of 10–20 years. Applying the concept to art might not give as much of an accurate timeline of its worth, but doing so is a meaningful exercise to contemplate the construction of allure. Painted by Leonardo da Vinci in the early 1500s, the *Mona Lisa* has been on display at the Louvre in Paris since 1804.[4] One could say that the acclaimed artwork has an indefinite shelf life as it continues to dazzle the millions of Louvre visitors every year.

What Does an Economist Know About Songwriting? 31

Swift's songs envelope the listener and take on a life of their own. In "You're On Your Own, Kid," she designates bracelet-making as a figurative piece of wisdom to revel in friendship and freedom. The simple line has since become a widespread trend at the Eras Tour, with fans accessorizing their arms with bracelets and exchanging them at the shows. Paris and London welcomed Swift with electronic edits of friendship bracelets encircling their landmarks of the Eiffel Tower and Big Ben, respectively. New Orleans marked the occasion with a huge inflatable friendship bracelet hung up on Caesars Superdome. National Football League (NFL) Kansas City Chiefs tight end Travis Kelce famously made a friendship bracelet with his digits on it to ask Swift out. Other fandoms have incorporated the practice in celebration of their favorite artists, including Fall Out Boy and Charli xcx.[5] Even though the *Midnights* era is past us, the friendship bracelets—and by association, *Midnights*'s fifth track, "You're On Your Own, Kid"—lived on. The album's 14th track, "The Great War," reaped a similar benefit. The song compares a specific situation of a fighting couple to the universal concept of war. When tickets to the Eras Tour were extremely difficult to obtain, people called the situation the Great War.[6] A shared experience was now ascribed to the song that was unrelated to, and much broader than, the literal subject of the song. As with "You're On Your Own, Kid," the shelf life of "The Great War" persisted through the Eras Tour. By writing figuratively and not literally, Swift's songs spawn detailed discussions and multiple interpretations. This allows people to draw parallels between phrases both in and out of the music as well as map connections over time (more on this in Chapter 4), which ties in with an economic principle known as *marginal utility*.

Utility is the economist's measure of happiness, satisfaction, or value derived from consumption of a good or service. Because every person has unique likes and dislikes, every person has their own utility function. According to microeconomic theory, humans aim to maximize their utility subject to certain constraints, such as income or product availability. Marginal utility is the additional utility gained from consuming one more unit of a good or service. Many products exhibit diminishing marginal utility over time, meaning that for each additional unit, the consumer's satisfaction increases by less.[7] Again, food gives a digestible example. Say you're craving something sweet. Your first chai sugar cookie will be quite delicious. Your 13th one, however, is likely to be less satisfying. At worst, your stomach might be feeling sick or at best, your appetite is already partially filled, and in either case, the benefit of consuming the 13th cookie is less than the benefit of consuming the first one. The law of diminishing marginal utility is behind bundle deals and progressive taxes. For "Buy 1 Get 1 X Percent Off" deals, sellers know that the second unit of the item brings less satisfaction, so they must price it lower to encourage buying. For placing a higher tax burden on the wealthy, the idea is that an extra $1,000 means a lot to someone who has $100 but does not mean as much to someone who has $1,000,000.

In some instances, marginal utility can be increasing. Say you collect autographed baseball cards. Your first one is sure to be exciting. Your seventh one, however, is likely to be more satisfying as each additional unit goes toward making the collection complete. This can be true even if the item isn't necessarily rare. Perhaps someone collects Hard Rock Cafe sweatshirts. Even though sweatshirts might generally have diminishing marginal utility, Hard Rock Cafe sweatshirts for this person do not due to personal reasons. Therefore, like utility, marginal utility is dependent on each individual. A beginner guitar player who has one guitar might not find that much use out of another one. A professional musician who has one guitar might find that owning another one for recording, practicing, and/or touring increases their productivity. It is also dependent on how the good or service itself is measured. Daily or weekly exercise has increasing marginal utility, because each additional day or week can go toward developing a healthy lifestyle. On the same day, for the average person, hourly exercise has decreasing marginal utility, because each additional hour can cause fatigue. In matters of the heart, playing hard-to-get while dating is driven by diminishing marginal utility. If you're too available, the other person will supposedly desire you less because additional time spent with you has diminishing returns. True love, though, tends to epitomize increasing marginal utility. As additional years pass, the involved people supposedly feel more deeply toward each other and the life they've built. If couples divorce, it's likely because they'd experienced an elongated upside-down U curve—increasing marginal utility for a number of years together and then diminishing marginal utility after working it out becomes no longer worth it.

What Does an Economist Know About Songwriting? 33

Clearly, these theories are interesting focal points for both concrete and abstract notions. Thinking of music simplistically, songs can have diminishing marginal utility, as people become bored of overplayed tunes. In practice, though, works of art can go either way, as shown in an experiment that examined opinions of art over the course of seven weeks. One group was exposed to the critically acclaimed pieces of English painter John Everett Millais, another group was exposed to the less renowned pieces of American painter Thomas Kinkade, and the last group was not exposed to any artwork. The Millais group had a higher opinion of the artwork by the end of the experiment compared to at the beginning of it, while the Kinkade group had a lower opinion by the end compared to the beginning. Hence, the marginal utility of good art can be increasing, while the marginal utility of poor art can be diminishing.[8] Of course, the quality of art is subjective and again, dependent on preferences. The challenge, then, is to create art that speaks to as many varied preferences as possible and invites the art consumer, regardless of preferences, to continuously enhance their appreciation for the piece. Swift's numerous accolades will tell you that she has risen to this challenge, and her compositions will tell you how.

Swift deftly employs every tool at her disposal to shape the narrative she wants to portray. Exhibit 3.1 displays the song structures present throughout Swift's discography, each structure complementing the thesis of the song it supports.

The *Pop Formula* is the one that you might be most familiar with. Songs of this type aren't restricted to pop but are named this way because of the structure's common usage in pop. Pop Formula songs follow a traditional layout: first verse, possibly a pre-chorus, chorus, second verse, possibly a pre-chorus, chorus, bridge, and chorus. Just in case this is jargon: verses typically contribute to the story and context of the song's situation; choruses typically spotlight the theme of the song and contain the memorable hook; bridges typically change pace or perspective to vary the song; and pre-choruses melodically differ from verses and choruses, can be the same or different each time they're repeated, and constitute creative choices by the songwriter that typically connect verses and choruses. "The Way I Loved You" (*Fearless*) and "Blank Space" (*1989*) are classic Pop Formula songs without pre-choruses, while "I Knew You Were Trouble" (*Red*) and

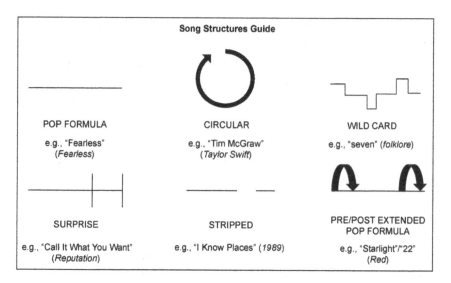

Exhibit 3.1 Song Structures Guide

"King of My Heart" (*Reputation*) are classic Pop Formula songs with pre-choruses. All of these tracks have two standard verses, three standard choruses, and a standard bridge.

Related is the Extended Pop Formula, which has two types: the *Pre-Extended Pop Formula* and the *Post-Extended Pop Formula*. Each type is the same as the Pop Formula with one key difference. The Pre-Extended Pop Formula starts with an extra chorus preceding the first verse. By starting with a chorus, "Midnight Rain" (*Midnights*) introduces the conflict of the song immediately, leaving the listener in suspense for the narrator's metamorphosis during the first verse's small-town setting. "Bad Blood" (*1989*) also kicks off with its chorus, alerting the listener to the battle. The nonverse beginning helps the song mimic the quick thinking needed for a catfight. As a variation of this, "Delicate" (*Reputation*) starts with the pre-chorus, clueing in the listener to the romantically hesitant theme of the song. The Post-Extended Pop Formula, which isn't as common in mainstream pop but is well-known in Swift's language, repeats the bridge after the end of the third chorus. Because a song's typical emotional center is the chorus, Swift uses the Post-Extended Pop Formula to transfer the listener's attention to the bridge. Just like when you don't want a party to end, the narrator of "22" (*Red*) doesn't stop at the last chorus, but continues for one last hurrah.

"Cruel Summer" (*Lover*) repeats the bridge in order to linger on the "desperation and pain" that Swift aimed to intensify: "This song is one that I wrote about the feeling of a summer romance, and how often times a summer romance can be layered with all these feelings of, like, pining away and sometimes even secrecy…there's some element of desperation and pain in it, where you're yearning for something that you don't quite have yet, it's just right there, and you just, like, can't reach it."[9] Later in the Eras Tour setlist comes "…Ready For It?" (*Reputation*), which does this as well. As the album's opening song, the bridge declares that the narrator is ready to pounce ("baby let the games begin"), and the second bridge furthers the anticipation for the rest of "the games" promised on the record.

Another one of Swift's favorites, borrowed from the country genre, is the *Circular* style. Like the Extended Pop Formula, there are two versions of Circular songs. With the first type, the songs start and end on the exact same line. "Guilty as Sin?" (*The Tortured Poets Department*) ends on the same few lines as the beginning, reinforcing the entire sequence of events as a risqué fantasy. "Invisible" (*Taylor Swift*) opens and closes with the same commentary on what another girl doesn't notice about the subject of the song, while the inside of the song points out that the narrator notices them. The identical bookends emphasize the narrator's futile efforts to be seen. Its more agonizing older sister, "tolerate it" (*evermore*), has this effect as well. The narrator begins a tale of silent suffering in a state of passiveness. In the climax, the narrator almost decides to break free—but the apparent resolution is broken as the narrator heartbreakingly concludes the song in the exact same state of passiveness. Ending at the same place as the beginning plays with the listener's emotions in the way a great tragedy does. It single-handedly underscores Swift's empathy for people in difficult relationships, and how hard it can be to leave. With the second type of Circular songs, the songs start and end on a similar, but not the same, line or verse. "I Almost Do" (*Red*) is a textbook example, starting with the narrator "bet[ting]" that the subject of the song wonders about her and ending with the narrator "hop[ing]" that the subject does. The one-word swap reveals the shift in mood that accompanies a passage of time. The narrator is confident at first, but as a rekindled relationship becomes less and less possible, the narrator becomes wistful about what was lost. The passage of time in "Mary's Song (Oh My My My)" (*Taylor Swift*), though, is endearing. The characters, aged

36   The Glory of Giving Everything

7 and 9 in the beginning and 87 and 89 at the end, regard each other in the same loving way at both stages of their relationship. Meanwhile, "Haunted" (*Speak Now*) opens with discussion of a connection the narrator believed would never break. The urgency of "Haunted" builds until its abrupt end right before the narrator can even say the word "break." As cliché as the advice is, this is "show, not tell" at its finest. The framing of the circular manner completes every one of these stories.

The *Surprise* song (not to be confused with the surprise songs on Swift's stadium tours) includes one or more unexpected elements. This element can take the form of an extra chorus, an extra pre-chorus, an extra verse, or an outro, and it breaks the audience's expectations to make a more fulfilling listening experience. A recurrent Surprise structure is when another lyrically different chorus is slipped in. In "Mine" (*Speak Now*), this extra chorus appears only in the second round, while in "You Belong With Me" (*Fearless*), it appears in both the second and third/last chorus round. Moving on to pre-choruses, the structure of "Out of the Woods" (*1989*) is as follows: first verse, chorus, second verse, pre-chorus, chorus, bridge, and chorus. The part between the second verse and the chorus (namely, the surprise) adds unpredictability, befitting Swift's motivation for the song: "The number one feeling I felt in the whole relationship was anxiety because it felt very fragile, it felt very tentative…it doesn't mean that it's not special and extraordinary just to have a relationship that's fragile and somehow meaningful in that fragility." This section of the song also boasts what has become a beloved symbol among Swifties—the flying pair of paper airplanes was an option at a tattoo parlor in Melbourne that was sold out the weekend Swift went down under.[10] "Daylight" (*Lover*) follows the same structure, breaking convention to convey a divergence of paths towards the brighter. The structure of "Never Grow Up" (*Speak Now*) is as follows: first verse, first pre-chorus, chorus, second verse, second pre-chorus, chorus, bridge, third verse, and chorus. The first two verses take place in a family home, while the third verse (namely, the surprise) sees the protagonist alone in her new apartment, thus completing the coming-of-age narrative. The structure of "The Other Side of the Door" (*Fearless*) is as follows: first verse, first pre-chorus, chorus, second verse, second pre-chorus, chorus, bridge, chorus, and outro. The outro (namely, the surprise) romanticizes the imperfections of the song's subject and offers a resolution through them. "Breathe (feat. Colbie Caillat)"

(*Fearless*), which details the loss of a friendship with a band member, has an outro that softly duplicates the word "sorry."[11] For a songwriter with a lot to say selling to an audience with declining attention spans—hit songs have shortened by around 40 seconds in length from 2000 to 2018[12]—outros provide anticipation and a motivation to listen to the entire song. On the reverse side, Swift's childhood-inspired track "Christmas Tree Farm" has an intro, which effectively sets up the rest of the song as a daydream. Besides individual songs, structures also elevate overarching storytelling. All three songs about the principal trio in *folklore*, which Swift has confirmed is a fictional teenage love triangle,[13] have Surprise structures. A cross between a third verse and a post-chorus appears in "cardigan," a self-assured yet underestimated Betty using the time to outline her proven predictions. An outro is present in "august," humanizing Augustine and pushing back on the usual "the other woman" arc. The pivotal moment of "betty" is when James, who yearns to show up at Betty's party to win her back, finally does it in the third verse. James also engages in an outro in the song "betty," which is used to tie him to Betty with three direct references to her narration in "cardigan."

Opposite of the Surprise is the *Stripped*, which eliminates one expected element of the song. "I Look in People's Windows" (*The Tortured Poets Department*) perfectly exemplifies this. Told succinctly in two verses and two choruses, the song feels unfinished because it depicts a missed connection. The song "illicit affairs" (*folklore*) ends without a full chorus, indicating that no matter where the narrator's moral compass points, the affair will always lack a sense of finality. "False God" (*Lover*) operates without a bridge, replicating the concept of falsity in the song itself. And while *folklore's* love triangle has been heavily broadcasted, *evermore* features its own pining high school couple: Dorothea, who visits home after having left town in search of something bigger, sings of her perspective using a Surprise structure with an extra lyrically different chorus in "'tis the damn season"; the nameless narrator of "dorothea" invokes a Stripped structure by way of leaving out a bridge, indicative of the missing romantic piece that he was on standby to welcome back.

The last umbrella is the *Wild Card*. Wild Card songs don't follow a conventional structure. "Is It Over Now?" (*1989*), a sister track to "Out of the Woods," is physically frazzled with roughly the following structure: first verse, first pre-chorus, chorus, second verse, bridge, second pre-chorus,

chorus, bridge, and a blend between the pre-chorus and the bridge. Also understandably frazzled are breakup jams "Death By A Thousand Cuts" (*Lover*) (roughly: chorus, first verse, pre-chorus, chorus, bridge, chorus, and a blend of the bridge and the first verse) and "right where you left me" (*evermore*) (roughly: first verse, first pre-chorus, chorus, bridge, second pre-chorus, and chorus). Since Swift knows that emotional rollercoasters are for the lowest and the highest moments of love, butterflies-rushed "So High School" (*The Tortured Poets Department*) is a Wild Card too, which has three distinct choruses that each repeat twice, a couple different verses, and a bridge in the middle of it all. The con artists of "cowboy like me" (*evermore*) get to know each other over a deceptive structure that mirrors their unraveling. The children of "seven" (*folklore*) live in a fragmented structure that reflects the imagination and brokenness of youth, with a long instrumental break to separate memories of the innocent friendship from memories of the abusive family.

Quite a few songs utilize a combination of these structures to productively make their points. "Don't Blame Me" (*Reputation*) is an Extended Pop Formula song in both senses, as it starts with a chorus before the first verse and ends with a double bridge. Swift's intention behind the song was to fuse the three things she believed could change a person—love, drugs, and religion—and the extensions are well-suited for a transformational song.[14] "Red" (*Red*) is both a Circular and Surprise song, ending with both an outro and on the first line of the song. "It's Nice To Have A Friend" (*Lover*) happens to be both a Surprise and a Stripped song with a third verse and no bridge. Exhibit 3.2 provides a breakdown of structures by album according to the categories outlined in Exhibit 3.1 and the subsequent paragraphs.[15] For songs with multiple structures, they are counted under each category (*Red*'s title track would have a tally for Circular and Surprise, for example) to create a holistic view of the albums' structure melding. While usage of these structures isn't exclusive to Swift, she wields each one to deepen her commitment to her musical products. Unsurprisingly, compared to the other albums, *1989* parades the highest number of classic Pop Formula songs, *Speak Now* tells the longest stories through Surprise structures, and *evermore* experiments the most through Wild Card songs.

Within these structures, Swift alters chorus lyrics and melodies that move the story forward in her songs. "White Horse" (*Fearless*) spends the

What Does an Economist Know About Songwriting?

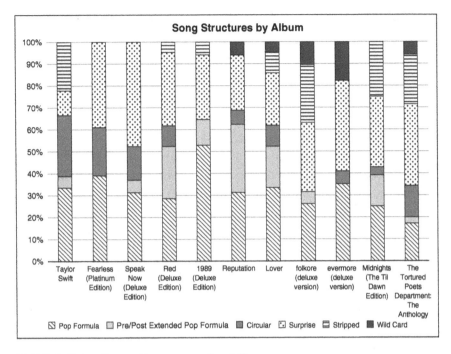

Exhibit 3.2 Song Structures by Album

song dwelling on the disappointment of a small-town romance, but the last chorus turns it around with the hope of a big-world romance. True to its title, "Timeless" (*Speak Now*) sets its choruses in different time periods leading up to the present. In "Maroon" (*Midnights*), Swift croons about her wine-splashed apparel in three different ways, emphasizing "shirt" in the second chorus and singing the line lower in the third chorus to signify a dark ending. The last chorus of "Say Don't Go" (*1989*) singles out the word "leave" by changing its note, accentuating the situation's hopelessness. Additionally, the stories in her songs are supplemented by other sonic devices; the tantalizing pen click in "Blank Space" (*1989*), the wailing police siren in "no body, no crime (feat. HAIM)" (*evermore*), and Swift's heartbeat in "Wildest Dreams" (*1989*) and "You're Losing Me" (*Midnights*) all place the listener in the setting. In "I Can Do It With a Broken Heart" (*The Tortured Poets Department*), Swift amplifies her staccato breathing between words of the broken promises that ignited the broken heart as if she were hyperventilating from crying. A number of tracks, including

40   The Glory of Giving Everything

"Stay Stay Stay" (*Red*) and "This Is Why We Can't Have Nice Things" (*Reputation*), feature Swift laughing. When performing live, she'll often switch notes, jump octaves, or adjust phrasing to make the experience unique.[16] She'll also mash up songs to connect old stories or invent new ones— "Back to December x You're Not Sorry x Apologize (by OneRepublic)" on the Speak Now World Tour, "Enchanted x Wildest Dreams" on the 1989 World Tour, "Bad Blood x Should've Said No" on the Reputation Stadium Tour, and the myriad of acoustic mashups on the Eras Tour. Because every part of the song is carefully crafted, she can seamlessly and intentionally mix and match them. These distinctions from the studio versions add to the songs' shelf lives, as the concert versions offer a fresh upgrade to what fans already know and love as well as prompt them to reconceptualize the original recordings.

Swift's songwriting also stands out due its use of bridges, with fans and critics alike dedicating time to ranking the bridges of her songs.[17] In fact, the prevalence of the Post-Extended Pop Formula in Swift's discography can be explained by her adoration of the bridge. During the *Lover* era on the Eras Tour, Swift expressed excitement at reaching the first bridge of the night, that of "Cruel Summer," and invited the crowd to prove that they knew the lyrics to it by singing along. During the *folklore* era on the Eras Tour, she sang only the bridge to "illicit affairs," but an extended version of it. In an Apple Music interview, she told Zane Lowe, "I really love a bridge where you tell the full story in the bridge, like you really switch gears in that bridge." Through her work, Swift reinvented the bridge to be a moment of revelation, realization, or reveal, unlike many pop songs that simply have bridges as earworms. "You Are In Love" (*1989*) and "the last great american dynasty" (*folklore*) are both stories about other people—the former told in second person inspired by her friend and collaborator Jack Antonoff's love story, and the latter, as we know, told in third person inspired by prior Holiday House owner Rebekah Harkness. In these, Swift inserts herself into the song using first person via the bridge—the bridge of the former explains how the love story constitutes her reason for being a writer, and the bridge of the latter shares that she was the one who bought Harkness's house and continued her legacy. The bridges of "Tim McGraw" (*Taylor Swift*) and "Getaway Car" (*Reputation*) lead directly back into the last chorus. With "Tim McGraw," the bridge makes it clear that

What Does an Economist Know About Songwriting? 41

the message of the chorus gets sent to the recipient. With "Getaway Car," the bridge changes the agency of the narrator from riding in the getaway car to being the one driving it. Critically, Swift's bridges are functional and directly serve the purpose of the song.

What truly levels Swift's art up to that of John Everett Millais, the painter for whom people had increasing marginal utility, is her proficient usage of figurative language. As with the friendship bracelets, Swift's construction of words allows listeners to glean new readings from it over time. For instance, plenty of her lyrics contain a double meaning. To Apple Music's Lowe, Swift elaborated on the "new me" in the song "happiness" (*evermore*), that it refers to the narrator after having reinvented themselves with new hobbies to get over a relationship and also to the ex's new significant other who replaces the narrator.[18] The wronged narrator of "my tears ricochet" (*folklore*) taunts that the subject of the song will "miss [her]," and the surrounding lyrics provide context for the double meaning. This follows a lyric discussing "aim," indicating that she'd be missed the way a hunter might miss their target. Yet the subsequent lyric, "in your bones," indicates that she'd be missed the way a friend might miss someone from their past. The crucial question in the second verse of "Blank Space" (*1989*) of "who is she?" comprises a double meaning depending on who utters the question. The lyrical setup points to the lover asking it, "second-guessing" where the narrator's insane patterns come from. However, the music video has Swift's character ask the question, acting on unfounded "jealousy." In "imgonnagetyouback" (*The Tortured Poets Department*), the narrator claims that she has the "upper hand" to touch the subject, where "upper hand" serves both as the idiom of having power and as a physical hand movement conducted by the narrator. Similarly, the "episode" in the same album's title track is both a metaphor—a loved one's poor conduct is compared to a favorite television show's filler episode—and a term for a psychotic breakdown. "Fifteen" (*Fearless*), a Circular song, revisits going through the high school doors at the end of the song, a moment that can be interpreted as the narrator passing the torch to the next class, reassuring her old self that everything will turn out alright, or mustering up the courage to now exit the school she'd known for four years.

Punctuation placement plays a part too, as seen on three *Midnights* tracks. In "Hits Different," the chorus can be written as either "oh my, love

42   The Glory of Giving Everything

is a lie" or "oh, my love is a lie," and the difference is whether the intention is general (love as a concept doesn't exist for anyone) or specific (love doesn't exist for the narrator only). Both achieve the same level of despair in alternate ways. In "Bejeweled," a comma can be placed between "don't" and "remember," changing the meaning from not remembering at all to remembering but not caring. Both versions relay a sense of self-confidence and flippance. "Maroon" as a whole captures the title's double meaning of dark red as well as isolation, and a comma (or lack thereof) in the bridge makes for an extra one. The Apple Music lyrics to the song suggest a "legacy to leave," while Swift's official lyric video denotes a "legacy, to leave."[19] The audience must decide for themselves if the legacy is being left, if the legacy is in the leaving itself, or a combination of both. To notice these double meanings, and then to analyze them, requires several listens of the song, hence making the value of consuming Swift's songs dynamic. Due to its layers of complexity, a consumer's 13th listen of a Taylor Swift song can be more satisfying than the first listen.

Besides double meanings, Swift has an aptitude for literary devices in her writing.[22] Metaphors apply words to an object or action when they are not literally applicable in order to say that they have the same qualities. In "Karma" (*Midnights*), the titular notion is referred to as a doting boyfriend, a revered god, an uplifting breeze, and a faithful cat, despite not literally being any of these. Similes imply shared qualities by making a comparison using "like" or "as." In "coney island" (*evermore*), a former relationship is compared to the mall prior to the internet as the center of activity. Hyperbole is composed of exaggerated assertions, such as when Swift sings of directly staring at the sun in "Anti-Hero" (*Midnights*). With alliteration (which is present in the premier part of the preceding paragraph), adjacent words begin with the same consonant, as the narrator of "mirrorball" (*folklore*) does on tall tiptoes and high heels. Personification assigns human characteristics to nonhuman things, like the city that screams in "Cornelia Street" (*Lover*). With a zeugma, a word is applied to two others in different senses. The first paragraph of this chapter, for instance, might have read "she played guitar and on her likings…" where "played" applies to two different things. In "The Smallest Man Who Ever Lived" (*The Tortured Poets Department*), the aforementioned smallest man crashes a party and a car. Symbolism is a method of representing something beyond a symbol's literal function.

What Does an Economist Know About Songwriting?

The famed scarf in "All Too Well" (*Red*) that the narrator never gets back is a symbol of her innocence.[20]

Swift's work benefits from an acute sense of scale in everything she does, musically or otherwise. When performing *Furious 7*'s "See You Again" with Wiz Khalifa on the 1989 World Tour, Swift commented that she and Khalifa hugged for "four years"—a perfect hyperbole because it created the illusion of believability and conveyed the warmth of the moment.[21] If she had said the hug lasted 100 years, it'd have been an easy exaggeration to mentally deconstruct and brush aside and wouldn't have had the same impact. Consequently, while some of these devices seem to be torn straight from a page in a grade school textbook, complexity emerges when Swift weaves these devices in intricate ways throughout her discography. The opening lines of "Sparks Fly" (*Speak Now*) connect a simile and a metaphor—one person moves like a rainstorm, the other is a house of cards—to say simply that one was blown away. The verses of *Red*'s title track are built upon a series of specific situational similes for passion—fast cars on dead end streets, crosswords with impossible answers. "Tied Together With a Smile" (*Taylor Swift*) laces a conceptual simile across a few lines—passing out love "like it's extra change," being stranded "like a penny in the rain," not being a desirable "price to pay." Some of her songs surround a central metaphor that is reflected in their titles: "Picture to Burn" (*Taylor Swift*), "Snow On The Beach" (*Midnights*), "The Albatross" (*The Tortured Poets Department*), to name a few.

Furthermore, richness is created through allusions, which connect the works of Swift to the works of others. "Love Story" (*Fearless*), of course, references Shakespeare's *Romeo and Juliet*, but also references Nathaniel Hawthorne's *The Scarlet Letter*, which tells the story of a woman who wears a scarlet letter as a mark of shame. Juliet, facing family disapproval, is Romeo's shame. The reference gets a reimagination in "New Romantics" (*1989*), where young people compare their "scarlet letters" in a contest of reckless behavior. F. Scott Fitzergerald's *The Great Gatsby* enjoys a few shoutouts as well. Swift sings of being her lover's "daisy" in "Don't Blame Me" (*Reputation*), calling to mind Gatsby's love interest, Daisy Buchanan. In hoping that the next woman would be attractive but ignorant, the narrator of "happiness" (*evermore*) echoes Daisy's sentiment for her daughter to grow up blissfully. The narrator goes on to channel the novel's famous green light on Daisy's

44   The Glory of Giving Everything

dock, symbolizing Gatsby's desperate devotion, to recognize a period of moving on. "This Is Why We Can't Have Nice Things" (*Reputation*) mentions Gatsby directly as a canvas for lavish parties. Classic characters Peter Pan and Wendy Darling are used in "cardigan" (*folklore*) to illustrate the maturity differences between Swift's love triangle characters Betty and James. The tale is utilized more extensively in "Peter" (*The Tortured Poets Department*) to discuss, allegedly, Swift's own relationship. Preceding "Peter" on the same record is another track whose allusion is made clear from the title: "Cassandra" likens the 2016 dismantling of Swift's reputation to Greek mythology figure Cassandra, who was cursed to forecast the future accurately with no one believing her. With the help of a rabbit hole and the Cheshire Cat, the lyrics of "Wonderland" (*1989*) paint a relationship as time spent provisionally in Lewis Carroll's children's fantasy *Alice's Adventures in Wonderland*. Robert Frost's poem "The Road Not Taken" makes an appearance in Swift's "The Outside" (*Taylor Swift*) and "illicit affairs" (*folklore*)—to ponder an ascent to fame in the former and a descent to immorality in the latter. Real-world figures Niccolo Machiavelli from the Italian renaissance and William Wordsworth from the Romantic age are revived in the twenty-first century in "Mastermind" (*Midnights*) and "the lakes" (*folklore*), respectively; moving forward in history, poet Dylan Thomas, singer Patti Smith, and contemporary artist Charlie Puth are name-dropped in "The Tortured Poets Department" (*The Tortured Poets Department*). Swift roots her work in a wide range of allusions, breathing life into her discography and establishing her credibility among esteemed creators.

As with the vault tracks from the re-recordings, glimpses into Swift's songwriting process serve as a case study. The first draft phone memo of "My Boy Only Breaks His Favorite Toys" (*The Tortured Poets Department*) synthesizes the concepts in this chapter. At the start of the memo, Swift acknowledged the song's Stripped and "abnormal" structure, and upon finishing the bridge, she stated that it would end like that without launching into another chorus. The story models a Stripped song, as the narrator—the metaphorical favorite toy—is too broken to return to the chorus and complete the expected route of the song. Exhibit 3.3 delineates the differences between the memo and the recording. In the final version, we can see that the language wholly commits to the overall metaphor of playtime. While the draft lyrics are emotionally valid, the changes made in the final

"My Boy Only Breaks His Favorite Toys"	
First Draft Phone Memo	Final Recording
"our midnight sighs"	"our days of wild"
"the kingdoms"	"sandcastles"
"been different this time"	"played for keeps this time"
"blew it up"	"smashed it up"
"that was the worst part"	"down at the sandlot"
"then in brief moments"	"when we played pretend"

Exhibit 3.3 "My Boy Only Breaks His Favorite Toys"

recording strengthen the narrator's communication through figurative language to form a cohesive storyline.

Many passersby would be quick to admire Swift's talent. They'd learn that in fourth grade, she entered a poem entitled "A Monster in My Closet!" into a national poetry contest and placed.[23] They'd see her accompanying herself on guitar singing the National Anthem at the NASCAR Cup Series Championship in Phoenix and the MLB World Series in Philadelphia— much before her SNL stunt in a tradition much older than SNL.[24] A reasonable reaction might very well be that Swift is a natural creative with a knack for catchy hooks. But this assumption undercuts her as an artist and impedes her ability to inspire growth mindsets in young dreamers. While she might have had the seeds of greatness, she has watered them until they sprouted. As with "My Boy Only Breaks His Favorite Toys," Swift diligently takes the time and makes the effort to craft her art. These are the products that live up to their potential and resonate with consumers; these are the ideas worth marketing. What's yours?

4

The Layered Musical Universe

If microeconomics is the study of consumers and firms, and if macroeconomics is the study of countries and governments, Swift's world also operates on a micro and macro platform. Queries of microeconomics revolve around the choices and constraints of individual units. Queries of macroeconomics revolve around the policies and behaviors of entire economies. For us, our singular unit is the song, and explorations at this micro level delve into the form, language, acoustics, and production techniques that sculpt a four-minute delight. Analogous to how the aggregate of smaller units influences broader economic indicators, Swift's songs build on each other. Lengthy shelf lives result in noetic layers that contextualize the universe of Swift, where every corner is a coded reference and every inhabitant is a willing sleuth.

A cultural commentator in *The New Yorker* dubs it the "Swiftverse," made up of a musical franchise akin to a four-dimensional chess game: "Why *do* we compare Swift with singer-songwriters like Grande and Beyoncé, and not with Bob Iger, the media executive who turned Disney into a 200-billion-dollar company?" Indeed, Iger and Swift both graced the cover of *TIME* in 2023—Swift as the Person of the Year and Iger as one of the 100 Most Influential People.[1] As the chief executive officer of the Walt Disney Company, Iger acquired the wildly popular Pixar Animation Studios (2006) and Marvel

48   The Glory of Giving Everything

Entertainment (2009), expanded the Disney theme parks to China with the opening of Shanghai Disney Resort (2016), and spearheaded the launch of the Disney+ streaming service (2019). He understood how to manufacture an empire while maintaining creative integrity as the heart of the company. Exceptionally, Disney's animators have been known to leave Easter eggs binding together their fictional worlds. Rapunzel, the *Tangled* (2010) princess with magical locks, is seen attending the coronation of Elsa, the queen with ice powers, in *Frozen* (2013). Alone in her tower, Rapunzel herself paints an apple symbolic of Snow White (*Snow White and the Seven Dwarfs*, 1937), a slipper symbolic of Cinderella (*Cinderella*, 1950), and a rose symbolic of Belle (*Beauty and the Beast*, 1991). French heroine Belle is also seen walking the streets of Paris in *The Hunchback of Notre Dame* (1996). And in *Beauty and the Beast*, a signpost spells out Anaheim, which houses Disneyland Park and Disney California Adventure Park, and Valencia, which houses the California Institute of the Arts, a common school among Disney animators.[2] The magic of Disney is captured in each film separately, on a micro level, but it soars in the broader Disney universe, on a macro level.

When the full-length 31-track *The Tortured Poets Department (TTPD)* emerged, some critics slammed it for the apparent lack of editing, minimal stylistic variety, and abundance of parallels to previous work. But as our friend at *The New Yorker* observes, "…without an understanding of the Swiftverse, very little of Swift's music…will ever make any sense." Not designed for a one-time reaction, the merit of *TTPD* lies in its place in Swift's musical family. As with her individual songs, *TTPD*'s home is furnished with figurative language that allows it to prosper. The opening track and lead single, "Fortnight (feat. Post Malone)," starts off with bold professions of needing to be sent away, presumably to a mental institution. The hyperbole does the job as a standalone, but it becomes effective in conjunction with the preceding album, *Midnights*. The closing song of the last edition of the album (*Midnights* spawned a *3am Edition* and *The Til Dawn Edition* on streaming and *The Late Night Edition* on CD), "Hits Different," desolately questions whether the authorities have come to take the narrator away. Immediately, "Fortnight" suspensefully positions fans at a particular spot in the timeline, where they know that a) the narrator anticipated being sent away, b) the narrator was not sent away, and c) the narrator, left to fend for herself in a functional society, still had the manic inclinations

The Layered Musical Universe 49

from "Hits Different." While Swift tinkered with "My Boy Only Breaks His Favorite Toys" to reach a centralized toy metaphor, the complete writing process actually extends back to another "Hits Different" overlap. The songs share an allusion to toy manufacturer Mattel, with the *Midnights* song discarding past lovers like Ken dolls and the *TTPD* song furthering it by recognizing that this time spent playing—even if it resulted in broken pieces—was meaningful because the subject wasn't like the other Ken dolls. You'll recall that one of the original "My Boy Only Breaks His Favorite Toys" lyrics referenced "midnight." Had this been kept, fans would've caught the blatant tie to *Midnights*, but the connection is more striking through the nuanced Ken metaphor. Some references are less obvious, making them more satisfying upon discovery. *TTPD*'s "loml" (whose title, short for "loss of my life," is a twist on the abbreviation for "love of my life") discusses a "get-love-quick scheme," which isn't present in any of Swift's old lyrics but rather appears in a poem she wrote for an exclusive *Reputation* magazine that was also recited on the Reputation Stadium Tour, "Why She Disappeared."[3] On the other hand, like the *folklore* love triangle, some references are self-contained, making for a delectable independent experience. "The Black Dog" mentions the band The Starting Line, and 10 tracks earlier, "Fresh Out The Slammer" uses a generic "starting line" phrase to indicate a new beginning.

Stunningly, *TTPD*'s "The Alchemy" is part of a metaphor that is more than a decade in the making. The connotation of 2012's "Red," which was written on a redeye flight to Nashville, is that intense love burns like the color red. The theme was influential enough to justify its own album, bringing us Swift's fourth record *Red* that labeled strong emotions of passion, frustration, joy, and rage as red-coded. In the album's prologue, Swift described red relationships as those that "went from zero to a hundred miles per hour and then hit a wall and exploded."[4] She contrasted it with real love that "shine[d] golden" and promised that she'd write an entire album about "golden" love if she ever found it. Swift's 2019 seventh record, *Lover*, was that album, with closing track "Daylight" explicitly stating that love was now golden instead of red. Aureate references slide in on other songs about that love, including the tattoo in "Dress" (*Reputation*, 2017) and the thread in "invisible string" (*folklore*, 2020). As fans went off in search of their own hue-reminiscent romances, Swift's *Lover* love exhausted its course. To situate her next serious relationship, she invoked alchemy, which is the chemical process of transmuting metals into gold.[5] Adhering to her established color symbolism, "The Alchemy" is a message to longtime listeners that not only is true love golden, but also that you can find, lose, and find it again.

Swift also facilitates mapping within her world visually. Behind the scenes of the "Fortnight" music video, she confirmed that "pretty much everything…is a metaphor or a reference to one corner of the album or another."[6] Among others, the video features a black dog to signify that song later in the record, a notebook with "us." on its cover to hint at a forthcoming (at the time) Gracie Abrams collaboration, and Swift's makeup in the style of silent film actress Clara Bow, whom one of the tracks is named after. Additionally, fans tracked down cinematographic equivalents to previous work, such as the traced silhouette of Swift's face matching that in the "Style" music video as well as the swirling papers matching that in the "The Story of Us" music video and in the "Lover" *Saturday Night Live* performance. While the "Fortnight" music video came out on the same day as its album, the "ME! (feat. Brendon Urie of Panic! At The Disco)" music video was released four months ahead of *Lover*, the album it carried. The video starts with a snake, a symbol reflective of previous record *Reputation*, bursting into butterflies to pave the transition to a new era. It also contained clues for the next single ("You Need to Calm Down"), which Urie exclaims to Swift in the video, and the album title (*Lover*), which is spelled out on a building's bright pink sign. The next two records mirrored the *Reputation/Lover* paradigm. The music video for *evermore*'s first track and lead single, "willow," opens with Swift wearing the cardigan and holding the gold thread from *folklore*, the precursor to *evermore*.

Continuity cements worldbuilding and increases content engagement. In 2013, tech corporation Microsoft updated its Internet Explorer browser, which was first introduced in 1995. To promote the new and improved version, Microsoft ran a '90s-themed advertisement full of nostalgic references to growing up in the 1990s, including fanny packs, water guns, and Lunchables.[7] Key to the effort was the tagline, "You grew up. So did we. Reconnect with the *new* Internet Explorer." Microsoft was moving its users through an evolving product line, reminding them of where they've been (à la the *Reputation* snake) and showing them where they're going (à la the *Lover* butterflies). The clip earned top prize in the film category at

The Layered Musical Universe   51

Ads of the World by Clios, which honors excellence in advertising, and a nomination for "Best Online Commercial" at the Webby Awards, which honors excellence on the internet. More importantly, the campaign captivated its millennial audience with seven million views in five days and 28 million views in three months. The agency who worked on it with Microsoft, Column Five Media, explained, "We wanted the audience to think, 'Maybe Internet Explorer can relate to me better than I thought; the new browser could exceed my expectations.'…[B]y sharing the video, they were sharing the story…a story that might not lead everyone to switch browsers that day, but that would linger and grow in a generation's mind… [T]hat's the impact we wanted more than anything: a reframing of [Internet Explorer's] relationship with Gen Y."

In addition, other forms of art benefit from continuity. Co-creator of nine-season CBS television show *How I Met Your Mother*, Craig Thomas, emphasized the importance of coherence and consistency "within the universe of a show" and how he brought that into the writers' room: "We have a good core group of people that have been there the whole time, so there's a good safety net for remembering what we said in episode 18. And now we're in episode 73 or whatever, and it's tracking those things. That stuff really matters to me as a fan."[8] Since the show was framed as a dad (Ted) telling a story to his kids, its unreliable narrator trope had a built-in protective measure in case of continuity errors. However, the writers remained remarkably invested in their cosmos. One character's (Lily's) necklace from season 1, for example, is worn again by a new character (Zoey) in season 6 because Zoey had purchased Lily's stuff online. A core personality trait of one character (Marshall) was his belief in the supernatural, and a flash-forward scene reveals, via a newspaper headline, that Marshall had captured the Loch Ness Monster. The elaborate proposal from one character (Barney) to another (Robin) occurs over seven seemingly insignificant episodes until Robin, along with the audience, sees Barney on his knee. The highest rated episode of the series, according to IMDb, is the 200th episode, "How Your Mother Met Me." With detailed overlaps from plenty of previous episodes, this season 9 gem beautifully weaves the main characters' storylines from the past eight years with the titular mother's (Tracy's). The show's layers are supported by other Swift-like elements. One scene hyperbolizes the length of a conversation by telling a couple's

52   The Glory of Giving Everything

entire story in the background, from their first date to their son graduating to the woman becoming a widow. The plot alludes to Ted's favorite book, *Love in the Time of Cholera* by Gabriel García Márquez. Throughout the show, two theories of love are symbolized with a yellow umbrella (the show's version of, some might say, serendipitous fate à la the gold thread from "invisible string") and a blue French horn (the show's version of, some might say, active choice à la the chemistry of "The Alchemy"). For ultra fans, various websites created by the characters exist on the real world wide web (such as http://tedmosbyisnotajerk.com), lending legitimacy to the universe of *How I Met Your Mother*.

In Swift's musical universe, she is simultaneously the creator, the main character, and the driving force. As she questions to herself, "how far is too far in advance…three years?," to plan her next moves,[9] her ability to narrate real life as it happens to her with details often reserved for fictional settings like movies or sitcoms is impressive. Her real life does play a role in making each detail leap out of its melody. Realizing that "Karma" addresses a business betrayal by Swift's former record label, the song's smartest lyrics become the monetary figure of speech in the second verse, not the stream of choral metaphors. The mention of Swift's "pennies" making her enemy's crown can be linked to the more common English idiom, "a penny for your thoughts." In this way, Swift insinuates that beyond her label free-riding off of the literal money she had earned, they profited off of her original thinking as an artist. Swift then cautions that payment wouldn't be as simple as cash (the standard language of businessmen), but rather karma. "The Great War," which was repurposed to encapsulate the Eras Tour tickets calamity, contains even another meaning when considering who the song is about. Although the couple survives the war in the song, fans learned of their eventual demise. In accordance with history, the Great War was synonymous with World War I and was followed by World War II—a second war that Swift and her lover did not survive. This final blow is depicted in "So Long, London," a song in which Swift strays from overt war imagery to avoid overuse but softly cites the slogan "Keep Calm and Carry On" that the British stood by in preparation for World War II.[10] The Starting Line, fans know, is a favorite band of the paramour that "The Black Dog" is supposedly about.[11] Hence, going beyond its neatly packaged cross-reference in "Fresh Out The Slammer," The Starting Line becomes an intriguing

The Layered Musical Universe   53

component of the Swift universe. In "The Alchemy," laced with football references for beau Travis Kelce, Swift sings of blokes warming the benches; "bloke" is a British slang term for a man, an unusual decision given that football screams American culture.[12] Prior to Kelce, Swift was with actor Joe Alwyn ("Daylight"; "Dress"; "invisible string"; "The Great War") and musician Matty Healy ("The Black Dog"), both British folks. While it's possible that "bloke" had simply become a part of Swift's vocabulary, it's more fascinating to interpret the usage as intentional. As one learns lessons from every relationship, Alwyn and Healy—the blokes in Swift's life—prepared, or warmed the benches for, her to be with Kelce. Finally, fans who remember that the working title of *Lover* was *Daylight* were given a complete picture three years (true to form) after *Lover*'s release. Depicting the breakdown of Swift's relationship with Alwyn, *Midnights* (2022) seemed to be the antithesis to *Lover* (2019), a link made stronger by the trivia of the latter's original title.

Returning to *How I Met Your Mother*, actor Josh Radnor ("Ted") kept the blue French horn after the show's conclusion but left the yellow umbrella on set.[13] This furthered the French horn's meaning of person-driven, as opposed to destiny-driven, love. During the show's run, the real-life significant others of Alyson Hannigan ("Lily"), Neil Patrick Harris ("Barney"), and Cobie Smulders ("Robin") appeared as recurring supporting characters. As each were given storylines separate from those of their partners' characters, this was a sweet detail treasured by fans of the comedy, adding depth to the artistic product. (Fun Fact: Harris was the host for Swift's *SNL* debut in January 2009, where she performed "Love Story" and "Forever & Always" and shared the stage with Harris for the "Save Broadway" skit.[14])

Like any civilization, the residents of the Swiftverse have inaugurated unique customs. Pioneered by Swift, there are three categories of lyrics, based on which pen Swift imagines writing them with. These are not the orthodox genres of country, pop, and alternative, but rather idiosyncratic categories that she shared upon being crowned Songwriter-Artist of the Decade at the Nashville Songwriter Awards in 2022.[15] To solidify these concepts, Swift made three playlists for Apple Music with songs that belonged under each umbrella. The first bucket of lyricism is the Quill Pen, written in the style of (imaginary) Emily Dickinson's great grandmother and designed to make listeners feel like a "nineteenth-century poet crafting

54 The Glory of Giving Everything

[their] next sonnet by candlelight." *Red*'s "Sad Beautiful Tragic" and *evermore*'s "ivy" are among those composed with a quill. The most common classification is Fountain Pen lyricism, which shares moments "where you can see, hear, and feel everything in screaming detail," akin to an anonymous letter writer. One example is *folklore*'s only duet, "exile (feat. Bon Iver)," a haunting depiction of a disintegrating relationship dueted with Justin Vernon of indie folk band Bon Iver. Lastly, like a drunk girl doling out compliments in a club bathroom, some songs are jotted down with a Glitter Gel Pen and put people in the mood to "dance, sing, and toss glitter around the room." Such an ebullient song is "Today Was A Fairytale," written for the movie *Valentine's Day* (2010), which Swift acted in alongside a star-studded cast. With these inventive groupings, Swift continued to drive a distinct dialogue between her and her fans, creating her own language to push forward the significance of her lyrics.

A dialogue, though, is a two-way street, and there have been occasions where it originated outside of Swift. Pioneered by Swifties, every album's fifth track has become a coveted slot for Swift's deepest cuts. In July 2019, while promoting *Lover*, Swift acknowledged the ritual: "Track 5 is kind of a tradition that really started with you guys because I didn't realize I was doing this, but as I was making albums, I guess…instinctively I was just kind of putting a very vulnerable, personal, honest, emotional song as track 5."[16] Track 5s mentioned in this book so far: "White Horse" (*Fearless*), "Dear John" (*Speak Now*), "All Too Well" (*Red*), "All You Had To Do Was Stay" (*1989*), "Delicate" (*Reputation*), "The Archer" (*Lover*), "my tears ricochet" (*folklore*), "tolerate it" (*evermore*), "You're On Your Own, Kid" (*Midnights*), and "So Long, London" (*The Tortured Poets Department*). Test yourself: which is the missing album? Answer: "Cold As You" (*Taylor Swift*) concedes to an imperious heartbreaker. Both the track 5s and the lyric-spilling pens reinforce a communal vernacular that distinguishes Swift-related spaces from non-Swift-related spaces.

Developing shared branches that stem from a central root—in Swift's case, lyrics—keeps consumers hooked. Quirky grocery store Trader Joe's, for instance, labels its products in a way that animates supermarket visits, like Hold the Cone! Mini Ice Cream Cones and Everything But The Bagel Sesame Seasoning Brand.[17] Some of its international items are affectionately named Trader Giotto's, Trader José's, and Trader Ming's. Its version of Oreo

The Layered Musical Universe   55

cookies are known as Joe-Joe's, Joe-Joe being not a human trader but a toucan. Its guacamole servings are called Avocado's Number as a play on the mathematical Avogadro constant. When the company faced backlash for stereotypical tagging, it took the chance to reassess feedback from customers, who turned out to still align with Trader Joe's vision of fun product marketing. Inside each store, shoppers can enjoy full-sized wall murals tailored to local landmarks, and kids can entertain themselves by going on a hidden stuffed animal scavenger hunt, where the plushie also differs by store.[18] Employees are referred to as *crew members*, consistent with the uncommercialized merchant atmosphere. And while *Fearless* has a specific meaning for Swift and Swifties, it adopts a different one for Trader Joe's frequenters. The brand's periodically released *Fearless Flyer* provides the scoop on their latest and seasonal products, all while maintaining its breezy tone through informative, entertaining descriptions.[19]

Keeping customers in your universe also makes the experience attract people on the exterior of it. Ubiquitous consumer electronics company Apple denotes its products with a lowercase "i"—distinct offerings like the iPhone (smartphone), iPad (tablet), and iMac (computer); various apps like iTunes and iMovie; and popular features like iMessage and iCloud. Software updates are called iOS (with OS standing for "operating system"). This branding is far-reaching, as kids who use tablets are called "iPad kids" regardless of whether their tablet is an Apple product or not.[20] Anecdotally, children themselves refer to their devices as iPads or their parents' devices as iPhones regardless of whether those are Apple products or not. The corporation also eases communication between Apple users through a number of methods, including seamless messaging (iMessage), photo sharing (AirDrop), and video calling (FaceTime) between iPhones. Between an iPhone and a non-iPhone, text messages become the color of the dreaded green (instead of the welcoming blue), and photo sharing and video calling require extra steps to complete. Of course, the emotions associated with green and blue messages aren't inherent; they have emerged culturally. Despite potential qualms about the morals of the Apple and Android battle, all can agree that Apple has effectively cultivated a lifestyle. Even though both smartphone brands have fairly high customer retention rates, 18 percent of iPhone users are former Android users, compared to the only 11 percent of Android users who are former Apple users. Almost half of people who switched from Android to Apple

56   The Glory of Giving Everything

cited user experience as the motivation, while a lower proportion of people (30 percent) who switched in the reverse direction were prompted by user experience. Daily, Apple users engage more with their devices, spending nearly five hours on the screen, sending 58 texts, and snapping 12 selfies, while Android users looked at their phones for under four hours, wrote 26 texts, and took 7 selfies.[21] Again, although there may be arguments raised for and against the health of these users when it comes to screen time, ultimately Apple's strategies to spur product usage are successful.

Like Apple's signature "i" mark and Trader Joe's trader buddies, Swift generates intertwining touchpoints that expand on each other via song, media, and community interactions. This makes the value of her universe exponential, not linear. While her stories do unfold in albums over time (linearly), fans and critics alike write and rewrite interpretations (nonlinearly), with Swift encouragingly perpetuating the act. Whether it's through layered symbolism as with lasting color metaphors or through shared practices as with functional roles of arbitrary tracks, Swift's evolution can, and deserves to, be viewed from multidimensional angles. Another commentator, this time at pop culture site *Uproxx*, underscores the précis: "She has, rather brilliantly, convinced the public that her past *and* present coexist *right now*…she gets to be a 'legacy act' and a 'relevant pop act' simultaneously."[22] Swift reflected on the idea of nonlinearity when penning "Lover" (*Lover*). *Speak Now*'s title track tackled the wedding scene by infusing a naive fantasy, but *Lover*'s title track, written around the time the average woman does seriously consider marriage, embraced a classic wedding scene: "I wanted it to sort of exist in a timeless era, where you wouldn't be able to guess if it was being played at a wedding reception in 1980 or 1970 or now. So, there were no instruments that we used that were new instruments since things that were invented post '70s."[23] With a chorus of "simple, existential questions" and a bridge suggestive of eternal vows, the song's 2019 release date has little bearing on its situational place in the world. Scaling this timelessness up to her discography, Swift has masterfully created a world to revolve around the musings of her and her followers.

5 | Fans: Consumer and Stakeholder

One of Swift's favorite songs she has ever composed is the lead single of 2022's *Midnights*, "Anti-Hero," which is a self-proclaimed map of her insecurities.[1] When it entered radio, casual pop enjoyers everywhere were alerted to her perceived misfit due to her towering height (5'10" or 5'11" depending on who and when you ask[2]), her fear of her benevolence being stripped down to a personality disorder, and her nightmare of a broken future family. Swift expressed her surprise at receiving Song of the Year for "Anti-Hero" at the iHeartRadio Music Awards in 2023, given that hit bops typically needed to be simple and stuck in everyone's heads.[3] On the surface, her choice of "Anti-Hero" as the first single, motivated only by an adoration of the song and not by a strategic selection, seemed to defy her usual pattern of putting out a radio-conforming lead single and reserving deep cuts for the rest of the album. In Swift's pop utopia, the lead singles tend to be armed with the definitive purpose of setting the tone of the forthcoming album. "Shake It Off," the musical introduction to *1989*, was catchy with two key messages: that of the song itself, which was to be free of negativity, and that of the larger cultural discourse, which was that Swift's genre reinvention was on the way. It was such a departure from the known Swift at the time that after its release, Ed Sheeran texted Swift to inform her

58 The Glory of Giving Everything

that clubbers were dancing to "Shake It Off," and she was ecstatic: "You know that's my only dream…for people to dance to one of my songs. Because usually people just cry to my songs."[4] Yet, the album treated fans who, like Zooey Deschanel's character in *New Girl* (a sitcom in which Swift guest-starred), still wanted to shed tears to Swift's music after a breakup. *1989* invited listeners to dance to "Shake It Off" but also to pine in regret ("I Wish You Would"), revel in serendipity ("This Love"), and emerge in rebirth ("Clean"). During an interview about *Speak Now* some years earlier, Swift had discussed the heart that goes into album creation: "I'm really, really in love with the idea of making an album. I don't really have much of an interest in having a few possible radio singles and then filling in the blanks with whatever you have. For me, putting out an album means that every song on that album has to be something that I thought was the best thing I've ever written when I wrote it."[5]

Upon closer inspection, the decidedly vulnerable "Anti-Hero" remains an innovative lead single but still follows in the footsteps of its predecessors. The sentiments of genuine despair are anchored by resounding self-deprecating identifications of Swift as a problem that is annoying yet approachable. The music video adopts a humorous take on the lyrics, with the graveyard shift depression manifesting as bedsheet-style ghosts and Swift's destructive habits being encouraged by a fun-loving doppelgänger. Size and color throughout the video are mystical elements rather than realistic representations, as a sparkly purple ooze serves as a substitute for the more unpleasant sensations of blood and puke, and a giant Swift altar ego appears at the end to join original Swift and doppelgänger Swift's rooftop party of acceptance. At Swift's imagined funeral, her future sons and daughter-in-law read her will and see that she has left everything to her cats. Despite the heavy subject matter contained within the track, the subject matter surrounding the track is more lighthearted and doesn't take itself too seriously. For newer listeners, "Anti-Hero" operates as an entry point that allows them to feel like they know Swift—a feature of her brand—but at the same time is unintimidating. If these listeners dared to venture further, they could check out the stories of 13 sleepless nights on the 13 songs of the standard edition of *Midnights*. Devoted fans, on the other hand, were more likely to stream *Midnights (3am Edition)*. This edition was a surprise arrival three hours after the release of the standard edition and featured

Fans: Consumer and Stakeholder

seven additional tracks, none of which were singles nor part of the Eras Tour setlist. The last of these seven was a cautionary tale entitled "Dear Reader," a letter from Swift at the pinnacle of her anti-heroism. "Dear Reader" discards the trust relationship between her and her fans, imploring them to find another role model to latch on to for their own good. Swift lays out pieces of advice that characterize human fight or flight responses, and then discredits the advice by discrediting herself. With no promotional materials, "Dear Reader" materializes as the true exposé of Swift's fragility. Here, Swift crumbles under the weight of loneliness, comparing her life to a game of solitaire that she is nonetheless losing. "Anti-Hero" states what her insecurities are; "Dear Reader" details the consequences of being consumed by them for herself and everyone around her.

The contrast of "Anti-Hero" and "Dear Reader" demonstrates the high-friction acquisition system of the Swift fandom, affectionately known as Swifties. Under this system, occupancy of the Taylor Swift universe is both broad and deep, and different layers of friction are applied at each level of being a fan. Casual listeners can be content with adding Swift's music into their playlists or humming along to her songs in public. At the same time, they're able to explore at a deeper level if they'd like. The next level might consist of listening to entire albums beyond the hits, watching her performances (in person or online), and/or joining in Swift-related trends like making friendship bracelets. Fans at this level might relate to several songs and feel uplifted by Swift's energy. At the penultimate level, people engage with all aspects of the Swift universe, navigating through its layers both spatially and temporally. Concrete actions at this stage include locating and interpreting Easter eggs in Swift's creations as well as staying updated on Swift's ongoing announcements, interviews, and current events in real time. A subset of these fans iterate on Swift's material to produce their own output, whether that's drawing up lesson plans in casual or formal settings or creating artwork in multiple media. Our friend at *The New Yorker* assigned "thousands of comments under Instagram posts, an additional 332 million dollars for the NFL, a worldwide run on bracelet beads, and the Fed wondering why inflation persists" as belonging to Swift's universe, observing, "[T]he music…serves a crucial purpose. But this purpose is different depending on whether you're a diehard Swiftie or a casual listener…Most musicians—and artists more generally—can only dream of their fan base

60   The Glory of Giving Everything

picking up on such subtleties." For a diehard Swiftie, this fandom is an essential component of their identity. Such a person dreams of making it to the transcendent level of Swiftiedom, where an in-person or virtual Swift interaction is within reach.

Broadly, Swift's universe has been continuously accessible over its 18 years of existence. To increase one's fandom at any given point, one need not (but is welcome to) go back to her debut album to deepen an appreciation for the current era. Every era parades radio singles and accompanying music videos that can get the attention of casual listeners, and every era provides avenues for advancement beyond those. The rollout of *The Tortured Poets Department (TTPD)* stunningly illustrated this. Approaching *TTPD*'s release date, Swift created five playlists of her songs on Apple Music that correlated with the five stages of grief: "I Love You, It's Ruining My Life Songs" for denial, "You Don't Get to Tell Me About Sad Songs" for anger, "Am I Allowed to Cry? Songs" for bargaining, "Old Habits Die Screaming Songs" for depression, and "I Can Do It with a Broken Heart Songs" for acceptance.[6] Each playlist was named after a *TTPD* lyric. Instead of having fans wait idly for her album, she used these playlists to direct attention to her previous music and place herself front of mind. By explicitly connecting parts of her discography to widely known psychological terms, she not only guided people's listening journeys to prepare for the new album, but also more permanently categorized her work, emphasizing her role as the narrator of humankind hardships. This was cultivated even further when after the album came out, each playlist was updated to include *TTPD* tracks. Still, pressing Play on the mood playlists in anticipation of *TTPD* would be quite frictionless for any fan level. Knowing this, Swift added another level as the world tiptoed closer to the release date of April 19, 2024. Within the lyrics of the songs on the playlists, certain letters were capitalized. Fans hunted for these letters, found in one song per day over the course of six days, and unscrambled it all at the end to spell out, "WE HEREBY CONDUCT THIS POST MORTEM," which ended up being a lyric on the record. For these triumphant fans, the playlists turned up the hype and set them up to truly savor the album upon its arrival, having felt like they were active participants in, as opposed to passive recipients of, its release.

All inhabitants of the Swift universe, whether they own a vacation cabin or live full-time in a manor, are equal and protected citizens who

Fans: Consumer and Stakeholder 61

roam as they please. In choosing their own adventure, those who occasionally whisk themselves to the outskirts of town opt to be proximal to Swift enthusiasm by liking some of her songs or albums, while those in the trenches of lunar valleys opt to succumb to Swift frenzy. When fans level up, they are rewarded for doing so, as each piece of knowledge immerses them in a culturally rich experience. In the case of *TTPD*, listeners would be able to catch themes of insanity and dramatism by virtue of the lyrics. Fans who pay closer attention would learn that Swift views the "Department" as a government municipal building where poets' minds and behaviors are studied.[7] Those who follow Swift's official social media pages would find themselves hooked on the concept with emblematic marketing efforts such as describing a performance as meeting minutes. The higher a fan goes, the more friction is applied, as it becomes more difficult to renege to nonchalance. Importantly, however, when fans decide not to level up, they are not punished. They are embraced with gratitude—"Shake It Off" and "Anti-Hero" were Eras Tour regulars, and "I Wish You Would," "This Love," "Clean," and "Dear Reader" were not.

By invoking this system, Swift appeals to a mainstream audience while preserving a sense of closeness with her most invested fans. Beauty brand Sephora structures its rewards program, called Beauty Insider Benefits, similarly. The Insider tier is complimentary to join and comes with perks like free shipping, a birthday gift, and 10 percent off at seasonal savings events. To be a VIB, or a Very Important Beauty Insider, a shopper must spend $350 on Sephora products a year. For VIBs, the seasonal discount is bumped up to 15 percent, and exclusive gifts are available in addition to the free shipping and birthday presents. Patrons who spend at least $1,000 a year at Sephora are eligible for Rouge status. Along with the rewards of the other two levels, Rouge Insiders get first access to products and a higher seasonal discount of 20 percent. Like Swift, Sephora has designed a system that is inviting to all consumers while offering opportunities for more exclusive involvement. It has paid off: 81 percent of Sephora's customers return (as of 2022), and the 17 million (as of 2018) Beauty Insider members constitute 80 percent of the retailer's sales.[8] Indeed, loyal customers generally spend an average of $61 more per month (as of 2023).[9]

Fans of Swift, then, take on two active roles beyond that of simple listeners. First, they become regular consumers of the Swift enterprise. Sephora

62 The Glory of Giving Everything

Beauty Insiders at the VIB or Rouge level frequently return to Sephora for cosmetic products; Swifties choose to hold up their end of the mutual connection with Swift through their resources, which are often, but not always, monetary. In terms of our civilization metaphor, fans renew the lease or continue to pay the mortgage on their property because they enjoy residence in the Swift universe. Upkeep of the environment is meticulously managed by Swift herself. While it's not uncommon for individuals and businesses to decide between quantity and quality, she forgoes that trade-off altogether and makes no sacrifice in delivering on both metrics. In regard to quantity, she has consistently kept her products on the market. With *Midnights*, she made history by becoming the first artist to claim all Top 10 spots on the Billboard Hot 100, a sweep made possible by her focused dedication. As it neared the end of the tracking week, she dropped a "Bejeweled" music video as well as "Bejeweled" and "Question…?" instrumental versions, securing their placements on the chart.[10] On a larger scale, since debuting in 2006, Swift has released music in some way, shape, or form every single year, as outlined in Exhibit 5.1. While this is not exhaustive because it doesn't include every remix or songs on which she has a writing credit but does not sing, we can already see that she is constantly creating.

Whenever she is presenting her current album on tour and at awards shows, she'll be vigorously plotting for her next album. With producer Nathan Chapman, Swift was beginning to record new ideas for *Speak Now* right after the launch of *Fearless*, posting online: "I've been in the studio all day (I know, I know. We JUST put out a new album. I think I have a problem, I cannot stop writing songs.)…I like dragging it out, that way you can be meticulous about every detail. Daydream about different ways to put the songs together, and then take them apart. I'm pretty obsessed with the whole process. So needless to say, it was good to be back in the studio with my redheaded producer who I missed terribly."[11] *Speak Now*'s "Long Live," Swift's show of appreciation to her crew and fans, was penned as the curtain closed on the last stop of the Fearless Tour in Foxborough on June 5, 2010. On June 9, 2010, the seed for *Speak Now*'s "The Story of Us" was planted when she ran into ex John Mayer at the Country Music Television Awards, where she was nominated for *Fearless*'s "You Belong With Me." Upon completion of the song the following week, Swift closed the writing chapter of her only entirely solo-authored album to date. *Speak Now* was released a

Fans: Consumer and Stakeholder

Year	Release
Musical Releases Over the Years	
2006	*Taylor Swift*
2007	*iTunes Live from Soho; The Taylor Swift Holiday Collection*
2008	*Beautiful Eyes; Fearless*
2009	"Crazier"; "Two Is Better Than One (feat. Taylor Swift)" by Boys Like Girls; *Fearless (Platinum Edition)*; "Half of My Heart" by John Mayer & Taylor Swift
2010	"Today Was a Fairytale"; *Speak Now*
2011	*Speak Now World Tour – Live*; "Safe & Sound (feat. The Civil Wars)"
2012	"Eyes Open"; "Both Of Us (feat. Taylor Swift)" by B.o.B; *Red*
2013	"Highway Don't Care (feat. Taylor Swift & Keith Urban)" by Tim McGraw; "Sweeter Than Fiction (From "One Chance")"
2014	*1989*
2015	"Bad Blood feat. Kendrick Lamar"
2016	"I Don't Wanna Live Forever (Fifty Shades Darker)" by ZAYN & Taylor Swift
2017	*Reputation*
2018	"September – Recorded at The Tracking Room Nashville" (cover); "Delicate – Recorded at The Tracking Room Nashville"; "Babe (feat. Taylor Swift)" by Sugarland
2019	*Lover*; "Beautiful Ghosts"; "Christmas Tree Farm"
2020	"Only The Young (Featured in Miss Americana)"; *folklore; evermore*
2021	"Gasoline (Remix)" by HAIM & Taylor Swift; *Fearless (Taylor's Version)*; "Renegade (feat. Taylor Swift)" by Big Red Machine; *Red (Taylor's Version)*
2022	*Midnights;* "Carolina (From The Motion Picture "Where The Crawdads Sing")"
2023	"The Alcott (feat. Taylor Swift)" by The National; *Speak Now (Taylor's Version); 1989 (Taylor's Version)*
2024	*The Tortured Poets Department;* "us. (feat. Taylor Swift)" by Gracie Abrams

Exhibit 5.1   Musical Releases Over the Years

short four months later. In 2024, she arrived at the Grammys, where *Midnights* was a nominee in a few categories, thoroughly prepared for *The Tortured Poets Department*.[12] Aside from a watch necklace subtly set to midnight, the rest of her outfit signified the upcoming record's color scheme with a white dress and nails and black gloves, shoes, and jewelry. Leading up to the awards ceremony, technology contributed as well. Swift, along with several folks in her inner circle, intentionally changed her Instagram profile picture to black and white. On the day of the Grammy Awards, she programmed

64 The Glory of Giving Everything

her website to glitch, leaving eagle-eyed fans to decipher the clues in the ensuing error message. All was revealed when she announced *The Tortured Poets Department* live on air when accepting the 2024 Grammy Award for Best Pop Vocal Album for *Midnights*. Even if she hadn't won, she would have announced the news at the next stop of the Eras Tour in Tokyo. These practices have created an endless loop of activity that persistently works in her favor.

Swift also fully commits to quality in every aspect of her career. The key to the success of her output velocity has been that each release simultaneously fits in with the other products and brings something new to the table. Her interpretation of positive feedback on one of her albums illuminates this, as she shared with the Recording Academy (the host of the Grammy Awards): "I didn't take that as, so I should make that again. I took that as great, awesome, now I want to make them like this new album just as much [as], if not more than, the last album. But I want them to like it for different reasons."[13] There is nothing that she hates more, as she notes in *The Official Taylor Swift | The Eras Tour Book*, than doing what she'd always done. When making *Red*, which came after *Speak Now*, Swift reached out to her musical inspirations to collaborate with her. Although she had initially planned to stick only with Chapman, she had a "sinking feeling" that *Red* was meant to go beyond her comfort zone.[14] Through reinvention, Swift keeps longtime fans invested while expanding her consumer base with various styles. Quarantine album *folklore* embodied cottagecore, a cozy vibe influenced by agriculture and nature and infused into interior design and clothing. Cottagecore gained traction in 2019 and exploded in popularity in 2020. With #cottagecore garnering more than nine billion views on TikTok, this trend has widely been implemented by Gen Z. After having captivated millennials through her relatability, Swift (a millennial) conquered the younger generation, who called *folklore* one of the best albums of 2020.[15] At the age of 22, Swift was already wondering what she'd be doing at the age of 30, confessing to *Vogue*: "I fret about the future. What my next move should be. What the move after that should be. How I am going to sustain this. How do I evolve. I get so ahead of myself."[16] From the current vantage point, some might say that she had no need to worry, but that would undermine the hard work that materialized out of the validity of her concerns, leading her to where she is today. (It was nice to see Swift, at the age of 30, celebrating the means by which happiness informs her art in another *ELLE* essay, "30 Things I Learned Before Turning 30."[17])

By sculpting eras, Swift elevates each of her albums beyond the direct elements, such as lyrics and production, that make up a musical body of work. Eras, in contrast to albums, consist of intangible components such as the concomitant backstories (recall *Speak Now*'s imaginary wedding disruption), emotions (recall *Red*'s short-lived, hot-burning portrayals), and colors (recall *TTPD*'s black and white). The force of these intangibles are at play every year when the days begin to shorten and an unusual trend occurs: *folklore* and *evermore* rise on the charts as listeners seek out cottagecore for the impending autumn.[18] Most recently, in October 2024, *evermore* jumped by around 60 percent on various Billboard charts and *folklore* jumped up by 13 spots (a number Swift would appreciate), designating seasons as part of the intangibles contributing to the sister eras. Swift drew on these intangibles to paint her nails 10 different colors while performing the Eras Tour.[19] Fans understood instantly that each one represented a specific era of her career (this was prior to her 11th album, *TTPD*), and more pertinently, which era each nail corresponded to. Eras also contain a multitude of tangible components like outfits, music videos, performances, honors, and interviews that enliven the music. During the photoshoot for *Speak Now*, Swift likened such tangibles to the pictures that supplement a storybook: "I try to approach each song differently when it comes to my albums. It has to fit within the general theme of the album in order to fit on the album. But as far as representing them in the album booklet visually, I just go straight to the lyrics. You have to make sure that every mood that you want to capture is somewhere…on [the photographer's] camera."[20]

All of these elements, tangible and intangible, made the 2023–2024 Eras Tour what it was and separated it from merely being a "Greatest Hits" tour. Distinguishing sets and costumes made the eras coruscate. *Lover*'s "Lover" was played on alternating guitars of pale pink, blue, and lavender shades, and *evermore*'s "champagne problems" was performed on a moss-covered grand piano. The *Red* era recreated 2013's "22" music video outfit of a fedora, sequined t-shirt, shorts, and Oxford shoes, and the *1989* era called back to the two-piece crop top looks of 2015's 1989 World Tour. A rustic cabin, one of Swift's favorite pieces, encapsulated the *folklore* era. Fans were not only engrossed in each distinguishing section, but they were incorporated in them. Every night, a lucky fan was picked from the crowd to receive the 22 hat, which Swift had signed on the inside. Overwhelmed with joy, these fans would often give Swift a friendship bracelet. During *Reputation*'s "Delicate," Swift looked forward to the fan-invented "1, 2, 3, let's go b*tch!" chanted by the crowd to lead in the beat drop. *Fearless*'s "Love Story" was not exempt, on this tour, from marriage proposals to the sound of Romeo proposing to Juliet, a longtime tradition Swift acknowledged in *The Official Taylor Swift | The Eras Tour Book*. Some 50 pages later, she credited the fans for turning "Enchanted" into "one of the most recognizable songs" from *Speak Now* despite it never having been a single, motivating her to select the six-minute track to stand alone on this era on the tour. As the Eras Tour swept the globe, the word "eras" itself became more widespread, with people fathoming their life stories and directions in terms of eras. The "in my... era" trend went viral on TikTok, the platform of choice for a generation known for identity explorations. The phrase was sometimes completed with Swift's eras but often self-coined ones, like "in my healing era" or "in my villain era." At the end of 2023, Dictionary.com unveiled its inaugural "Vibe of the Year" award (its "Word of the Year" award has been running since 2010), and "eras" was rightfully the winner.[21] In 2024, actress Anna Kendrick was proclaimed to be in her "soft girl era" after she made her directorial debut with *Woman of the Hour*, a crime thriller based on the true story of serially murdered women.[22]

The juxtaposition of the *Reputation* and *Lover* albums exemplifies the distinct packaging of eras as well. The 2017 and 2019 records had opposite aesthetics, the former a defensive dark and the latter a feminine pastel, and ran parallel to opposite career markers, the former Swift's retreat from the public eye and the latter Swift's foray into politics. However, the two are more closely related than they appear. Lyrically, they both contemplate the beauty of a fulfilling romance and are primarily inspired by Joe Alwyn. Thematically is where they differ, and taken together, the two albums convey the message that love is for both the tough and the soft. The sheer number of eras and their distinguishing features allow ample people to find themselves in the star's varied facets that complement their diverse preferences. Considerable amounts of online discussion have centered on the personality of each Swift era,[23] and fans eagerly attach their breadth of experiences to handpicked eras. A couple who is in love and in their *Reputation* era has

Fans: Consumer and Stakeholder   67

different energy from their friends who are in love and in their *Lover* era. A broken heart that replays memories cathartically while blasting *Red* heals differently from a broken heart that finds solace in the mournful wisdom of *evermore*. A person in between, not quite in love and not quite broken-hearted, might ruminate in a backward-looking manner via *Speak Now* or forecast in a forward-looking manner via *1989*. Overarchingly, the same people undergo transformations and express their biological, societal, or idiosyncratic milestones by moving between eras, as Swift has done. More than a series of songs, every era is a collection of maxims.

Perhaps one of the most fascinating case studies is that of a fan whose life could not have turned out more disparate from Swift's—a prisoner in Los Angeles County Jail named Joe Garcia.[24] Garcia's exposure to her was slow but steady, interspersed between noisy celebrity gossip during television privileges. Tracks from *Red* reminded Garcia of his sweetheart prior to the murder he committed, and tunes from *1989* gave him and his fellow inmates something to bond over, something that tied them to the "world [they] had left behind." Most prominently, Garcia felt seen in his days and nights by "Daylight" and *Midnights*. When Swift wrote the "Daylight" chorus of an agonizing 20-year slumber, she likely didn't imagine that she would appeal to locked-up convicts. But for Garcia, that took on a specific meaning. Under a California law passed not long after *Lover's* release, those above the age of 50 who had served 20 consecutive years in jail would be eligible for parole. For the first time in a long time, Garcia saw daylight. As he approached his parole hearing, he pondered the existential crises of "Anti-Hero" in his own life, posed the cosmic questions of "Karma" to himself, and wondered about the ways his sleepless nights mirrored Swift's.

While it may seem that mood and vision boards are only advantageous to products that lend themselves to touching lives, such as the creative arts, that isn't true. The marketing savants behind the beloved M&M candy designed a crew of "spokescandies," breathing life into classic M&M colors. Customers who visit M&M's website are introduced to Red, Yellow, Orange, Purple, Green, Brown, and Blue, who each have their own greetings and profile picture poses and answer a few icebreaker questions in a way that showcases their personalities.[25] The spokescandies have been at the forefront of several successful campaigns, but the most famous one is the "They Do Exist" Christmas commercial. In the 16-second ad set to Pyotr Ilyich

Tchaikovsky's *Dance of the Sugar Plum Fairy*, Red and Yellow are about to put a bowl of M&Ms (humorously, a treat of their own kind) under the Christmas tree for Santa. They come face-to-face with Santa, who is already at their house. In shock, Red exclaims, "He does exist!"; equally in shock, Santa responds, "They do exist…" Red and Santa faint on the spot, leaving Yellow with the bowl of candy unsure of what to do next. The clip then ends with the tagline "Always Fun." The commercial has aired every year since premiering at the Christmas Tree Lighting in Rockefeller Center in 1996, and even earned a sequel. In 2017, "Faint 2: A Very Yellow Sequel" aired. As the last man standing, Yellow believes it is his duty to save Christmas. He mounts Santa's sleigh and distributes the presents on Santa's list. Come Christmas morning, everyone has received a gift, but the wrong one. As Yellow fears that he has done more harm than good, neighbors are seen exchanging gifts and sparking the holiday spirit, and Red tells him that he made the holiday even better. "Bring Everyone Together With M&M's" is the tagline that closes the commercial.

The spokescandies' storylines in these commercials reflect their personalities. Charismatic, perfectionist Red is unequipped to handle surprises like meeting Santa. Naive, endearing Yellow doesn't faint because he hasn't grasped the extremity of the situation. When he gives out the gifts, he messes up the recipients, but his good intentions shine through as he turns out to amplify the people's Christmas cheer. Red, quickly assessing the verifiable effects of Yellow's actions, is able to instinctively comfort his buddy. The character development of Red, Yellow, and the other colors through M&M's advertisements positively impacts consumers' relationship with the chocolate brand. When snacking on the colorful candy, people are inclined to remember the associated personas. They might chuckle to themselves, or they might take it further by discussing with friends which M&M they identify with. Aided by the multitude of online "Which M&M are you?" quizzes, the spokescandies become archetypes, or representations of universal patterns in the human psyche. Blue is the chill friend you'd grab a beer with; Brown is the professional colleague you'd run ideas by. Like classic characters, archetypes conceptualize the familiar tropes that people encounter recurrently. Swiss psychiatrist Carl Jung defined 12 archetypal figures that reside in our collective unconscious: the Innocent, the Everyman, the Hero, the Caregiver, the Explorer, the Rebel, the Lover, the Creator, the

Fans: Consumer and Stakeholder   69

Jester, the Sage, the Magician, and the Ruler. He also acknowledged that the fusing of primary archetypes is possible and should correlate with the realities of life: "There are as many archetypes as there are typical situations in life. Endless repetition has engraved these experiences into our psychic constitution, not in the forms of images filled with content, but at first only as forms without content, representing merely the possibility of a certain type of perception and action."[26] Many of us have a dominant archetype, but over the course of our lives, access and channel the other ones depending on the, for lack of a better word, era that we are in.

More mythical than technical, the Jungian archetypes have not necessarily been proven or debunked. Nevertheless, they constitute a striking place in the psychology literature and a philosophical framework to examine Swift's catalog. Her writing is specific yet ubiquitous—not all of us are insecure about our height, but we all certainly have had moments of considering ourselves the problem. Her eras supply a guiding light as to how the phases of her life coalesce in ways that are flexible for fans to emulate. In "I Think He Knows" (*Lover*), Swift excitedly skips down 16th Avenue, which is part of Music Row in Nashville and hence significant to her own lore. The song omits the district or city name, though, to let the listener think of their own personal geographic signifier of elation (another city, San Francisco, boasts a landmark of a mosaic staircase on its own 16th Avenue[27]). The people, places, and desires that Swift sings about transcend mere objects and become archetypal characters, signs, and qualities. Caught between the sweet nerd and popular cheerleader (both played by Swift in the music video) in "You Belong With Me" (*Fearless*), the male football player makes a predictable decision that we all nonetheless root for because it calls a moral code into question. The addressee in "Would've, Could've, Should've" (*Midnights*) is not only about John Mayer (who is over a decade older than Swift), but represents the pain of a loss of youth, no matter what or who the cause. The detractor for whom "Mean" (*Speak Now*) was written is not just a music critic in our collective discourse, but an oppressor that we all must face at some point. The music video supports this rewriting, as it shows a fashion-interested boy being bullied by the football team, a fast food employee being taunted by the patrons, and a girl ostracized at lunch by her pink-ribboned classmates for wearing a blue ribbon. By the end of the video, the boy is acclaimed in the fashion industry, receiving recognition

70 The Glory of Giving Everything

from peers and fans; the fast food worker, who had been saving up for college, is a big-time executive; and the blue-ribboned girl is the only invitee to Swift's concert.

These all summon the listener to interweave their own stories into Swift's work. Fairy tales and their magic have endured in our culture due to their mutability,[28] and in a parallel manner, this sheds light on why Swift's music has lasted. Fans become consumers not because they want to follow her, but because they want to be her. A less dramatic claim—those deep within the high-friction acquisition system remain locked in because she provides a backdrop to not only know her, but to know themselves. It isn't a parasocial fixation on Swift's personal life; it's a healthy interest in their personal lives. Key to Swift's business mind is that she encourages this, not just through digital media like songs and music videos, but through purchasable items. To accompany the album *Lover*, she put out four diaries that recorded her thoughts from the ages of 13 to 27. The handwritten booklets were filled with insights on public events ("September 18, 2009, 19 years: [I]f you told me that Kanye West would have been the number one focus of...my part in the VMAs, I would've looked at you crossed-eyed. If you had told me that I would win the award I was nominated for, I wouldn't have believed you. And if you had told me that one of the biggest stars in music was going to jump onstage and announce that he thought I shouldn't have won on live television, I would've said 'that stuff doesn't really happen in real life.' Well...apparently...it does."); references to career catalysts ("January 25, 2014, 24 years: "...the Grammys are tomorrow...Never have I wanted something as badly as I want to hear them say 'Red' is the album of the year."); and musings on everyday occurrences ("October 15, 2003, 13 years: I really have decided school is a big disappointment...I guess I'm just not good enough for people my own age. Or maybe I'm not bad enough?"; "January 5, 2014, 24 years: Dating is awful. Love is fiction/a myth. I'm over it all."; "January 3, 2017, 27 years: But it's senseless to worry about someday not being happy when I am happy now."). The year 2016 has only one short entry ("August 29, 2016, 26 years: This summer is the apocalypse.")—it seems that the incidents of that year not only distanced her from the public, but from the tender version of herself she treasured even in private. Most notably, though, the journals included blank pages at the end, pages meant for the buyer to draft their

Fans: Consumer and Stakeholder

own feelings. "Emotion," according to communication and culture scholar Margaret Rossman, "is translated to currency, something that can be performed for a return on investment."[29] By creating space for fans to journal alongside her after years of attention on her own musical diaries, Swift was aligning herself with her consumers, and capitalizing on it.

Swift packaged the *Midnights* vinyls similarly, in a collectible set of four. When put together, all four vinyls—the Jade Green Edition, the Blood Moon Edition, the Mahogany Edition, and the Lavender Edition—formed a clock. *Midnights* was the highest selling vinyl of 2022, making up one out of every 25 vinyls sold in the United States and surpassing the vinyl sales of the next two artists combined, Harry Styles and The Beatles.[30] Fans, most of whom were ingrained in the streaming age, were going out of their way to buy not only one vinyl but four. This can be attributed in part to the innovative clock design. Rossman noted the "central" role of collection in fan status, with items such as the journals and vinyls intended not solely for writing in or listening to but also for being a "specific way of showing their fandom to the rest of the fan community." Another driver of this era's vinyl purchasing is, again, fans striving to understand themselves. Out of all the album prologues, the prologue to *Midnights* is the only one written entirely in the second person. In it, Swift hounds the reader: "What keeps you up at night?...*What must they all think of you*...You've gotten lost in the labyrinth of your head, where the fear wraps its claws around the fragile throat of true love. Will you be able to save it in time? Save it from who? Well, it's obvious. From you." The other prologues see Swift comment on the making of the record from her unique perspective, but *Midnights* refrains from any mentions of "I" or "me." Pronouns are all an ambiguous "you" or a general "we": "Isn't it mystifying how quickly we vacillate between self love and loathing at this hour?...We lie awake in love and in fear and in turmoil and in tears...hoping that just maybe, when the clock strikes twelve[,] we'll meet ourselves." Swift put herself on the backburner, asking fans to take the lead on introspection this time, to "keep the lanterns lit and go searching." Fans' consumption is the result.

The patterns of Swift and the Swiftie become salient when extricated from immediate economic ties with each other. Swift's clean versions of albums demonstrate her impulse to cater to fans, even when it isn't meant for consumerism. For every record marked as explicit, Swift prepares a version for those with children or clean preferences. She makes the effort to record new versions of explicit songs replacing the swear words with actual words instead of bleeping them out. Examples are *evermore*'s "gold rush" replacing "contrarian sh*t" with "contrarian wit" and *TTPD*'s "Down Bad" replacing "f*ck it if I can't have him" with "what if I can't have him." Clean listeners can then thoroughly enjoy these albums, without having to be reminded of the explicit versions during those songs. On the Swifties' end, they echo her habits and values, even when it doesn't directly involve her. In the United States and the United Kingdom, half of beginner guitar players are women, an unprecedented phenomenon labeled the sustaining "Taylor Swift factor" by guitar brand Fender, which has since strengthened its relationships with female artists.[31] Evidence can be mined from the bold signs in the audience at the Fearless Tour, fan declarations of "I PLAY GUITAR BECAUSE OF U" and "I WANT 2 B LIKE TAYLOR!!" Swift's acoustically accessible compositions help facilitate this trend, layering complex melodies over manageable chord progressions. For instance, when she performed a genre-mixing mashup of "Getaway Car" (*Reputation*), "august" (*folklore*), and "The Other Side of the Door" (*Fearless*), she used the same four chords (D, A, Em, and G) in the same order throughout. While she often plays intricate strumming patterns and incorporates decorative techniques (such as hammering on or pulling off strings, or alternating variations of basic chords), new guitar players can still get through quite a few of her songs, straightforward sing-along style, by knowing a handful of chords. Swift was able to write her first song, "Lucky You," at the age of 12, after she learned three chords (C, G, and D). The song remains unreleased except for a leaked demo, but she maintained this viewpoint throughout her career. Imogen Heap, who co-wrote "Clean" (*1989*) with Swift, blogged about the writing process: "[W]e tried a few things out. One of which had me going over to the keyboard to suggest a slightly 'odd' chord progression as I do like a bit of that on my own records. I played it to Taylor and she quite clearly said 'I think we're going to lose them at this point' and I said[,] '[W]ow... that is why you sell millions of records and I don't!'...I learned that lesson again, keep it simple. I just never seem to remember it!"[32] For the final cut of "Clean," instead of the "odd" chord progression, Heap created tension and a woosh right before the last chorus.

Fans: Consumer and Stakeholder 73

Speaking of guitars, in 2024, a bride-to-be put up her autographed-by-Swift guitar for sale on Facebook to fund her wedding.[33] A guitar player herself, the instrument had been a focal point of adolescent memories, but it was a necessary resort, and she believed it could bring value to others. The outpouring of responses she received was unexpected. Swifties, drawing on their own experiences with regard to Swift, knew the sentiments behind such a piece without even knowing the bride personally. They insisted on contributing to the wedding expenses out of pocket so that she wouldn't need to part with the guitar. A GoFundMe was set up with a goal of $1,813, and the couple raised $9,251 by the time of their special day. The signed guitar, as it should, continued its reign over significant moments in the bride's life. In this way, the connection that Swift fostered between her and her fans extends to the acts of kindness within the fan community. Although she might not hear of this specific story, she thanked all her fans at the end of the Eras Tour for embodying "joy and acceptance" at the shows and conveyed the hope that they would continue that practice in their lives, schools, and jobs.[34]

Besides creating the canvas for fans to paint their own colors on, Swift invests in her fans. Recall the $1.50 hot dog from Costco, an item first offered in the mid-1980s that is no longer profitable for the retail warehouse. Comparably, Swift prioritizes the people who consume her products. For the Eras Tour, she deliberately opted out of the dynamic pricing model, which increases price in response to demand (more on the resale market, where this did happen, in Chapter 7). "Because she was considering her career in the long run," wrote *The Economic Times*, "she was prepared to make choices that might reduce her income."[35] She also allocates time to meet with fans, even though she could be spending that time in the studio or on the stage, both places that contribute directly to her monetary gain. In 2016, she surprised a couple at their New Jersey wedding, performing the groom's favorite song, "Blank Space," on the keyboard during the reception and gifting the happy couple a framed card saying "So it's gonna be forever" with their names and wedding date.[36] She posed for photos afterward and sweetly posted them on her own Instagram account. While this was a surprise for the bride, groom, and guests, the visit had been planned for months leading up to the big day by the

74   The Glory of Giving Everything

sister of the groom. She had written to Swift to share about their mother's passing. The couple had tied the knot in the hospital to include her and set the groom's last mother–son dance to "Blank Space." Evidently, Swift was touched and agreed to the appearance.

Additionally, she has forged intimate spaces to conduct relationship building with fans. Before she was playing back-to-back over-three-hour-long concerts and before the pandemic raised health concerns worldwide, she devised special meet and greets to hang out with fans backstage after her shows. At every headlining tour prior to Eras, attendees were handpicked by Swift's team based on their Swiftie zeal either on social media or in the audience. The meet and greets were known as the T-Party for the Fearless Tour and Speak Now World Tour, Club Red for the Red Tour, Loft '89 for the 1989 World Tour, and the Rep Room for the Reputation Stadium Tour. In 2010, she hosted a "13 Hour Meet & Greet" at the Country Music Association Festival (renamed CMA Fest in 2018) in Nashville.[37] Her vision for the event was a free-entry, all-day, all-encompassing hub where fans could meet Swift, chat with Swift's band members, get a behind-the-scenes look at the Fearless Tour buses and outfits, and of course, watch Swift perform. She wanted fans to be entertained at any given moment, not just when they were meeting her. "I didn't take any breaks throughout the day," she shared, which made sense given that she met over 2,000 fans. "The only break that I took was to go grab my guitar so that I could play the performance. I didn't sit down. And somehow I was wearing painful heels. You know, the fans weren't sitting down, so why should I? But it was so much fun! The fans kept my energy high all day because every time I turned around a beautiful emotion was shown to me." Reflecting on these emotions, Swift recalled a fan named Gavin who had her write "Taylor loves Gavin" on his ribs. Gavin immediately got it tattooed and returned to the festival to show Swift. She was delighted and impressed with its permanence, especially because his mom was present and had approved of the tattoo. Thirteen years later, the mother and son were still fans and attended the Eras Tour in Philadelphia. Family is unquestionably important to Swift, as epistolized in songs like "The Best Day" (Fearless) and "Never Grow Up" (Speak Now). Her parents and brother Austin, who were in charge of bedazzling her Fearless guitar for the Eras Tour, have been closely interrelated with her operations. At the concerts, Swift's mom, Andrea Swift, was the chief of the team choosing

Fans: Consumer and Stakeholder 75

fans for the meet and greets. At the 13 Hour Meet & Greet, Swift's dad, Scott Swift, strolled the venue with Swift's Fearless Tour guitar and gave festivalgoers photo opportunities with it.

On the other side of the album process, Swift has held Secret Sessions in advance of a new release.[38] These sessions were exclusive listening parties, where Swift would press Play on the upcoming record and tell the stories behind the songs from beginning to end. Fans would get to try Swift's famous baked goods, meet her precious cats, and take pictures holding her prestigious awards. "This is something where you can't buy a ticket," she explained. "There's no real way to try and figure out how to get in other than maybe you made a video that made me laugh...Or maybe you did some really grassroots marketing with post-it notes...Or maybe you had been fiercely defensive of me on Twitter." For the *1989* Secret Sessions, the first instance of these, she spent months on social media choosing diehard fans, "people who had been so supportive and had tried and tried to meet [her], had been to five shows or however many events but had never met [her] before." Describing them as a sleepover or a party, Swift initially implemented these sessions to keep the rapport between her and her fans as she embarked on a new musical direction: "I think if you respect, admire, and love...a musical community, you'll be honest with them and very upfront about what's happening...There was this huge fear that they may be about to hear an album from me that sounded alien to them." The warmth-exuding Secret Sessions were one way for her to allay those concerns. They were also a rare chance for Swift to witness the emotional impact her music had on her fans and connect with their stories as well. She continued Secret Sessions for *Reputation* and *Lover* and logically stopped with quarantine project *folklore*.

Although it may seem counterintuitive, these actions cement her lasting value and have helped transform her fans into consumers who regularly buy her products. Fitness YouTuber MadFit's Maddie Lymburner, who hit 10 million subscribers in 2024, choreographs workouts to specific songs on her channel.[39] The revenue for these videos go to the artist or the label of a song, not to Lymburner, due to the copyrighted music. But the song workouts—which target a variety of areas like abs, arms, and cardio— are immensely popular, with subscribers commenting that these videos motivate them to exercise or lift their spirits after a long day. So,

The Glory of Giving Everything

Lymburner keeps making them because, like Swift, she sees and cares for the people who use her offerings. In the long run, this increases exposure to her YouTube channel and expands the community of at-home workout enthusiasts, who might start off enticed to exercise to one of their favorite songs (e.g., ballet sculpting set to *folklore* and *evermore*; abdominals set to "Message In A Bottle"; cardio set to *Midnights*), but stay to follow along to her other, nonsong videos, for which she does make money. She celebrated reaching 10 million subscribers by re-creating some of her choreographed workouts with big "10" balloons in the background, including her most viewed routine to Billie Eilish's "bad guy" (and her dance workout to "Shake It Off"). Again, these didn't add to Lymburner's income directly, but commemorating a milestone with them united her with her subscribers and viewers, who are akin to customers in today's digital world. Indeed, the success of MadFit has spurred the launch of a MadFit app, which requires a paid subscription and features workout classes, programs, and individualized plans, as well as nutritionist-advised recipes. The community-centric approach to business is worth assuming, as 82 percent of consumers care whether a brand's values line up with their own and will "vote with their wallet" accordingly.[40]

As the world becomes increasingly interconnected, Swift leverages social media to promote borderless online communities and heighten the public's consciousness of her music and personability. Going back to "Anti-Hero" and its palpable humor, Swift invited fans to participate in the #TSAntiHeroChallenge exclusively on YouTube Shorts to share their anti-heroic traits. Her anti-heroic traits included self-imposed isolation and treating her cat, Benjamin Button (adopted on the "ME!" music video set and named after a 2008 film), like her son (her other cats are named after media characters too, Meredith Grey from *Grey's Anatomy* and Olivia Benson from *Law and Order*). Swift even made a short video from the perspective of Benjamin, whose anti-heroic trait was letting a human (Swift) sleep in his bed and enabling her codependency. The prompt listed examples, like inputting the same word first on the daily *New York Times* Wordle or putting your feet on the car dashboard. To market her next lead single, "Fortnight (feat. Post Malone)," she employed a similar strategy with #ForAFortnightChallenge on YouTube Shorts.[41] A fortnight (not to be confused with video game Fortnite) is a British term indicating a period of

Fans: Consumer and Stakeholder   77

14 days. In her short video, she showed fans a glimpse of her life from the past two weeks and encouraged fans to do the same. These trends stoked the shift from Swift as the main character of her music to fans as the main characters, all the while strengthening engagement with the songs. Even when these arrangements aren't explicitly allocated, she has reached a point where the archetypal nature of her songs easily emerge. This was made clear when a single mother shared via TikTok that Swift's music was a savior to her and her nine-year-old daughter, for whom "Mean" was helping get through schoolyard bullies. To her astonishment, Swift saw the video and left comments: "I'm so moved by what you said. It reminds me of me and my mom and the memories we made at that age...Being vulnerable enough to share your true emotions is a beautiful thing."[42]

More than consumers, the other active role that Swifties take on is that of stakeholders. Fans are stakeholders of the Swift entity because they have a vested interest in the decision and outcomes of causes related to Swift. The two causes of recent prominence have been Swift's re-recordings, also known as the Taylor's Version projects, and concert ticketing legislation, referred to "The Great War" situation in Chapter 3. Under her contract with her first label, Scott Borchetta's Big Machine Records, she inherently owned the intellectual property for the music she made, but she did not own the masters. Owning the masters meant owning the copyright to the original sound recordings. (She has owned the masters to her music, as part of her current contract with Universal Music Group, since her *Lover* album.) In 2019, Big Machine Records was acquired by Scooter Braun's company, Ithaca Holdings, and Swift's catalog was effectively sold to Braun. Swift took to Tumblr to tell fans of her plight, stating that Borchetta and Braun didn't give her the courtesy of informing her of the sale.[43] She'd heard about it on the news. Although she had been aware that Borchetta might have sold her masters eventually, it was to the worst possible buyer, one who was in cahoots with Kim Kardashian and Kanye West: "Never in my worst nightmares did I imagine the buyer would be Scooter. Any time Scott Borchetta has heard the words 'Scooter Braun' escape my lips, it was when I was either crying or trying not to." Since then, Swift has painstakingly re-recorded *Fearless, Speak Now, Red,* and *1989. Fearless (Taylor's Version), Red (Taylor's Version), Speak Now (Taylor's Version),* and *1989 (Taylor's Version)* contained near-identical versions of the original tracklists along with songs "From the

78   The Glory of Giving Everything

Vault," which were created during the writing process for but left off the original albums (some of these vault songs aided our case study in Chapter 2). While re-recording is not an endeavor unique to Swift, she has achieved unparalleled success with her *Taylor's Version* albums.[44] Her fans, who dub the original versions "stolen versions," made *Fearless (Taylor's Version)* the first re-recorded album to top Billboard. *Speak Now (Taylor's Version)* was the most streamed country album in a day; *Red (Taylor's Version)* was the most streamed female-made album in a day on Spotify. The value, and hence the sales, of the stolen versions declined as re-recorded ones were put out, and *1989 (Taylor's Version)* sold more copies than the stolen *1989* within the first week of coming out. Fans' fierce support of *Taylor's Version* recordings reflect the harmonious journey that Swift and Swifties undertake together—the artist gifts fans with songs to contextualize their lives and the fans gift the artist with commercial boosts. As an extra savvy move, Swift's *TTPD* grief playlists on Apple Music had only featured "Taylor's Version" songs. Fans would be curious to see if Swift adds songs from *Taylor Swift (Taylor's Version)* and *Reputation (Taylor's Version)* when those are released.

With the Eras Tour, many people who attempted to buy tickets on Ticketmaster's Verified Fan presale failed due to poor infrastructure on Ticketmaster's part resulting in website crashes and extended waiting periods.[45] To add fuel to the fire, Ticketmaster canceled the general sale because of "extraordinarily high demand" and "insufficient remaining ticket inventory." Frustrated, Swift took to social media here too, this time Instagram: "It's really difficult for me to trust an outside entity with these relationships and loyalties…I'm not going to make excuses for anyone because we asked them, multiple times, if they could handle this kind of demand and we were assured they could. It's truly amazing that 2.4 million people got tickets, but it really pisses me off that a lot of them felt like they had to go through several bear attacks to get them." Her personal statement, while lacking concrete next steps, reinforced the importance of the fan experience to the Swift entity and helped mobilize Swifties to take action. After a lawsuit spearheaded by Swifties, the Department of Justice opened an antitrust investigation into Ticketmaster and its parent company, Live Nation. In this way, fans recognized their derived power as stakeholders in the already-influential establishment of Swift.

Fans: Consumer and Stakeholder

Outdoor apparel and gear corporation REI, or Recreational Equipment, Inc., turns its customers into stakeholders as well. REI is structured as a co-op, where customers become lifetime members with not only discounted prices but also a share in the company and voting rights.[46] In addition to selling clothing and equipment, the brand offers classes, events, and trips. These experience-based services complement REI's innovative business model, as they shape the perception that outdoor adventures should be actively driven by customers as opposed to passively stumbled upon. Berkeley pizza joint The Cheese Board Collective is noteworthy for its singular fresh pizza of the day, turn-the-corner long lines, and employee model. Cheese Board is owned completely by the workers, who democratically manage every part of the place.[47] Whether it's the traditional customer or employee that is developed into a stakeholder, their steadfast interest in the business can translate into enduring success. Stakeholders, unlike shareholders, do not necessarily own a piece of the company (although they can), but are certainly impacted by and impact a company's outcomes.[48] Shareholders tend to be financially motivated, while stakeholders wish success upon a company for a variety of composite reasons, including but not limited to social, environmental, and political rationales.

For Swift, this has also manifested in ways that received less attention than the re-recording remarkableness and the Live Nation fiasco, but were equally as crucial. During the *1989* Secret Sessions, she asked the invitees to respectfully keep the album's song titles and lyrics a secret until the record's release. *1989* ended up being leaked a couple days before it was meant to come out, but the fans prevented it from trending on Twitter (now known as X), which was what had happened with all the other leaks Swift had faced in the past.[49] They flocked to the posts originating the leaks to protest the unfair and devaluing acts of distributing art illegally. Fans feel compelled to tackle Swift's issues because she listens to their needs. At the Eras Tour in Minneapolis, she honored a fan's request to play "Daylight" as the surprise song. The fan had posted on X (formerly known as Twitter) that the show date coincided with the fifth anniversary of her late brother's passing. She reportedly fell to her knees sobbing when Swift played it.[50] ("Daylight," it seems, can take on a lot of meanings: romantic comfort for Swift, a chance at freedom for the prisoner, and healing from

80   The Glory of Giving Everything

grief for this Minneapolis attendee.) With this in mind, Swift has high-lighted the need for marketing strategies to be tailored: "I think that what we need to start doing is catering our release plans to our own career, to our own fans, and really get in tune with them. I've been on the internet for hours every single night figuring out what these people want from me."[51] This philosophy is what allowed her to say with confidence that the 10-minute version of "All Too Well," which fans had long been clamoring for and finally got with *Red (Taylor's Version)*, would be well-received. She elaborated to Jimmy Fallon on *The Tonight Show* that she felt like she knew the fans and believed the 10-minute version would become the new standard version of the track for them. The song ended up dethroning Don McLean's "American Pie" as the longest song to top the Billboard Hot 100.[52] And for times when Swift's products aren't as well-received, she's there to fix it. When absorbing the ethereal "Snow On The Beach (feat. Lana Del Rey)" from *Midnights*, fans noticed that Swift's vocals were dominating the track. In response, Swift gave them "Snow On The Beach (feat. More Lana Del Rey), in which Lana Del Rey (real name Elizabeth Grant) sings the second verse and has intensified vocalizations in the cho-rus. In speaking about the collaboration, Grant shared that Swift did want her to sing on the song: "I can mimic almost anyone, so I layer and match [Swift's] vocals perfectly, so you would never even know that I was com-pletely all over that first song."[53] Even though Swift could have simply resorted to this explanation, she took the fans' feedback seriously and took it upon herself to go to the studio and record another version.

As with fans-as-consumers, fans-as-stakeholders extend past what directly involves Swift. Leading up to the 2024 United States presidential election, a Donald Trump news account (unaffiliated with Trump) spread false news on X (formerly known as Twitter), using a photo of Swift in tears with the headline that she was losing money after endorsing Kamala Harris for President. This photo was actually from the year 2012. Around that time, Swift had come across the blog of a mother, Maya Thompson, who had lost her four-year-old son, Ronan, to neuroblastoma. Moved, she penned a heartbreakingly beautiful tribute, "Ronan," and listed Thompson as the co-writer.[54] It was first released as a charity single with proceeds going toward cancer awareness and research and was part of *Red (Taylor's Version)*. Per-forming "Ronan" for the first time at the annual Stand Up to Cancer

Fans: Consumer and Stakeholder

81

Telethon made Swift emotional, which was when the photo in question was taken. Understandably, Thompson was shocked and angry at the misuse of the photo and expressed that on X (formerly known as Twitter). Swifties were outraged at the blatant disrespect, and one way or another, within a day, the Trump news account deleted the post. Thompson updated her followers of the deletion and thanked them for making it happen.

The active roles that Swift's fans step into are the result of career-long efforts. A pivotal moment in forming her country music dream was when she attended her first concert, LeAnn Rimes, at eight years old.[55] Swift sent letters and pictures to Rimes's hotel room the night before the show. From the audience, Swift asked Rimes if she got the package, and Rimes responded, "I sure did, Taylor!" From that young age, Swift knew that she wanted to make people feel the way Rimes made her feel. By the age of 24, she foresaw a music industry future in which fandoms weren't only key to sustaining a career but to launching one: "A friend of mine, who is an actress, told me that when the casting for her recent movie came down to two actresses, the casting director chose the actress with more Twitter followers. I see this becoming a trend in the music industry. For me, this dates back to 2005 when I walked into my first record-label meetings, explaining to them that I had been communicating directly with my fans on this new site called Myspace. In the future, artists will get record deals because they have fans—not the other way around."[56] On Myspace, a social networking platform from the early 2000s, Swift shared sassy, goofy parts of herself.[57] Her profile picture was of her sporting a spelling bee champion shirt. In the bio she posted at age 18: "I like to read up on weird medical problems." To those who read the bio she posted at 20: "I love you like I love sparkles and having the last word. And that's real love." One of the more iconic social media interactions started when someone posted a high school photo of Swift on Tumblr, claiming that it was their friend Becky, who was happy until she died from marijuana usage.[58] A user commented that they were "pretty sure that's Taylor Swift," to which the original poster chirped, "no its becky." To fans' delight, Swift was aware of it and wore a yellow T-shirt stating "no its becky" soon afterward. Her personability was undeniable in every space she assumed, from the radio to the internet.

They're also the result of Swift's personal projections onto her fan base. She has always loved buying a vinyl at a record store, putting it in a record player, and listening to it because "[i]t makes music more of an activity."[59] Ever since her debut album, engaging with Swift's music has been a full-blown activity, as we saw with the *TTPD* rollout. From *Taylor Swift* to *1989*, she capitalized certain letters in the physical lyric booklets to spell out a secret message that revealed information about the song. Some hidden passages referenced other songs, like the one in "Last Kiss" (*Speak Now*) spelling out "forever and always," a song on *Fearless*, or "Dear John" (*Speak Now*) spelling out a lyric from "Superman" in the same album. Others were more subtle references that fans would need to look up for context, like Hyannis Port in "Everything Has Changed" (*Red*). The best ones gave insight into Swift's feelings surrounding the song or pointed pieces of advice—"Jump Then Fall" (*Fearless*) sharing that "last summer was magical" or "Picture to Burn" (*Taylor Swift*) reminding people to "date nice boys." The songs on *1989* adopted a fresh take by connecting each song's secret message into one cohesive story of a doomed relationship in New York that ends with the girl losing the boy but finding herself. Because she was most proud of her lyricism, she instilled the behavior of scrutinizing lyrics in her listeners, just as she had once done as a child for the music she was consuming.[60] As physical lyric booklets dwindled with the rise of streaming, Swift put this on hiatus starting with *Reputation*, but began to more intentionally utilize other forms of media for cryptography, and identified "Look What You Made Me Do" as the first "crazy video" to implement Easter egg culture on a massive scale. By involving fans in Easter egg culture, fans are inclined to cherish the end product more because they feel like they were involved in the decoding of it.

"I think that is perfectly reasonable for people to be normal music fans and to have a normal relationship to music," Swift stated. "But, if you want to go down a rabbit hole with us, come along. The water's great! Jump in! We're all mad here." And so the fans went and never looked back.

6

Friends: Candid and Strategic

"You're not going to understand this text for a few days, but...," Swift rattled off in a message to Este Haim, one of three sisters who comprise the rock band HAIM. "Which chain restaurant do you like best?"[1] Haim picked Olive Garden, and we know what happened next: the Italian eatery made its way onto the sixth track of 2020's *evermore*, "no body, no crime (feat. HAIM)." In the fan-favorite murder mystery, Swift avenges her friend "Este," who was allegedly murdered by her unfaithful husband, by killing the husband and framing the mistress. The two friends, according to the first and second verses, regularly had dinner at Olive Garden until Este's disappearance. HAIM sings backup on the song, and Danielle Haim serves as the narrator's alibi ("She was with me, dude").

The song flagged the musicians' first collaboration after a years-long friendship that included casual girl hangouts, backstage meetups at star-studded events, and HAIM performing on select dates on the 1989 World Tour.[2] When Swift had the idea for the true crime twist, she imagined Este Haim in it because that was the friend she knew "would be stoked to be in a song like that," and Haim's reaction was viscerally affirmative. The relationship between Swift and HAIM, while always tight, was then thrust further into the public eye in ways that benefitted both parties. In 2021, HAIM put out a remix of "Gasoline" from their 2020 album *Women in*

Music Pt. III that featured vocals from Swift, who had named "Gasoline" her favorite from that record. In 2022, the trio acted as evil stepsisters in Swift's Cinderella-themed "Bejeweled" music video (Lady Este, who wants the prince for his title; Lady Danielle, who wants the ring; and Lady Alana, who wants the d★★★). As the sisters leave for the ball, where they can earn the prince's hand by entering a talent competition, their "I'm gonna be hungover" tune is a comedic nod to one of their viral videos in the real world. Meanwhile, "House Wench Taylor" wants to win the contest for the castle. She secures it by the end, even though she declines a proposal from the nonchalant Prince Jack, played by Jack Antonoff, another friend whose alliance with Swift has been heavily documented. (Swift cold-called actress Laura Dern to cast her as the evil stepmother. Dern agreed right away and later good-naturedly shared an anecdote where she was recognized for being "the girl in the Taylor Swift video" instead of for her breakout role in *Jurassic Park*.) In 2023, HAIM was one of the openers for the Eras Tour, and none other than Olive Garden weighed in on the situation, posting online that they would find comfort in their unlimited breadsticks if "no body, no crime (feat. HAIM)" was not on the setlist for those shows.[3] Thankfully, it was. Swift's self-proclaimed status as the fourth HAIM sister was not only a testament to their personal friendship but also to a cultural relationship perceived, for better or for worse (arguably for better), by millions worldwide.

If fairy tales are known for their mutatable tropes, and if real estate is known for its "location, location, location" mantra, then the supreme law of business is that your network is your net worth. Maintaining relationships is a valuable asset to sustainable growth, whether it's with another community member who increases word-of-mouth marketing, an expert outside of your field who elevates your offerings, or even an apparent competitor who joins forces with you to create a stronger product. The best part about strategic partnerships is that they're not a zero-sum game. One partner's gain doesn't necessitate the other person's loss—in fact, the opposite is true, and like healthy personal relationships, healthy business relationships enhance everyone involved.

Quite a few of Swift's partnerships have been with companies that, like the songstress herself, have faced standout success but are nevertheless constantly seizing opportunities to enlarge their customer base. Eighth studio record *folklore* was accompanied by *folklore: the long pond studio sessions*, a

Friends: Candid and Strategic

85

soothing documentary concert recorded at Long Pond Studio in New York. The film streamed exclusively on Disney+ in November 2020, four months after the album came out. With performances of all the songs in tracklist order and discussions of the creative process throughout, fans were given a peek behind the cottagecore curtain and a unique way to connect during a time when artists' tours were automatically on hiatus. For nonfans who hadn't come across "cardigan" on the radio, here was another entry point to joining the high-friction acquisition system during the *folklore* era. Much like how the album reached Gen Z, the at-home concert attracted new fans by becoming available to Disney+ subscribers who may not have been knowledgeable of or keen on Swift's music. This worked in the opposite direction as well, with Swift's fans newly subscribing to Disney+ to watch *folklore: the long pond studio sessions*. In the fall of 2020, Disney+ was at its one-year anniversary; after letting go of 28,000 jobs due to theme park closures, the Mickey Mouse company had clearly been strategizing its streaming content.[4] Its most recent blockbuster at that point was the original Broadway production of *Hamilton*. During *Hamilton*'s streaming debut in July 2020, Disney+ app downloads increased by 72 percent.[5]

While exact statistics in this vein aren't published for *folklore: the long pond studio sessions*—which swaps out Alexander Hamilton for James, Elizabeth Schuyler for Betty, and Maria Reynolds for Augustine—the enduring alliance between Swift and Disney+ has proven to be a smart move. In the midst of the Eras Tour and after a movie theater spotlight, Swift also released *Taylor Swift | The Eras Tour (Taylor's Version)* movie exclusively on Disney+. The *Taylor's Version* indicator differentiated this offering from the theater version, which cut a few songs ("The Archer," "no body, no crime [feat. HAIM]," "Long Live," "cardigan," and "Wildest Dreams") due to length constraints. The Disney+ version, or rather *Taylor's Version*, kept these songs and featured additional acoustic songs ("I Can See You" and "Death By A Thousand Cuts" on guitar, "You Are In Love" and "Maroon" on piano). To signify the monumental streaming premiere, the platform arranged its content according to Swift's eras: "Fearless (Disney's Version)" movies included *Moana*; "Speak Now (Disney's Version)" included *Enchanted*; "Red (Disney's Version)" included *Big Hero 6*; "1989 (Disney's Version)" included *The Little Mermaid*; "Reputation (Disney's Version)" included *Avengers: Endgame*; "Lover (Disney's Version)" included *Robin Hood*;

"folklore (Disney's Version)" included *The Chronicles of Narnia: The Lion, the Witch, and the Wardrobe*; "evermore (Disney's Version)" included *Into the Woods*; and "Midnights (Disney's Version)" included *Cinderella*.[6] Just like the Eras Tour, there was no official debut section. *Taylor Swift | The Eras Tour (Taylor's Version)* became Disney+'s most-viewed music film to date in an opening weekend, with an astounding 4.6 million views in its first three days.[7] Comparably, *Hamilton* had garnered 2.86 million views in its first 12 days, accomplishing this with less than half the subscribers that Disney+ had at the time of Swift's Eras Tour movie (60.5 million versus 149.6 million).[8] With Swifties flocking to Disney+ and subscribers tuning in to Swift's concert films, the two entities continued to thrive. Perhaps, in four years after the Eras movie, Disney+ will shell out another $75 million, as it did for *Hamilton* (2020) and *Taylor Swift | The Eras Tour (Taylor's Version)* (2024), for another major hit.

Besides maximizing her outreach through partnerships, Swift has leveraged outside resources to enable her biggest clue-searching fans. In the days leading up to *The Tortured Poets Department*, Apple Music wasn't the only music streaming service she used to generate buzz. She also teamed up with Spotify to offer a three-day pop-up at The Grove in Los Angeles. Aptly set up as a library, Spotify's label partnerships manager emphasized the desire for it to be "thoughtful and ornate" to "literally take fans inside Swift's new era."[9] The library was packed with lyrical and symbolic references that people figured would all be revealed at the time of release. However, after downloading and listening to the 16-track album, fans were quick to notice that lyrics at the pop-up hadn't appeared on the album. The ensuing hour was riddled with speculation, until the imminent surprise hit the internet at 2:00 a.m.—*The Tortured Poets Department: The Anthology* arrived, making for a total of 31 "tortured poetry" tracks. Because of the Spotify exhibit, whose clock set to 2:00 was another foreshadowing, fans were primed for devouring the surprise double album. Considered together with the Apple Music secret message (spelled out in Chapter 5), some raised the point that a post-mortem examination takes around two hours to perform on average (the secret message, too, was a lyric that appeared on *The Anthology*). To mobilize the public in advance of her already hotly anticipated *1989 (Taylor's Version)*, Swift partnered with their favorite search engine, Google. With a consistent market share

Friends: Candid and Strategic   87

of approximately 80–90 percent from 2015 to 2025 (for perspective, the next highest one was Bing with 4–12 percent over the same time period), Google's visibility matched Swift's steady omnipresence. In September 2023, the time of Swift and Google joining forces, Google's market share was 83.84 percent, while Bing's was 8.66 percent.[10] Googling "Taylor Swift" would yield a word puzzle to solve, and fans collectively needed to complete 33 million puzzles (representative of Swift's age at the time) to unlock the vault and reveal the "From the Vault" titles. It took Swifties 19 hours to finish the 89 unique, 33 million total puzzles (the number of hours being an unplanned nod to the album title).[11] As with Disney+, these relationships were two-way streets despite being short term. Swift extended her platform, into a practically unavoidable space, for consumer sleuthing. At the same time, Google and Spotify maintained their relevance within the contemporary zeitgeist. Their consumer engagement toolkit already included regular quirky Google Doodles, which are artistic takes on the Google logo that reflect current events, and the yearly anticipated Spotify Wrapped, which is a personalized compilation of users' listening statistics that gets widely shared on social media. By booking the Swift train, Google and Spotify ensured that their hold on society was not only up-to-date, but justifiable.

Perhaps her longest-term corporate partner is retail giant Target, which has exclusively carried her physical products—including deluxe album editions, vinyl editions, DVD footage, and magazines—since the *Fearless* era in 2008. The eras of the Target commercial have mirrored the eras of the studio, from the fourth-grade crush storyboard in the *Speak Now* advertisement to the music-set polaroid montage of the *1989* advertisement. Worlds collided wonderfully in the *Red* commercial, with Swift parading Target's signature color. She's even been known to drop by the store to buy copies of her albums and surprise fans (or passersby: "'I live across the street and just came to get this for dinner,' said a man in one of the videos as he stood next to Swift, holding a jar of spaghetti sauce…"), per Target's territorial claim of being the "only place to get more Taylor." As Swift's prominence has steadily increased since *Fearless*, Target has continuously reaped the seeds they had planted, with the Phantom Clear vinyl of *The Tortured Poets Department*, for instance, being their biggest music preorder in history and *The Official Taylor Swift | The Eras Tour Book*, on another instance, being the fastest-selling new release book of the previous four years.[12] The singer's appointment of the trendy yet affordable Target as an axis for her fans to gather reinforces her relatability.

Part of what makes Swift special is her double function as an entity and an individual—someone who produces art and someone who unwittingly, at times, becomes the art herself. Her relationships are no different, as she seeks them out with specific people in addition to larger-scale corporations. While one aspect of Swift's community is her pulsing fan base, the other part is her matrix of colleagues, which she cultivates with precision and care. These efforts serve to augment work products as well as build genuine connections, occasionally achieving more of one than the other but always achieving a combination of both. For the music video of "I Can See You," the main promotional tool of *Speak Now (Taylor's Version)* (2023), Swift recruited old friends from the original *Speak Now* (2010) era. Actress Joey King, who played the blue-ribboned heroine of the "Mean" music video, starred alongside actor Taylor Lautner, who inspired the apology ballad "Back to December." On *The Tonight Show*, Lautner reflected on Swift's reaching out: "We had been out of touch for a while, so it was a real cool full-circle moment for both of us."[13] King and Lautner not only pleased fans in the heist-centered music video, but also surprised the audience on stage in Kansas City the night the re-recorded album dropped, making it nostalgic for Swift's teammates and supporters alike. In another full-circle moment, the music video for "Everything Has Changed (feat. Ed Sheeran)" (2013) told the story of two elementary school-aged children, and the music video for "The Joker And The Queen (feat. Taylor Swift)" (2022) by Ed Sheeran brought back the actors, now grown up, for a sequel.

When embarking on projects, Swift has had a keen eye for harnessing the qualities of others, whether they were old or new associates. During the making of the second music video of her career, "Teardrops On My Guitar," she explained that she chose to keep director Trey Fanjoy from her first music video, "Tim McGraw," because it had been a positive experience.[14] Her "Teardrops On My Guitar" co-star, musician Tyler Hilton, had given an interview prior to ever meeting Swift sharing his love for her music. As soon as Swift read that article, she reached out to Hilton through her manager to return the sentiment. The two then met up at one of Swift's shows in California, where she asked if he wanted to be in her music video

Friends: Candid and Strategic 89

and received an instantaneous yes. In a conversation with filmmaker Martin McDonagh as part of *Variety*'s "Directors on Directors" series, Swift described her thought process into casting actress Sadie Sink in *All Too Well: The Short Film*: "Sometimes, you see an actor and you see the work they've done, but you can kind of see how it could have gone further, and you can kind of see flickers of how they could really be excellent in a part they hadn't been cast as. I had seen Sadie in *Stranger Things* and I thought, she has such a presence, she has such an empathy to her. You can just see microemotions flash across her face, in a way that I just don't usually see in performances. It's rare. And I thought, she's never been a romantic lead." Sink, 19 at the time, found the offer unexpected and thrilling: "You would never think that our paths would really cross, someone being in the music industry and then in the film industry. It was like two different worlds...but everyone was very excited."[15] The fact that she had never been that much in love or equally heartbroken in real life made the critical acclaim for the short film's acting all the more impressive. Within the music sector, Swift is just as observant. After working with Antonoff on '80s pop jam "Sweeter Than Fiction" for the 2013 movie *One Chance*, she enlisted his talents for *1989*, and on many endeavors that followed. For her trek into the folklorian woods, she sent a cold text to Aaron Dessner of alternative rock band The National, who ended up tremendously contributing to her new sound during quarantine. Dessner helped Swift reach out to Justin Vernon to sing on "exile" because she was too nervous to do so herself, exemplifying the ripple effects of solid networking (Vernon agreed, and dueted with Swift again on *evermore*'s title track). Besides serving as key sculptors of Swift's musical trajectory, both Antonoff and Dessner have since experienced higher profiles, with Antonoff crediting Swift for kickstarting his production career and Dessner pointing out that he'd been approached by more people post-Swift-collaboration.[16] Antonoff and Dessner made guest appearances on the Eras Tour and continued to make music with Swift on a number of instances.

Through it all, the glue that keeps these folks in Swift's corner is the positive feedback loop of authentic appreciation.[17] On her first radio tour promoting her debut album, she brought homemade cookies for the DJs who were taking the time to listen to her play in conference rooms (more recently, Dessner spoke about Swift cooking meals for house guests).

90 The Glory of Giving Everything

On *Fearless (Platinum Edition)*, Swift covered "Untouchable" by Luna Halo, trading the original's punk rock for pared-down acoustics, because Luna Halo was one of Scott Borchetta's favorite bands (recall Borchetta of Big Machine Records, Chapter 2 friend and Chapter 5 foe). Although her only goal was to delight Borchetta, she was granted a co-writing credit due to the intricate arrangement. Down the road, when the fallout with Borchetta happened, Kelly Clarkson was adamant in her support of Swift. She was the first one to publicly suggest that Swift re-record her music and promised to buy all of the new versions. Even though Clarkson believed that the idea didn't originate with her—she herself had proposed it based on Reba McEntire's re-recording initiatives—and that Swift would have done it irrespective of her comment, Swift acknowledged Clarkson in her 2023 TIME Person of the Year interview and has sent Clarkson flowers and gifts with every re-recording release. Charlie Puth, who Swift declares should be a household name in *TTPD*'s title track, has admired Swift for years, once obsessing over the chords of "Teardrops On My Guitar" on Instagram and being one of the first people to welcome her to TikTok when she joined the platform. Swift's shoutout was more than a kind gesture, as it actually pushed Puth to release a single entitled "Hero": "Sometimes I get a little nervous being overly honest in my music, which is why this has been sitting on my hard drive for a while. But I think someone out there was giving me a sign that I needed to release it." In a separate announcement, he thanked Swift explicitly. The "The Tortured Poets Department" nudge, which likely started out as a pure tribute of Puth's work, went beyond by unintentionally blessing more fans with more music. Swift's relationship with pop rock band Train emerged in somewhat of a reverse fashion. Swift mashed up "Fearless" with Train's "Hey Soul Sister" and Jason Mraz's "I'm Yours" on the Speak Now World Tour, and included, out of all the surprise cover songs on that tour, her cover of Train's "Drops of Jupiter" on the *Speak Now World Tour – Live* album. Train's lead singer, Pat Monahan, later invited Swift to collaborate on one of his projects, and she reciprocated the request. The two wrote "Babe," which went on to be recorded by country duo Sugarland with backing vocals from Swift. Swift provided her rendition of the Top 40 Country Airplay hit by making "Babe" a vault track on the re-recorded *Red*.

Whether your default mode is a profit-maximizing business mindset or an individual growth perspective, know that interpersonality sparks productivity.

Friends: Candid and Strategic 91

Two community hubs on the same street in Berkeley, the Berkeley Playhouse and Mrs. Dalloway's Bookstore, jointly hosted a Dr. Seuss reading event during the theater's run of *Seussical*.[18] In addition to Seussical Storytime led by the Playhouse actors portraying Horton the Elephant and Gertrude McFuzz the girl-bird, the bookstore offered a 15 percent discount on all Dr. Seuss books for the second month of the production. Such a crossover was meant to widen the overlap between families of theatergoers and bookworms and draw in customers at both places. Capitalizing on the social media "Get Ready With Me" (GRWM) trend, where content creators talk to the camera while going through their beauty routine, cosmetics brand e.l.f. (eyes lip face) released *Get Ready With Music, The Album*.[19] The album, with lead single "Hairpin" by Charlotte Rose Benjamin, was an investment in emerging artists, who now had heightened exposure via distribution under a major entity. It was also the first product launched under the makeup company's entertainment branch, e.l.f. made, and a new way for e.l.f. to inscribe itself into the makeup tables of girls in bathrooms everywhere, whether they hum along to themselves or to millions of followers on the internet. By marrying complementary strengths, e.l.f. was able to cater to the more than three quarters of women who view makeup and music as a means of community and self-expression. For a longer-term example, take the relationship between camera producer GoPro and energy drink manufacturer Red Bull. Although they differ in products, they share a vision of inspiring adventurously challenging lifestyles. In exchange for equity in GoPro, Red Bull has GoPro as its exclusive videographer for all of its events, like Red Bull Rampage, an invitation-only mountain bike freeride competition.[20] Such content is then posted across both companies' social and promotional avenues, augmenting each one's brand awareness and continuing to cement their shared larger-than-life philosophy.

While Swift invoked partners Disney+ and Target to aid in distribution of the two successful Eras Tour spinoffs, she did not contract with entities that would hinder the terms she wanted. For both *Taylor Swift | The Eras Tour Concert Film* and *The Official Taylor Swift | The Eras Tour Book*, she decided to forgo the middleman. After unsatisfactory discussions with potential studios, she chose to give her movie directly to AMC and Cinemark Theaters. Under this deal, she earned 57 percent of the movie ticket profits and AMC got 43 percent, neither of them needing to split with a studio. Moreover, she got to release the film at a time she deemed desirable—on her lucky number (the 13th of October) and importantly, while the Eras Tour was still in full motion, in order to include fans who weren't able to get tickets. Swift encouraged moviegoers to deck out in Eras Tour attire, bring friendship bracelets, sing along, and dance in their seats to promote the film as an alternative to the concert experience, something she would not have been able to do had she been following the slower timeline of a Hollywood studio that was likely managing other movies at the same time. In "betting on [her]self," [21] she inadvertently caused other releases set for October 13, 2023, to shift with cheeky Swift-themed announcements: "Look what you made me do. *The Exorcist: Believer* moves to 10/6/23, #TaylorWins"; "So we'll take our time...Are you ready for it? Meg Ryan ends her 14-year rom-com hiatus and the #Megaissance begins with #WhatHappensLater, now happening...later. Coming only to theaters November 3!" For the book, Swift bypassed traditional publishing routes and instead self-published under Taylor Swift Publications, which appeared to be a new subentity. This ensured that she wouldn't have to share the revenues with a publishing house, but as with the concert film, monetary gain was not necessarily her goal. "People often greatly underestimate me on how much I'll inconvenience myself to prove a point," she remarked at the Tribeca Film Festival in 2022, the point in this case being securing control over a product's creative direction and ultimate delivery.[22] As she mentioned in her Ticketmaster statement, she has done "so many elements of [her] career in house" for this reason.

Like in life, choosing the right partners is essential. Because Swift spent time developing alliances that mattered, from pals to businesses, she was able to cut relationships that wouldn't have served her. Conversely, because she took charge of her own timeline, she was able to focus her energy on investing in meaningful relationships in a variety of ways. Through song, she has memorialized not only her experiences but those of her close friends.[23] In *Fearless*'s coming-of-age "Fifteen," Swift touched on her high school best friend, Abigail Anderson, who was proud that millions of girls could learn from her story. From helping Swift choose a prom date in a 2008 episode of MTV's *Once Upon a Prom* to watching Swift dedicate "Fifteen" to her "beautiful redheaded high school best friend" in 2023, the pair have stayed friends. In *Speak Now*'s "When Emma Falls In Love," Swift described all the ways in which she admired her friend Emma, theorized to be actress

Friends: Candid and Strategic   93

Emma Stone. Over a decade after that song was written, Stone introduced Swift to choreographer Mandy Moore (not to be confused with singer and actress Mandy Moore of *A Walk to Remember*, *Tangled*, and *This Is Us*). Moore, who had choreographed the Oscar-winning 2016 film *La La Land* starring Stone, received rave reviews for her work on the Eras Tour.

While putting reverence to melody is one form of action, Swift is aware that lasting impact is also fostered through accessible public support, since not all consumers would sift through an album's songs and research their subject matters. By conducting her career the way she has, she has paved the way for future music industry foragers to be more involved—whether in the process of creating more personal music or on the front of defending deserved rights, and whether she interacts with them or not—but Swift has opted for direct interaction when possible. Take singer-songwriter Ryan Adams, who released a track-by-track cover album of *1989* a year after the original came out. Swift could have simply gushed about it online, but instead she sat down with Adams to discuss songwriting. During the interview, she likened Adams's cover to when actors change emphasis within their scripted lines to change meanings.[24] In her 30s and "eras era," Swift began to more consciously fertilize a newer crop of musicians. Two notable meteoric rises linked to an association with Swift were those of moody songwriter Gracie Abrams and pop princess Sabrina Carpenter, who were both Eras Tour openers. Carpenter, who opened for Swift in Latin America, Asia, and Australia, saw a 117 percent spike of monthly listeners in the months during and following her Eras gig; Abrams, who opened for Swift on both North American legs, enjoyed a jump from 10 million monthly listeners to more than 30 million monthly listeners just before the second segment.[25] A spontaneous middle-of-the-night collaboration resulted in "us. (feat. Taylor Swift)" on Abrams's second studio album, *The Secret of Us*, which debuted at #2 on the Billboard 200, after Swift's *TTPD*. Then, she scored her first Billboard Hot 100 Top 10 hit and #1 on the U.K. Singles Chart with "That's So True," a song from the deluxe edition of *The Secret of Us*. The song became popularized on social media as content creators competed to make the best edits of Swift to the bridge (recall: Swift's favorite part of a song). Videos of Swift were hence being circulated as well, stoking conversation about her that wasn't the result of a Swift product but rather came out of Swift's investment in young talent. "I am inspired by Taylor in

94   The Glory of Giving Everything

a million ways, but especially by the pace with which she puts things out into the world," Abrams commented, with regard to her friend's output velocity mentioned in Chapter 5. "There's less pressure the more you release—that's how I consider it for myself. I want to just keep it coming while I'm in this period of writing as frequently as I am."[26]

Carpenter's first Billboard Hot 100 Top 10 hit and #1 on the U.K. Singles Chart, "Espresso," came during her run as Eras Tour opener, and set the stage for her first #1 album on the Billboard 200, *Short n' Sweet*. In New Orleans, Swift surprised the audience by having Carpenter join the acoustic section to sing a mashup of "Espresso," "Is It Over Now?" (which flowed due to its lyrical measurement of time in takeout coffees), and "Please Please Please" (Carpenter's blockbuster follow-up to "Espresso"). This marked the only time on the Eras Tour that Swift performed a song by another artist who had zero musical collaborations with her. "It's so cool for me to get a perspective on this whole process from her...stuff that you can't just ask the internet," Carpenter shared of being in Swift's corner. Taking a page from Swift's relentless need to address matters in song, she continued, "[W]henever I start to think, 'Maybe I'll get on Twitter and say something about this,' I'm always like, 'Maybe I'll write a song instead.'"[27]

Both Carpenter and Abrams made the most of their coveted opening slots on the Eras Tour by solidifying their own brands—raw, emotionally charged Abrams and flirty, energized Carpenter—to flurries of hyped Swifties. Fans' eagerness to decode just about anything helped Swift fully indoctrinate her protégés into her universe. Both of them donned a white dress when performing with Swift in the acoustic section (Carpenter for the aforementioned song trilogy, Abrams for a mashup of "us." and "Out of the Woods" in Toronto), and in both instances, Swift wore an orange dress. While these stylings were more likely a consistent fashion choice with no bearing on future announcements, they still served as a speculatory rabbit hole. Fans remained entertained by melodies and lyrics, packaged eras, and now, partnerships. Truly, working together to expand, rather than divide, the pie has far-reaching benefits for producers and consumers. The only reason that the technique of networking has worked so stunningly for Swift? She does it all completely genuinely.

7

Reaching Your Billionaire Era

By the end of 2023, Swift had amassed 1.79 percent of the United States recorded music market, higher than any other artist. At that point in time, which was the near midpoint of the Eras Tour, more music listeners were consuming the genre of "Taylor Swift" than were consuming the genres of gospel (1.7 percent market share), jazz (1 percent), and classical (0.9 percent).[1]

The data was published fresh off the crowning of Swift as a billionaire and the world's richest female musician in October 2023. In August 2017, her net worth was reported to be $280 million; that number shot up to $740 million by June 2023. Come October 2024, she was valued at $1.6 billion. At #2 on the list of wealthy musicians, sandwiched between Jay-Z ($2.5 billion as of October 2024) and Rihanna ($1.4 billion as of October 2024), Swift was the first (and only at the time of writing) billionaire to make her fortune primarily from songwriting and performing. Exhibit 7.1 categorizes her estimated earnings, totaling just over a billion dollars, as of October 2023.[2]

Swift's music catalog was hence valued at approximately 40 percent of her wealth at the time she hit the billionaire mark. In contrast, Jay-Z's (real name Shawn Carter) music catalog was worth $75 million, or 7.5 percent of $1 billion, when he was named the world's first hip-hop billionaire in 2019.[3] Carter earned his status through a number of ventures, including

Taylor Swift's Wealth Breakdown as of October 2023	
Source	Net Earnings ($ in millions)
Music Catalog	400
Concert Tickets and Merchandise Sales	370
Spotify and YouTube Partnerships	120
Real Estate	110
Royalties from Record Sales	80
Total	1,080

Exhibit 7.1 Taylor Swift's Wealth Breakdown as of October 2023

owning stock in music streaming service Tidal and liquor brands Armand de Brignac and D'Usse, founding and selling clothing line Rocawear, and collecting valuable works of art. Also a part-owner of Tidal, Rihanna (full name Robyn Rihanna Fenty) has been lauded for her business instincts outside of music. In 2021, she became the youngest self-made female billionaire largely due to her cosmetics line, Fenty Beauty, which was worth $2.8 billion.[4] The ownership of Fenty Beauty is split 50/50 between Fenty herself and LVMH (Moët Hennessy Louis Vuitton), which houses many luxury companies including Dior and Tiffany & Co. Situated in a previously untapped niche of diversity within makeup, Fenty Beauty became a household name.

In some ways, Swift's approach to business mirrors that of Fenty, who developed a recognizable brand of inclusivity by featuring BIPOC models and catered to consumers' needs by offering 40 shades of foundation to complement different skin tones. (Their musical overlaps, on the other hand, are mere trivia—long before she penned "This Is What You Came For," a teenage Swift covered "Umbrella (feat. JAY-Z)" in a live iTunes performance promoting her debut album.) Swift, however, directly applies entrepreneurship to the core product classification of music, resulting in the unique building of her empire. Like the collectible *Lover* diaries and *Midnights* vinyls, everything manufactured and sold by Swift has a tangible connection to the music she writes. Dabbling in goods outside of her music or official lyric- or photo-adorned merchandise has been no exception. Her fragrances, for instance, were named after song lyrics.[5] About the fruity

Wonderstruck released in 2011, Swift expressed a hope for the perfume to play a role in wearers' first impressions, just like the instant "wonderstruck" infatuation she pined about in "Enchanted." The woody, musky Incredible Things, released in 2014, was a physical manifestation of the "incredible things" Swift promises to show in "Blank Space." The bottle displayed a silhouette profile of Swift reminiscent of the one in the music video for "Style," the single after "Blank Space." In the realm of apparel, Swift worked with British fashion designer Stella McCartney on a reasonably priced special edition clothing line to accompany the *Lover* era.[6] This was a tie to the *Lover* track "London Boy," where Swift declares her love for all things London and refers to herself as a "Tennessee Stella McCartney." When Swift played the song for McCartney, McCartney proposed the collaboration. As Swift has never formed a stand-alone entity separate from music-related activity, possession of such limited releases functions as actors within the layered musical universe.

Purchasable items associated with Swift fall under two buckets: the *Taylor Swift Experience* and the *Taylor Swift Good*. These categories, while discrete, are bound to one another, absorbing the movement toward experience-based product promotion.[7] The live concert is the quintessential example of a purchasable event, à la the former, and includes expenses ranging from the ticket, which provides access to the Taylor Swift Experience, to the outfit, which ensures maximum utility derived from the Taylor Swift Experience. In performing, Swift holds herself to the same standards of excellence as in songwriting. Famous for frolicking at rain shows, Swift makes sure to put on the concert despite weathering conditions: "I know I'm going on that stage whether I'm sick, injured, heartbroken, uncomfortable, or stressed. That's part of my identity as a human being now. If someone buys a ticket to my show, I'm going to play it unless we have some sort of force majeure." (The Vienna shows were canceled after Austrian authorities were alerted to a planned terrorist attack. Swift publicly expressed gratitude to the authorities that everyone was "grieving concerts and not lives.") She reassured attendees that the magic of the rhinestoned Versace bodysuit, the first costume of each Eras concert, could "pull [her] out of any funk, fix any headache, [and] heal sore muscles"—performing when she felt suboptimal wasn't a burden, but rather an antidote.[8]

The Glory of Giving Everything

Even as a big-name stadium act, she has a history of constructing a sense of individuality for each show. The Red Tour, the 1989 World Tour, and the Reputation Stadium Tour all featured a surprise song from her discography on acoustic guitar that was not part of the main setlist.[9] On the Speak Now World Tour, she added excitement to touring her solo-authored songs by paying homage to other artists. While the "Fearless x Hey Soul Sister x I'm Yours" mashup remained a staple, she covered a different song each night by an artist from the city she was in: Bruce Springsteen's "Dancing In the Dark" in New Jersey; Britney Spears's "Lucky" in Bossier City; Bryan Adams's "Summer of '69" in Vancouver. On that tour, fans also looked forward to seeing which lyric would be on Swift's left arm, which she scribbled with a Sharpie about five minutes before she took the stage each night. The ritual began when Swift spontaneously wrote "You've got every right to a beautiful life," a lyric from "Who Says" by Selena Gomez & The Scene (Gomez is a September 2024–billionaire largely because of her cosmetics company Rare Beauty), on her arm as a mood booster during a tough rehearsal.[10] The arm lyrics included a range of Swift's favorite artists, some revered (Melbourne: "All romantics meet the same fate somehow" from Joni Mitchell), some contemporary (Detroit: "You better lose yourself in the music" from Eminem), and some of whom she would go on to record with (Washington, D.C.: "I guess to build yourself up so high you had to take her and break her down" from Keith Urban). On the 1989 World Tour, Swift brought out guest stars each night to intentionally keep the suspense for fans who had looked up the setlist prior to attending, explaining, "The things that I try to really focus on when bringing out people as surprise guests is what do my fans really want to see, what would they lose their minds over?"[11] Each surprise duet was performed as a fully choreographed number; for a Halloween show in Tampa, Idina Menzel joined an Olaf-dressed Swift for a rendition of "Let It Go" from Disney's animated hit *Frozen*. On the tour that for Swift, was all about inclusivity, non-musical guests were part of the action too. In Los Angeles, basketball champion Kobe Bryant of the Lakers walked the catwalk during "Style" and gave Swift a sweet surprise of his own: a banner commemorating her record-breaking sold-out shows. When the Eras Tour came to Los Angeles eight years later and three years after Bryant's passing, his daughter Bianka

Bryant was the recipient of the 22 hat. With the tailored efforts made on what could have plainly been commercial tours, fans at each stop felt that they got a worthwhile experience.

As we know, the Taylor Swift Good is anchored by, and driven by, the music first and foremost. Specifically, within the context of the Swift economy where Swift is the producer and Swifties are the consumers, the Taylor Swift Good is inextricably linked to a Taylor Swift Experience. For instance, collecting any of the 11 variants (at the time of writing) of the *folklore* cardigan brings the wearer back to the comfort of listening to "cardigan" in quarantine. Tightening the bond between experiences and goods is a system that effectively capitalizes on the societal shift toward experiential spending, which can include traveling, dining out, and attending live events. Spearheaded by millennials, a generation that Swift claimed "no one's prouder" to be part of, the trend has accelerated since the 1990s and become the fascination of modern consumer research. From 2014 to 2016 in the United States, experiential expenditures increased almost 4.0 times faster than material expenditures, and over 1.5 times faster than overall consumption expenditures. Millennials, of whom over 75 percent would choose to pay for an experience over a good, spent more than Gen X and baby boomers on entertainment and fitness memberships in 2016. Since experiences are translatable into shareable content on social media, which focuses on what users are doing rather than buying, millennials' spending habits are likely to trickle down to Gen Z, whose grip on the digital lifestyle is starting to outpace that of millennials. In line with that, a 2017 report by McKinsey & Company predicted that the change toward experience-based spending behavior would not be transient.[12]

Importantly, investing in experiences isn't only born out of a fear of missing out as people attempt to one-up peers via social media posts. Consumers' experiential purchases have been linked to higher levels of happiness than material purchases. Recall (from Chapter 3) that the economist's unit of layman's term—happiness is utility, and that each consumer has a utility function determined by their idiosyncratic preferences. The roots of utility theory were planted by Swiss mathematician and physicist Daniel Bernoulli in the eighteenth century and advanced by Hungarian-American mathematician John von Neumann and German economist Oskar Morgenstern in the twentieth century. At the turn of the twenty-first

100 The Glory of Giving Everything

century, economists began to dice utility further, defining *anticipatory utility* as the value derived from looking forward to an upcoming event, *experienced utility* as the value derived from the real-time undergoing of an event, and *remembered utility* as the value derived from retrospectively evaluating a past event.[13] According to a 2020 study conducted by researchers at the University of Texas at Austin, the University of Pennsylvania, and Cornell University, experiential purchases led to increased utility on all three fronts. Simply put, people were happier before, during, and after consuming an experience compared to consuming a material good or consuming nothing at all, after accounting for price and across every experiential and material category.[14] The experience of romance might lend itself to these three kinds of utility. *The New York Times* journalist Taffy Brodesser-Akner commented on Swift's depiction of such an experience: "Her songbook is really only minimally about romantic love, and the best part of romantic love, which is its moment of revelation. It's maximally about the other things that happen to a person in life: about the sometimes-questionable, sometimes-great, sometimes-tragic aftermath of that revelation…"[15] Anticipatory is "Electric Touch," a four-and-a-half-minute pep talk before a first date dueted with Patrick Stump of rock band Fall Out Boy; in-the-present is "Paper Rings," a shout-from-the-rooftop declaration of love; remembered is "Holy Ground," a no-longer-bitter tribute to the kind of dancing that would never be the same.

While Swift might not be acquainted with the minutiae of utility types, she does pronounce a familiarity with ancient Greek philosopher Aristotle ("So High School"). Aristotle considered two conceptions of human happiness—hedonia, which correlates with pleasure, and eudaimonia, which correlates with fulfillment—that went on to be popularized in psychology and the social sciences.[16] Arguably, the arete (borrowing another Greek term) of the Eras Tour appealed to all the aforementioned kinds of well-being. With the average Eras Tour attendee spending around $1,300 (a figure Swift would appreciate), Swift knew that basking in the glory meant giving everything she had: "[Fans] had to work really hard to get the tickets. I wanted to play a show that was longer than they ever thought it would be, because that makes me feel good leaving the stadium."[17] Her desire to celebrate both the four new albums since her last tour and ongoing re-recording project matched fans' craving for live events after lockdown. Indeed, large-format shows, not only Swift's,

Reaching Your Billionaire Era

enjoyed a 70 percent increase in 2022–2024 compared to 2015–2019.[18] As an immersive spectacle with 16 costume changes, hydraulic platforms, and visual effects including a simulated swimmer's dive into the stage, the Eras concert was as exhilarating as it was entertaining; in other words, it was hedonic. As a reminiscent journey through career- and life-defining musical arrangements, the Eras concert was awash with nostalgia and belonging; in other words, it was eudaimonic. These sensations made up concertgoers' in-the-moment experienced utility. Brodesser-Akner described her Eras experience in Santa Clara, the California town redubbed Swiftie Clara where Swift was named the mayor, as an all-encompassing trance not unlike that found in temples. The tradition of surprises from past tours ran wild at the Eras Tour: two to five surprise songs on guitar and piano, announcements of endeavors like re-recorded albums and music videos, guest appearances from those who had a hand in writing and/or recording tracks with Swift, and setlist adjustments. Like the Speak Now World Tour covers, Swift cemented the distinctive feel of each night with location-specific twists, whether it was through the welcome—she learned to say "Welcome to the Eras Tour!" in 15 languages; during the acoustic section—she mashed up "Paris" and "Begin Again" (whose music video was filmed in Paris) on piano in Paris; or with the help of dancer Kameron Saunders, who counted off in the local language for "I Can Do It With a Broken Heart" and swapped the "like ever!" in "We Are Never Ever Getting Back Together" for a culturally significant phrase—he exclaimed "Ew, David, ew!" as a reference to Canadian sitcom *Schitt's Creek* in Toronto.[19]

The Eras Tour reigned as the epitomized Taylor Swift Experience not only because of its experienced utility, but also for its intensified anticipatory and remembered utility. For some, the Eras Tour was folded into vacation plans. These fans attended in a city where tickets were more accessible, where they wanted to visit as a tourist, or where they felt was important to Swift and predicted to be the bearer of extra surprises, such as Nashville or London, or opening or closing nights. (The Nashville weekend included the reveal of *Speak Now (Taylor's Version)* and live debut of "Nothing New" with featured artist Phoebe Bridgers; the closing night of London included the live debut of "Florida!!! (feat. Florence + the Machine)" with Florence Welch as well as an acoustic performance and re-enactment of the writing

The Glory of Giving Everything

session of "Getaway Car" with Antonoff.[20]) But whether your show was local or global, preparation was required. Fans who had long been emotionally embodying the songs, albums, and eras of Swift's career seized the opportunity to physically personify those. They thoroughly re-created tour and music video looks or artfully mixed pieces to dress as a lyric. They devoted hours to stringing beads together to spell out titles, lyrics, and inside jokes on friendship bracelets. These pre-concert practices were part of fans' Swift-recounted identity-seeking voyage, and helped mold arenas into fervent spaces to deepen their connection to Swift, other Swifties, and themselves. The era you came dressed as or the friendship bracelet you chose from an outstretched hand weren't merely fashion statements, but rather tangible trinkets of the self.

Since consumers gravitate toward shared experiences, even if it sacrifices the quality of said experience,[21] getting ready for the Eras Tour was as collective as it was individual. Social media was wielded to spin a cohesive narrative that documented every part of the tour, from unexpected surprise song updates to fans' detailed costumes. Swift's marketing and management team, Taylor Nation, encouraged online conversations with a stream of real-time information, reposts of creative attire, and hashtags for each stop. Bill Gates, co-founder of software company Microsoft with a net worth of over $100 billion, cited the absence of social media as critical to his billion-dollar ideas; ever-adaptive Swift found a way to make it advantageous to her billion-dollar ideas.[22] Continuous engagement with Eras Tour content when fans were not yet at the stadium heightened excitement for when the magical night would be theirs.

The mentally evocative steps that concertgoers took to coordinate for the show—which might have involved, for longtime fans, digging through recollections to settle on their current era, or for newer fans, discovering Swift's past work—coalesced into the singular extravaganza of the live Eras concert. This catapulted all of the remembered utility that had been derived from participating in previous Taylor Swift Experiences over the years into the remembered utility for the Eras Tour. Swift had once shared with fans that the song "All Too Well" had "two lives": "There's the life of this song that was born out of catharsis and venting and trying to get over something...and then there's the life where it went out into the world...You turned this song into a collage of memories of watching you scream the words to this song, or seeing pictures that you post to me of you having written the words to this song in your diary, or you showing me your wrist and you have a tattoo of the lyrics to this song underneath your skin." "All Too Well" was transformed from Swift's lone emotional processing to her consistently highest rated, most impactful song. Reciprocally, she wished for her hits to be reborn at the Eras Tour: "These are songs I have written about my life or things I felt at one point in time, whether I was a teenager, in my 20s, or a couple years ago. But after tonight, when you hear these songs out and about in the world, my dream is that you're gonna think about tonight and the memories we made here together." For Swift, this was an accomplishable dream, as explained by our pop culture buddy at *Uproxx*: "She's dismantled the former 'new work vs. old work' binary for artists and replaced it with the 'Eras' paradigm, where her songs are parceled into different concurrent channels that are equally accessible. It's the same logic that streaming platforms have taught us, where all of music history exists in the same bucket. And Taylor Swift has figured out how to reprogram the public's internal algorithm better than any of her competitors, so that her historical fame doesn't count against her contemporary fame."[23] The addition of *The Tortured Poets Department* to the setlist, starting with the European leg, demonstrated this. The Eras Tour had become a fluid exhibition of her classics and her moderns, all of which were now remembered as having been part of the tour along with the actual periods of time they had been released. For the majority of fans who attended a show prior to closing night, they returned to the handheld screen to keep up with the rest of the tour, making social media a pragmatic tool for feeding both anticipatory and remembered utility. As a quantitative testament to these utility types, the median secondary-market ticket price for the Eras Tour steadily increased as it progressed, a phenomenon not observed in comparable tours.[24] Those who weren't planning on going noticed others' anticipatory utility and felt the need to partake, and fans who had already gone acted upon their remembered utility to attend again.

Embarking on a perennial tour, coupled with knowledge of experiential spending habits, might discourage a producer from selling material items. But completely abstaining or pivoting away from doing so would squander potential. A more adroit strategy would be to procure goods from the sought-after experience (top-down). If goods are the starting point, illuminate them by designing experiences around them (bottom-up). Retailer Williams-Sonoma offers an assortment of in-store and virtual events to complement its kitchenware and home furnishing products. With cooking classes, book gatherings, and a private event space, the high-end brand is inviting rather than repellent. Even on an unscheduled basis, mini experiences of demonstrations, tastings, and advice sessions greet patrons who wander in. This was all in line with founder Chuck Williams's mission to make premium French cookware accessible for Americans. Williams opened the first shop in Sonoma, California, in 1956, and the entity has remained profitable.[25] To illustrate the top-down method, enter the Taylor Swift Good. While every show was treated to their own surprise songs, New Jersey was in for a purchasable surprise: a *Midnights* CD featuring the vault track "You're Losing Me," exclusively available at the Metlife Stadium stands. Fans lined up far in advance of the stands' opening, as possession of the special edition, branded as *Midnights (The Late Night Edition)*, would reflect their specific New Jersey Eras experience. A digital copy of *Midnights (The Late Night Edition)* was soon made available on Swift's website for a limited 24-hour period, still relying on consumers' sense of urgency to buy without hesitation. Nearing the end of her tour, Swift put out the coffee table–style *The Official Taylor Swift | The Eras Tour Book*, prompting fans to purchase the book to hold on to the cherished experience they had at the show. She also dropped the Acoustic Piano Collection on her website, which included a holiday stocking decorated like the acoustic piano on the Eras Tour, to remind fans of the portion of the concert that was special each night. If consumers are happier when they spend on experiences, there's a likelihood that they'd be willing to spend on mementos that connect to those experiences. For them, utility from these goods might be pocketed into the remembered utility of the experience it attaches to. At the Eras Tour—the first tour to gross $1 billion, then the first tour to gross $2 billion—a collective $862 million was spent on merchandise.[26]

The money spent on a Taylor Swift Experience, a Taylor Swift Good, or any experience or good stems from a consumer's *willingness to pay* (WTP), which is determined by that consumer's utility function. Consumers are willing and able to spend up until their WTP, or the maximum dollar amount they'd pay for that experience or good (we'll now refer to both experiences and goods as "goods" for this discussion). The WTP of all the

Reaching Your Billionaire Era

105

consumers in the economy make up a downward sloping demand curve, where generally speaking, higher prices lead to lower demand and lower prices lead to higher demand. Goods that are inexpensive tend to be bought in larger quantities and be demanded by more people due to their affordability. However, as people flock to these goods, the goods' value increases and prices rise accordingly, provoking the other demand relationship that helps balance prices at equilibrium: high demand (relative to supply) drives higher prices and low demand (relative to supply) drives lower prices.[27] Goods that are more desirable are demanded by a larger number of people, by people with deeper pockets, or a combination of the two. Either way, these items move from producer to consumer at a faster rate compared to items that are less desirable. As these goods are more valuable, they are more expensive, partly due to increased production costs that come with distribution on a greater scale. For example, general admission to Swift's 2007 concert at a gym at Alabama's Saks High School cost $20.[28] She played five songs off of her debut album and had proceeds go toward the school's football team. Admission to the Eras Tour was priced higher because of her accumulated value as well as her crew's laborious effort to set up multidimensional stages. On the flip side, less desirable goods are demanded by fewer people, by people with more scarce monetary resources, or a combination of the two. Either way, these items do not fly off shelves. As these goods are less valuable, they are less expensive, partly because sellers of these items must find a way to entice buyers, and lower prices can be attractive.

WTP reveals preferences but does not always dictate specific actions. Let's consider a shopper named Cory with a WTP of $15.00 for any copy of *The Tortured Poets Department*. Cory has the following options: the digital download of *The Tortured Poets Department* for $11.99, the digital download of *The Tortured Poets Department: The Anthology* for $14.99, the vinyl of *The Tortured Poets Department* with bonus track "The Manuscript" for $34.99, or the vinyl of *The Tortured Poets Department: The Anthology* for $59.99. Cory will definitely not purchase either vinyl because $34.99 and $59.99 are over $15.00. However, his $15.00 WTP does not necessitate that he will buy the digital copy of *The Tortured Poets Department: The Anthology* for $14.99. Even though he's willing to spend up to $15.00, it's possible that he will opt for the standard edition for $11.99 and take the remaining $3.01 as consumer surplus. There are also multiple ways for consumers to

106 The Glory of Giving Everything

arrive at the same utility level, represented visually by an indifference curve that graphs the different combinations of goods that give a consumer the same utility. Cory likes all the albums, but his favorite is *Taylor Swift*. Let's say that his WTP for an Eras Tour ticket is $105.00 (on the lower end because of the tour's exclusion of the debut album). Alternatively, for $105.00, he can watch the Eras Tour movie for $19.89, buy *The Official Taylor Swift | The Eras Tour Book* for $39.99, and order a debut-themed Eras Tour T-shirt from Swift's website for $45.00.[29] When the opportunity to snag a $105.00 Eras Tour ticket arises, Cory might go for it, but he also might opt for the series of purchases; the economist would say that he is indifferent between the two routes.

Because many aspects of the globetrotting Eras Tour could not be easily replicated, most consumers would not easily find an equatable experience to live along their indifference curve. Many Swiftie concertgoers, then, had a higher WTP than Cory for an Eras Tour ticket (or multiple—one 27-year-old fan attended 20 Eras concerts[30]). Many of them also had a higher WTP for an Eras Tour ticket than for all other purchasable forms of entertainment, like tickets to attend a sports game, see a circus, or watch live theater. With a total of over 10 million attendees, Eras Tour tickets cost $218.90 on average, more expensive than the live entertainment industry average of $131.00 for the top 100 worldwide tours in 2023 and $135.92 in 2024. This data did not include secondary markets on platforms like StubHub and Vivid Seats. On the resale market, the average ticket price shot up to $839 in North America. For the closing weekend in Vancouver, Eras Tour tickets were resold for $2,952 on average. The spokesperson for StubHub, for whom the Eras Tour was their highest-selling tour since its launch in 2000, emphasized the consumer-initiated price-setting of the secondary market: "This is truly a market-driven platform. So this is really about what sellers think that the price, the value of the ticket is, and what buyers think the value of the ticket is, and they effectively agree on it with a purchase." Had Swift squeezed fans out based upon their sky-high valuation of her products, she would have made an extra $50 million per stop.[31]

The secondary market was influenced by patterns from behavioral economics that explain exacerbated value perceptions.[32] Coined by economist Richard Thaler in 1980, the *endowment effect* states that people value something they own simply because it is theirs. Thaler, along with psychologist

Reaching Your Billionaire Era 107

Daniel Kahneman and economist Jack Knetsch, conducted an experiment where participants were randomly assigned to a seller group, which was given mugs, or a buyer group. Each group was instructed to price the mug, and participants in the seller group consistently priced the mug higher than those in the buyer group, with the median selling price around twice as much as the median buying price. The endowment effect was a display of *loss aversion*, developed by Kahneman and psychologist Amos Tversky in 1979. Loss aversion deals with an asymmetrical value perception of gains and losses. The disutility from losing a good is greater in magnitude than the utility from gaining an equivalent good; for instance, winning $50 is nice, but losing $50 tends to come with a sense of pain that is felt more strongly than the joy of winning. Related is the concept of *status quo bias*, originated by economists William Samuelson and Richard Zeckhauser in 1988, which affirms that people have a preference for the status quo over a change. A 2006 National Bureau of Economic Research working paper investigated the role of defaults on employees' retirement plans and demonstrated that more employees saved for retirement when their paychecks were already set up to contribute to a designated account. They were not likely to change the status quo by opting out, even if they wouldn't have voluntarily opted in to save for retirement had the default been not to contribute. Applying these effects to an already-tantalizing tour, resellers of Eras Tour tickets (whether they bought them intending to sell or were reluctantly parting with them due to unforeseen circumstances) considered their tickets particularly valuable and priced them accordingly. Aligning sellers' higher-than-average prices with buyers' higher-than-average WTP, the ensuing effects on the secondary market were expected.

Given the plethora of goods associated with this Taylor Swift Experience, including ones not produced by Swift herself, Swifties' WTP extended beyond the ticket.[33] Orders from Georgia-based fashion designer Loren McManus blew up when she started making custom Eras Tour outfits, with McManus discerning that some were spending even more on the costumes than they did on the tickets. One of McManus's clients acknowledged that she "thought long and hard about what [she] could pay to have somebody make something that nobody else would have," deciding on the mirrorball-esque outfit from the 2018 American Music Awards. Replicas of Swift's Reputation Stadium Tour green sequin jacket, the most requested item,

108 The Glory of Giving Everything

ranged from $450 to $1,500. Notably, this was the jacket Swift donned while playing the acoustic surprise song during that 2018 tour, and re-creating this outfit naturally reminded fans of their exclusive stadium experience via the distinguishing surprise song. In anticipation of Swift's shows in Seattle, crafts store Bead World, which has been open for as long as she has been alive, underwent their biggest sales period in history. Bead World found that they were busier than during Christmastime, which was their usual peak of the year. The shop was left scrambling to reorder merchandise, a problem for which they were likely thankful. For the Miami stop, fans flocked to the city without Eras Tour tickets, hoping to snatch some last minute but knowing that even if they didn't, they would enjoy the zest nonetheless. Miami had a carousel of Swift-themed activities, organized for visitors in a dedicated event guide, to honor the star's arrival. On both nights in Munich, an estimated 50,000 people congregated at a park behind the stadium Swift was playing to listen to the shows. In fact, at virtually every stop on the tour, legions of ticketless fans gathered in the outdoor vicinities of the stadiums in a convention known as "Taylor-gating" to sing along and dance to the concert in real time.

Entertainment research shows that for a typical concert, a $100 ticket bought by a tourist would generate an additional $334.92 in spending, making for a total spending impact of $434.92.[34] Exhibit 7.2 calculates the total spending impact of an average-priced concert ticket both for the Eras Tour and across the live entertainment industry.

The positive economic chain reaction happened for the Eras Tour not only at a higher average ticket price, but also in larger waves of attendees. The Federal Reserve Bank of Philadelphia noted that hotel revenue when Swift came to Philly was the strongest since the COVID-19 pandemic. Pittsburgh, another city in Swift's home state, gained $46 million from concertgoers, of whom 83 percent were visitors to Allegheny County, with hotel stays averaging $309 per night. When the Eras Tour, along with other events, came to Chicago, the place reached a high for most hotel rooms occupied in their history, not just after the pandemic. In Cincinnati, downtown hotels made over $2.6 million and county hotels made over $5.3 million, which the city attributed to Swift. Los Angeles, where Swift announced *1989 (Taylor's Version)*, enjoyed a rise in employment of 3,300 workers and earnings of $160 million. Although the United States

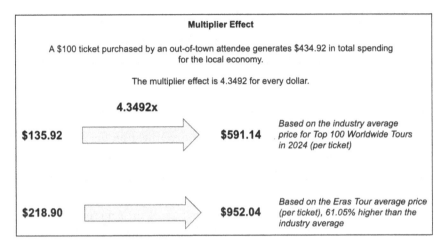

Exhibit 7.2 Multiplier Effect

reaped the most benefits from the tour of self-proclaimed Miss Americana with $4.98 billion from both U.S. legs, every country Swift graced experienced a bump. The United Kingdom, with $1.26 billion in growth, was second after the U.S. Japan, with $230 million in growth, ranked higher than European countries France, Italy, Germany, and Ireland. Spain, with $26 million in growth, served as the lower bound of the list. Overall, the Eras Tour boosted the global economy by over $9 billion.[35] If we multiply our calculated average spending per person of $952.04 with the 10,168,008 people in attendance, we'd get an aggregate spending on the Eras Tour of $9.68 billion.[36] Such economic growth exemplifies the *multiplier effect*, which is the effect of a change in economic activity on total economic output. When Bead World owner Nicolette Stessin makes more money, she can then spend more on consuming other products and supporting other businesses. Alternatively, she can save or invest the money to secure her future. Swift's donation to the Cardiff Foodbank in Wales nourished 925 people, and those 925 people not only had food, but they could also allocate the cash they had toward other necessities.[37]

Swift's employees benefited from the multiplier effect as well. Reportedly, the Eras Tour truck drivers, who each received $100,000 in bonuses in July 2023, put those earnings toward homeownership and their children's education, both investments with a high rate of return. With the end of the first leg of the tour in August 2023, bonuses for the whole crew totaled

110 The Glory of Giving Everything

$55 million. At the end of the tour in December 2024, Swift shelled out another $197 million in bonuses for the whole crew, nearly 10 percent of the tour's overall gross. Whether the lighting staff, security guards, physical therapists, and every other Eras crew member splurged or saved, Swift took care to reward the hard work of her team.[38] Widely recognized coffee chain Starbucks refers to this as "relational capital," with former CEO Howard Schultz writing in his memoir, "We can be extremely profitable and competitive, with a highly regarded brand, and also be respected for treating our people well. In the end, it's not only possible to do both, but you can't really do one without the other."[39]

A kind of intangible capital, whether it ends up spurring monetary capital or not, may very well make up the heart of the fandom. The Swiftie community includes—and welcomes—international fans, who reside in countries where Swift isn't able to tour, and budget-sensitive fans, who don't have the means for a Taylor Swift Experience or a Taylor Swift Good. Take the popular game Mastermind as a sample economy. The game united fans worldwide by giving out prizes for correct predictions of outfits and surprise songs on each night of the Eras Tour. Mastermind was hosted on a free app called Swift Alert, and the prizes, which consisted of bundles of Taylor Swift Goods, were fan-donated. For a one-time $1.99 fee, users could download an All-Access version of the advertisement-free app, which concatenates all Swift-related activity, including trivia quizzes, ranking games, and a pipeline to Taylor Nation, in one place (Mastermind was available on the free version). Swift Alert celebrated all participants by sculpting its role as a Swiftie-centric hub, publishing data of users' guesses to its hundreds of thousands of social media followers and topping it off by setting up Mastermind Live, an in-person meeting point at the last Eras stop in Vancouver. During its run, Mastermind had 1,240,004 players; the app overall (as of 2024) has users from each of the 195 countries in the world, most densely the United States (732,697), the United Kingdom (239,638), and Brazil (150,611).[40]

Like Mastermind, a thriving economy has a variety of players whose contributions balance out in equilibrium. A broader adoption of the WTP framework might examine fans' willingness to spend time, among other non-monetary constructs, on Swift. Out of pure enthusiasm, fans heavily discuss Swift content with other Swifties or Swiftie-adjacents in online and offline spaces. This expands the community, in which there are fans who would be willing to pay dollars on experiences or goods. Additionally, with the time that Swifties spend listening to her music, Swift has broken a myriad of streaming and viewing records, which have cultivated her status as an icon. Spotify Wrapped, after all, isn't just a fun feature that users look forward to each year, but it's a measure of how much artists' music has stuck with listeners that year. Journalist Daniel Griffiths took to industry resource MusicRadar to explain that a high Spotify Wrapped ranking was an artist's "passport to festival headline slots, movie soundtrack offers and cameos, and celebrity endorsements from soft drinks to soft play...everywhere you can make money from music, that isn't actually music, because...nobody makes money from music except for Spotify."[41] As a thank you gift to fans for making her Spotify's most streamed artist of 2023, Swift released "You're Losing Me" on streaming platforms everywhere.[42] It was an acknowledgement not of money spent on her, but of the spirit.

8

Impact, Implicated

The moxie of the Eras Tour is part of the fabric delineating the role of entertainment in the public's lives, Swiftie or not. Beyond providing leisure, pop culture increasingly permeates our society to shape attitudes, opinions, and behavior. From 1998 to 2004, cosmopolitan HBO series *Sex and the City* attracted a cult following by boldly championing female independence, sexuality, and fashion. When viewers tuned in to its 2021 reboot, *And Just Like That...* (named after the original's commonly uttered punchline reveal), they were stunned at a death in the first episode. Main character Carrie Bradshaw's love interest, known as Mr. Big, collapsed in a heart attack upon finishing a ride on his Peloton stationary bike. Although this was fictional, the exercise company faced real-world repercussions; its stock plummeted 11.3 percent right after the first episode aired and continued falling more than 5 percent the next day.[1] Peloton, which knew about the bike's appearance in advance but not the details of the storyline, responded promptly. Dr. Suzanne Steinbaum, a member of Peloton's health and wellness advisory council, commented on Mr. Big's "extravagant" diet and lifestyle—habits that were visible within the world of the *Sex and the City* franchise—that likely contributed to his demise. Instead of invalidating those whose perceptions were influenced by a television show, the brand alleviated consumers' fears by meeting them where they were. (Peloton also released an advertisement featuring Chris Noth, who plays Mr. Big, about

114   The Glory of Giving Everything

to get on a Peloton bike, purporting that he was alive.) Despite the potential grounds for litigation—HBO was technically in violation of nominative fair use under trademark law, which states that products must be shown in a manner consistent with the original trademark—Peloton's nonconfrontational handling was more effective.

A few years prior, a parallel incident occurred with NBC drama *This Is Us*, which was groundbreaking for its time-jumping portrayal of complex family dynamics and ran from 2016 to 2022. In the second season, a faulty Crock-Pot sets the primary family's house on fire the night of the 1998 Super Bowl, and the father, Jack Pearson, suffers cardiac arrest from smoke inhalation. By the next morning, the slow cooker company was under intense scrutiny. Like Peloton, Crock-Pot took action by working with, not against, the instigator. Crock-Pot, along with show creator Dan Fogelman, produced a video featuring Milo Ventimiglia ("Jack") inviting viewers to come together for the 2018 Super Bowl with food from their Crock-Pots. Crock-Pot also immediately joined the online discourse with Twitter handle @CrockPotCares and circulated #CrockPotIsInnocent. The account grew more than 2,000 percent in its first 48 hours, and the hashtag won best "Hashtag, Real Time Response" at the Shorty Awards, which recognizes outstanding digital content by brands. As a testament to Crock-Pot's strategy, sales for the slow cooker jumped by 3.1 percent in the year following the episode. For an appliance whose popularity peaked in the 1970s as a way for working women to prepare meals, pop culture revitalized its relevance.[2]

As a fulcrum of the modern cultural zeitgeist, Swift is no stranger to these stratospheric effects.[3] After being romantically linked to Kansas City Chiefs tight end Travis Kelce, Kelce's jersey sales shot up by 400 percent, and the NFL had its highest female viewership (2023 season) since 2000. With the Chiefs' home game ticket sales increasing by almost three times, the football team's fan base expanded by 30 percent. When Swift was reported to be eating chicken with ketchup and "seemingly ranch" at one of the games, food processing company Heinz quickly developed a limited edition condiment called "Ketchup & Seemingly Ranch." The product had the same ketchup–ranch mix concept of its 2019 predecessor, Kranch, yet Ketchup & Seemingly Ranch sold at a rate 320 percent faster than Kranch. Similarly, the Pirouette Skort from activewear brand POPFLEX sold out in 15 minutes after Swift was seen donning it in her #ForAFortnightChallenge video.

Impact, Implicated   115

At times, the impact has been on a structural, rather than consumerist, level. Instagram's feature that allows users to ban comments containing designated emojis or words kicked in after Swift's pre-*Reputation* battle against snake emojis. The filter was first tested on Swift's account, then piloted with other celebrities facing cyberbullying, and finally made available to the general public, as a step toward instilling more positivity in online spaces.

Unintentional byproducts on a scale this massive beg the question of how much more fruitful intentional efforts would be. During the 2018 midterm elections, Swift made her first political statement, endorsing Phil Bredesen over Marsha Blackburn for the United States Senate from Tennessee.[4] The decision to do so after an apolitical career was a clear one for Swift personally, but it was one riddled with tension for Swift as an enterprise. Threats to business and safety were among her team's considerations when advising her, as she had dealt with harassment even during political silence. Despite voiced concerns that the move would "halve" any future tour audience, Swift felt strongly about speaking out, as Blackburn's values clashed with what she believed her home state should encapsulate. In her Instagram post, she implored people to vote not for who she wanted to be elected, but for who they wanted to be elected: "Please, please educate yourself on the candidates running in your state and vote based on who most closely represents your values." This was a complete and delightful surprise for Bredesen, who then shared photos of him and Swift working together to fight online predators in 2007 and raise money for flood victims in 2010. Although Blackburn was ultimately elected, there was a measurable impact on voting turnout. In the 24 hours after Swift's statement, 65,000 new voters registered to Vote.org, the site Swift directed followers to in the post's caption. In five days, 434,000 new voters registered, with 65 percent of those being people under the age of 30. The voting turnout of Tennessee, the 17th most populous state, was within the top 10, an impressive feat since voter registrations tend to mirror a state's population.

In the 2020 U.S. presidential election, Swift publicly favored Joe Biden and denounced Donald Trump, speaking on *V Magazine*'s Thought Leaders Issue and baking blue-frosted "Biden Harris 2020" cookies. For the 2024 U.S. presidential election, the Biden campaign's open social media position was overwhelmed with applications detailing a strategy to get Swift's endorsement once again. When Biden stepped down and Kamala

116   The Glory of Giving Everything

Harris stepped in as the Democratic candidate, Swift took to Instagram to share that she would be voting for Harris. Again, she emphasized the importance to followers of deciding their own stances: "I've done my research, and I've made my choice. Your research is all yours to do, and the choice is yours to make." The ensuing 24 hours saw 405,999 visitors to Vote.org, a stark uptick from the average of 30,000 daily visits the site had garnered in the week prior to Swift's post.[5]

Like Bredesen, Harris—whose campaign produced Swift-inspired friendship bracelets that sold out within hours—did not win the election. Interestingly, in a poll conducted by Quinnipiac University in Connecticut, 9 percent of poll respondents felt "more enthusiastic" about Harris's candidacy after Swift's post, but a higher amount, 13 percent, felt "less enthusiastic." The same pattern occurred with Elon Musk's endorsement of Trump, where 13 percent of respondents felt more enthusiastic after it, but 21 percent felt less enthusiastic. The majority of respondents, 76 percent in the case of Swift/Harris and 64 percent in the case of Musk/Trump, stated that these endorsements had no effect on their viewpoints.[6] Survey data from business intelligence pollster Morning Consult demonstrated that a large portion of Swift's fan base was already young, female, and Democratic. Other parts of her fan base were international or under the age of 18 and had no bearing on the U.S. election. Additionally, Trump supporters already had a less favorable view of Swift compared to Harris supporters. Therefore, it's plausible that neither side would significantly sway based on a post from her. It's also possible that Swift simply expedited the process for some who already planned on voting, but were reminded to do so while scrolling social media and thus switched tabs from Instagram to Vote.org. For some, a political endorsement from Swift wasn't a criterion of ethics but a means of validation of aligned beliefs, thus adding to the simulated sense of closeness with her. For example, Philadelphia-based 38-year-old Jacob Phelps asserted that he would not change his vote because of Swift but expressed relief over the candidate she chose to speak out for.

Anecdotal evidence reinforces the prospect of impact on an individual level.[7] Texas-based 67-year-old Michael Dee: "I think she could, potentially, absolutely change my mind politically, because she is a strong woman who is a role model to my 24-year-old daughter...It is time we prepare the next generation of women for leadership." Utah-based 29-year-old Noel Drake:

Impact, Implicated

117

"With this sense of community that I have established through interacting with other Swifties online, it has really changed the way I interact with politics this election cycle." Perceptibly, Swift is able to alter the brain chemistry of possibly agnostic members of society. With her framing not as a superstar, not as an activist, but as a responsible citizen, they are informed that basic civic duty is worth exercising. Higher participation both quantitatively and qualitatively in a system as fundamental as democracy, which conceptually functions only as well as its contributors, has long-lasting productive spillover effects. Bredesen's communications director, Laura Zapata, noted that efforts like Swift's are "always worth the swing" no matter the outcome of a given election. For fans Emerald Medrano and Irene Kim, founding advocacy group Swifties for Kamala was worth the swing. The grassroots organization, which focused on voter education and raised $235,000 for the Harris campaign, was started prior to Swift's post. Kim clarified that executing this mission would have been done "regardless" of Swift's endorsement. Swifties for Kamala garnered the attention that it did because the group harnessed the communal capacity of Swift's fans: "We are used to sharing information together as a community. So now, instead of doing it around Taylor, we're doing it around voting and this election, and I think it's helped make it really accessible." Swift's political power might not always stem from the singular statements she posts at singular moments in time, but rather from the messaging she inculcates in her fan base of consumers and stakeholders. Another immediate effect of Swift's Harris endorsement was an expansion of that fan base, as she gained 1.85 million followers on Spotify following it, contrary to the previously predicted effect on her number of fans. It's no surprise that the AI-generated images spread by Trump's campaign spelled out "Swifties for Trump" instead of "Swift for Trump" in an attempt to misinform the public of Swift's (nonexistent) support for Trump.

Along the spectrum of sentiments, people have expressed other opinions, from ambivalent to oppositional. Colorado-based 58-year-old Geoff Lusk: "I think she would be far more effective if she didn't endorse a candidate but instead told her fans to study the issues and make up their own minds." California-based 34-year-old Leigh (last name ungiven): "If Taylor Swift endorsed a presidential candidate, I would be angry. Americans do not need more noise in their already noisy election. We do not want musicians having that much power that they could sway a political election to one side

118   The Glory of Giving Everything

or another." Given the range of beliefs, both politically and on what celebrities' political involvement should or shouldn't be, satisfying every single person might prove impossible. Exemplifying this was one of *Lover*'s singles, "You Need to Calm Down," an LGBTQIA+ anthem.[8] The song's music video featured queer icons as well as a link to sign a petition she created to get the Equality Act to pass in the U.S. Senate. (The law, which aimed to combat discrimination on the basis of sex, sexual orientation, and gender identity, had already passed in the House, but did not end up passing in the Senate.) After the video, the Gay & Lesbian Alliance Against Defamation (GLAAD) expressed gratitude for the singer's shoutout, as it drove a surge of donations to the organization. Psychologist Kevin Nadal, who researches discrimination against LGBTQIA+ folks, stated that "anytime" a celebrity spoke out on social justice using their platform was overall positive. However, Swift was also accused of exploiting and capitalizing on the struggles of a marginalized community. Some were adamant that the move was a trendy latch onto performative, rather than pure, allyship, while others pointed out that any one song shouldn't be expected to carry the weight of entire advocacy movements. But when Swift cast transgender model and actor Laith Ashley as her love interest in the music video for *Midnights* single "Lavender Haze," contention quieted. Feedback was decidedly positive, with Ashley receiving thousands of messages from trans people affirming the importance of representation for the community through Swift's video.[9] Here, there was no flashy (as perceived by detractors) pro-gay lyricism or bandwagon (as perceived by detractors) petition, no noise that could be cited as a purported distraction from the true cause; there was only visibility enacted through action. Unlike a spike in voter registration or monetary contributions, the extensive reach of such representation isn't readily quantifiable. Medrano, our Swifties for Kamala co-founder, is a Latinx trans man, who may or may not have been empowered by Ashley. *Vogue*'s Abbie Aguirre wrote that prior to *Lover*, Swift's pro-LGBTQIA+ gestures were "subtle, but none insignificant," noting a number of signals dating back to "at least 2011" from the *Speak Now, 1989*, and *Reputation* eras.[10]

For a celebrity like Swift, gently leading by example is a valuable form of advocacy. Among the numerous reasons that explain why adolescents look up to famous people, from athletes to politicians to content creators, character attributes are the most cited cause.[11] A 2011 study conducted by

Impact, Implicated   119

the University of Pittsburgh School of Medicine showed that ninth graders who frequently listened to music with references to cannabis were more likely to use the drug compared to those who weren't as highly exposed to cannabis-laced music.[12] Music can work wonders both negatively and positively. In 2021, World Wildlife Fund conservation scientist Jeff Opperman discovered that *folklore* and *evermore* featured nature seven times more than a similarly sized sample of "Today's Top Hits"—1.68 percent compared to 0.24 percent. Of the 0.24 percent of nature-themed words from the 32 analyzed hit songs, almost one-third came from Ed Sheeran's "Afterglow" (removing the cozy Sheeran tune would have brought Swift's statistic to ten times as opposed to seven times). Nature on Swift's isolation records wasn't only prevalent by recent standards, as the declining nature in song lyrics was stated to have gone from 1.1 percent in 1950 to 0.4 percent in 2010 (as determined by a loosely comparable method). Opperman believed that this was noteworthy not because lyrical mentions are meant to save nature, but because they highlight nature as an interactive backdrop for moments of life: "Ms. Swift's songs aren't going to reverse climate change or the decline of wildlife. But they are a step toward reversing the decline of nature in pop culture, and that matters. If we want to change the world to safeguard nature, and ourselves, we first have to see it. Art can do that."[13]

Politics, too, has weaved its way into Swift's writing, unsurprising for someone who reads political news every day.[14] Her first overtly political song, *Lover*'s "Miss Americana & The Heartbreak Prince," is set in a metaphorical high school, vividly characterizing her transition to deeper involvement in current events while retaining her authentic perspective. She chose it as the opening song on the Eras Tour. The title track of *evermore*—whose nature references include frost, waves, and a wild winter—begins in a gloomy November, a month known to Americans as the time of elections (and Thanksgiving). Swift confessed that she wrote the track while holding her breath for the results leading up to the 2020 election and viewed "evermore" as symbolic of the "process of finding hope again." More explicit is "Only The Young," the single accompanying Swift's 2020 documentary *Miss Americana*, in which Swift discusses, among other things, her decision to be politically outspoken. The song, written around the time of the 2018 midterm elections, places faith in youth to enact change. After Trump won the 2024 presidential election, "Only The Young" earned its highest-streamed

120   The Glory of Giving Everything

day on Spotify with a 159.28 percent increase from the previous day. Streaming of "The Man" and "mad woman," feminist anthems from *Lover* and *folklore* respectively (the latter of whose nature references include a scorpion and a bear), rose by 10.62 percent and roughly 24 percent, respectively. "The Smallest Man Who Ever Lived" and "I Hate It Here" streaming jumped by 19.14 percent and 36.22 percent, respectively.[15] Although neither song from *The Tortured Poets Department* is expressly about politics, recall that fans are adept at ascribing layers of meaning—a song about an anticlimactic ex can be attributed to a controversial president-elect and a song about favoring mental fantasies over actuality can be applied to any reality. Evidently, people gravitated toward Swift's music in times of need, an intersection sometimes overlooked when assessing the sufficiency of her engagement with global affairs.

A similar intangible is invoked by her charitable giving. On the Eras Tour, Swift donated to local food banks in the cities that she performed in, who commended not only the cash contributions but the attention that came with it.[16] Mark Coleman, spokesperson for Seattle's Food Lifeline, remarked that the "real lasting gift" was the awareness that Swift raised for hunger relief causes, and Michelle Beck, chief development officer of Las Vegas's Three Square Food Bank, called the association "priceless." Shobana Gubbi, chief philanthropy officer of San Jose's Second Harvest of Silicon Valley, observed that more people were interacting with and donating to the organization after Swift's contribution. Furthermore, Swift has been beneficent long before acquiring the Midas touch at the level granted by the Eras Tour.[17] In 2012, Swift partnered with learning platform Chegg to give $10,000 to the music departments of the top five colleges in an online voting competition. The school in first place, Harvey Mudd College in Southern California, was treated to a live acoustic concert. Swift's personal investments in education included a $70,000 (equivalent to 6,000 books) donation to her hometown library in Reading, Pennsylvania, and a $50,000 (generated from proceeds of "Welcome To New York") donation to schools in her adopted home of New York City, New York. The earnings from the music video of another *1989* single, "Wildest Dreams," went to the African Parks Foundation of America. For animals within the country, Swift donated a "sizable" amount to pet rescue foundation Beth's Furry Friends. She contributed to disaster relief efforts, including $1 million in the wake of a

Impact, Implicated 121

2016 Louisiana flood, $1 million each for both Tennessee tornadoes in 2020 and 2023, and $5 million to aid with rebuilding after Hurricanes Helene and Milton swept Florida in 2024. Like her political voice, her generosity extends to individuals: $10,000 for medical bills for a fan battling stage four osteosarcoma; $13,000 for rent for a single mother who lost her job due to COVID-19; $30,000 for college tuition for an aspiring mathematician. For two fans who set their plea video to "Only The Young," Swift gave $1,300, and inadvertently a spotlight boost, toward haircare and skincare products for people of color in Minneapolis.

While philanthropy does not equate advocacy, it is often a related stepping stone. A 2018 Center for Effective Philanthropy survey reported that over 40 percent of foundation leaders in the United States planned to further their focus on advocacy and public policy, and a 2016 Independent Sector poll discovered that 78 percent of voters would have liked the charitable sector to work more closely with the government to solve problems.[18] Well-placed munificent gifts are one of the highest-yielding forms of currency of advocacy work, as it mitigates the financial barriers to reform. Philanthropic efforts tied with one organization can elevate the broader conversation around sister entities and related causes. Donating to a library, for instance, might call attention to students who seek mentorship in free-to-enter after-school spaces. Apparel basics brand Bombas epitomizes the momentous leaps taken from a small desire to tackle problems in the community. For co-founders Randy Goldberg and David Heath, charity defines and guides their business model. The catalyst for starting the company was learning that socks were the most requested item in homeless shelters. After giving socks to those in need individually, the pair came up with the buy-one-give-one philosophy and pitched it on *Shark Tank* in 2014, a time when social awareness of brands wasn't as commonplace. With the support of *Shark Tank* investor Daymond John, the mission-centric business exceeded $1 billion in retail sales at the same time as Swift, in October 2023. More importantly to Goldberg and Heath, Bombas has been able to donate more than 150 million essential clothing items. Besides information on products, the Bombas website contains a detailed impact report that offers the consumer insight into the distribution process and the effects of their purchases.[19] The site also includes a directory of welfare recipients, known as Bombas Giving Partners, and welcomes organizations to become part of the network.

For others, the opportunity to actively empower individuals or groups comes with experience—that is, wisdom in the industry—or experiences—that is, the collective passage of events involving the producers, consumers, and passersby who might positively or negatively affect the buyer–seller relationship. Such was the case with athletic apparel and footwear brand Adidas's Here to Create Change campaign, which highlighted the legacy of tennis champion Billie Jean King.[20] King, who consistently won women's tennis games but earned smaller amounts of prize money than comparable male winners, fought for equal pay on the court. The journey's turning point was the 1973 worldwide-watched Battle of the Sexes. King, aged 29 at the time, was accepting the challenge of 55-year-old Bobby Riggs, a retired tennis player who believed women's tennis was inferior. Starting with the U.S. Open that year, male and female players would go on to earn equal prizes for games well played. On the 45th anniversary of the iconic match, Adidas worked with King to re-create the blue pair of Adidas shoes she was wearing when she defeated Riggs. At the Adidas location in the U.S. Open, King invited patrons to join her in spray painting her shoes blue. It was a visual attestation to Adidas's efforts to encourage girls to stay in sports, as they were dropping out at a rate faster than boys were. The brand has continued to promote inclusivity and gender equity in athleticism, with initiatives like the Breaking Barriers Project and a commitment to having more females fill management positions. Adidas might have started off in the 1900s with the primary goal of making excellent equipment, but as societal needs evolved, the company's focus rightfully expanded to address what consumers cared about.

Taking this notion to Swift's career, perhaps the most potent impact she has is within her chosen field of expertise. In 2015, when Apple Music stated that it would not be paying royalties to artists during the free three-month trial period, Swift decided not to release *1989* on the streaming platform. She then composed a respectful open letter to Apple: "This is not about me…This is about the new artist or band that has just released their first single and will not be paid for its success….the young songwriter who just got his or her first cut and thought that the royalties from that would get them out of debt…the producer who works tirelessly to innovate and create, just like the innovators and creators at Apple are pioneering in their field…but will not get paid for a quarter of a year's worth of plays on his or

Impact, Implicated   123

her songs." Virtually overnight, Apple Senior Vice President Eddy Cue pledged to pay artists for the trial period, and only after this change did Swift make *1989* available on the service. But Apple's quick turnaround wasn't covering a bluff on Swift's part. With other streaming giant Spotify, Swift withheld her music catalog for three years, starting in 2014, to protest unfair compensation to artists. In 2017, Spotify adopted a windowing policy, under which new music would be accessible only by paid subscribers before it was released to all general subscribers, and increased its royalty rates. Spotify co-founder and CEO Daniel Ek was also making the effort to meet with Swift's team to discuss the advantages of the streaming model for the music industry. At the same time, the Recording Industry Association of America declared that Swift had sold 100 million songs. She put her catalog back on Spotify as a celebration. In both instances, Swift advocated for the rights of artists who didn't yet have the upper hand to walk away from an undesirable situation.[21]

Paving the way for rising artists to make music and thrive while doing so might be Swift's version of self-actualization. While Gracie Abrams and Sabrina Carpenter had Swift to look up to, Swift once told Billboard that she was scared of the fact that she had "very few" female role models. Nevertheless, instead of shying away and succumbing to her fears of the industry, she took charge, knowing precisely when standards needed to direct her prospering, when norms needed to be challenged, and when the torch needed to be passed. Entertainment brand strategist Marcie Allen of Marcie Allen Consulting, who managed a couple of Swift's early deals, credited Swift with solving the "biggest problem in the music business" by anointing new stars.[22] But back when Abrams and Carpenter were just over a decade old, Swift was already planting seeds in young people. During a visit to the headquarters of media company Scholastic in 2010, she encouraged children to read to enrich their perspectives and dispensed the sage nugget that smart kids were the coolest kids. Like her music, Swift knows that her actions will undoubtedly appeal to the future generation of a cornucopia of world leaders and thought engagers, dreamers and doers: "My hope for the future, not just in the music industry, but in every young girl I meet [] is that they all realize their worth and ask for it."[23]

The lenses that lend themselves to Swift's undertakings as an advocate are as varied as her artistic personas. From the vantage point of pop culture,

124 The Glory of Giving Everything

any move that Swift makes is profoundly discussed by the general public and bound to be replicated by a subset of enthusiasts. Through meaningful songwriting and impactful philanthropy, she continuously wields this rare power for good. From the perspective of business, genuine public engagement—whether it's serving a community need, mobilizing patrons to rally, or teaching budding entrepreneurs—keeps the industry alive and more often than not, ensures longevity within it. So it goes, the response to any one operation can be varied as well. Loyal consumers might become instinctive proponents; intrigued onlookers might be inspired to conduct more research. Casual customers might disagree on the cause of choice or the method of aid; some might prefer businesses to stay out while some might suggest that the efforts aren't enough. In assessing the right strategy, consider the worst outcome from both decisions, and weigh being alienated for doing something against being alienated for not doing something. The key lies in knowing, like Swift before she pushed the post button on her 2018 statement, the difference. With an effusive nature balanced by firm boundaries, Swift embodies the principle of pouring your heart and soul into your work—and doing it justice.

9

For the Critics

For a songstress whose veneration originates from art but ventures into realms beyond it, criticism arrives as an equally dominating force. Because Swift's songbook (the music of her career) and Swift's playbook (the management of her career) are knit together by personal matters, detractors have taken the liberty of assuming that every facet of her relationships, perspectives, and initiatives are fair game for condemnation. Like a good challenge, though, criticism can be empowering, and criticism directed at you signals that you're worth discussing. The method by which negative commentary can fuel your private or entrepreneurial life depends on whether it takes the form of constructive or deconstructive criticism.

Constructive criticism calls attention to a valid issue, is given out of care for long-term success, or a combination of both, and acting upon it can lead to humble reflection and avenues of improvement.[1] For example, fast food industry staple McDonald's took action toward sustainability, including replacing plastic straws with paper straws and making Happy Meal toys returnable and reusable, following customer complaints. Instead of waiting for complaints, mortgage servicer Valon continually seeks feedback from customers through surveys. In implementing the results from the survey, Valon clarified elements of the online process that were deemed confusing and overwhelming. When a manufacturing defect caused the Galaxy Note 7 to heat up and explode into flames, electronics company

126   The Glory of Giving Everything

Samsung not only recalled the phone but also adopted preventative measures. A newly built lab of 700 researchers investigated the defect, and more thorough safety and quality controls were developed for all products that came after. For Swift, a frequent but affectionate observation from fans is that she isn't a skilled dancer. While she has embraced this by awkwardly attempting different styles of dance in the "Shake It Off" music video, she has also admitted that she wasn't strong at choreography. After three months of dance training in preparation for the Eras Tour, some noticed higher ease in Swift's dancing, and others have reminded bashers that her dancing isn't the point of the show.[2]

Deconstructive criticism, on the other hand, is doled out in a way that emulates mockery or attack, and typically has the effect of disparaging its recipient. Although one strategy is to keep your head high and ignore it (which has its own power), a more impactful scheme is to conduct your own critique of it. Assuming the criticism is untrue or exacerbated, a simple technique would be to break it down and argue against it using cogent evidence. In our dancing example, a factual response might look like compiling the top reasons people admire Swift and noting that dancing isn't among them. A logical response might look like mentioning that pop's influential princess, Britney Spears, is known for choreographing her own stellar dance moves but not writing her own hit songs, and questioning why it isn't proper for Swift to be known for the reverse.[3] Thinking through these responses, whether to be verbalized publicly or internalized privately, can reaffirm both your confidence and understanding of yourself with respect to the criticized component (it can also alert you as to whether this was constructive criticism disguised under poor delivery). More complex techniques would involve incorporating the criticism in acts of defiance or celebration. "Blank Space" superbly accomplished this: "The media have... paint[ed] me as like this psycho serial dater girl...Every single article...had these descriptions of my personality that were very different from the actual personality. My first reaction was...this isn't fun for me, but then my second reaction ended up being...that's actually kind of a really interesting character to write about...I can use this."[4] The critically acclaimed *1989* single satirizes the media's depiction of Swift by crafting a riveting story from the perspective of a seductive woman cycling through men who try to escape her craze.

For the Critics

A version of this serial dater criticism has existed throughout Swift's career, with some online discussions in the early 2010s purporting that she might be the problem causing her breakups and suggesting that she write a song called "Maybe I'm the Problem"; while unconfirmed by the singer-songwriter, fans were quick to establish a link between these posts and "Anti-Hero" upon release of the also critically acclaimed *Midnights* single.[5] When touching on the same album's "Mastermind," Swift thought it would be fun to write about the elaborate plots women must undertake to achieve success in romance and business: "[Being calculative] is something that's been thrown at me like a dagger, but now I take it as a compliment."[6] In light of accusations that she practices witchcraft and brainwashes her cult of fans into partaking as well, Swift singles out the "narcotics" in her music that supposedly drive listenership in her exploration of industry corruption in "Who's Afraid of Little Old Me?" from *The Tortured Poets Department*. She also relents to being burned at the stake in *Reputation*'s "I Did Something Bad." Outside of music, she ditched the theatrics and instead mirrored the ridiculousness of the criticism. When a plane coincidentally flew overhead at the Eras concert in Buenos Aires during a lyric about a plane, Swift posted the clip with the caption, "Never beating the sorcery allegations."[7] The quote became a running joke among Swifties, who repeat it whenever serendipity favors Swift (like with the perpetual appearance of her lucky number 13). By creatively claiming these stereotypes rather than squashing them out of sight, Swift acquired the upper hand both personally and professionally.

It is also possible to overshadow the cacophony of criticism with positivity. When Hector Mkansi, a South African man, proposed to his now-wife Nonhlanhla Soldaat at popular fast food joint Kentucky Fried Chicken (KFC), a journalist found the video online and scorned Mkansi (and, unnecessarily, all South African men) for supposedly being broke and classless. The comment made the KFC proposal go viral and actually induced heartwarming reactions. KFC South Africa then gifted the couple with a wedding planner and posted updates about it on social media. Other brands jumped on the bandwagon, including luxury vehicle manufacturer Audi helping with honeymoon travel, technology corporation Huawei providing devices to photograph the moments, and various South African companies offering items like jewelry and home furniture. Mkansi, who had initially

128   The Glory of Giving Everything

planned for a modest event to fit his budget, described their special day as the wedding of their dreams.[8] Swift's procedure of filtering the noise, and subsequently spreading joy, is charting her constellation of music—songs that, much like the celestial beauties, guide those who need to see them and mesmerize those who want to see them. "[T]he difference," according to Swift, "between those who can continue to create in that climate [of criticism] usually comes down to this: who lets that scrutiny break them and who just keeps making art."[9]

That scrutiny includes the two career-long jabs that Swift plays the victim and that she only writes about ex-boyfriends. Executive coach Caren Kenney stated that leaders often fall back to a position of victimhood to shift responsibility from themselves onto others, "undermin[ing] their ability to take risks, make difficult decisions, and mobilize energy to find constructive solutions."[10] People's common assertion that Swift painted herself as the victim of a standard music contract failed to take into account that she sought constructive solutions, first by attempting to negotiate a deal to purchase her masters outright and, when that didn't work, by re-recording her albums. (These opinion holders also often miss the memo that Swift wasn't upset by the sale itself but the identity of the buyer of her music, as mentioned in Chapter 5.) Those who maintain that her victimhood mindset is prevalent in her work might not have perused her discography. The sincere apologies in "Back to December" (*Speak Now*) and "Afterglow" (*Lover*) stand out, but her mature portrayals of endings are just as compelling: Swift falling out of love in "We Were Happy" (*Fearless*), understanding that two good people hurt each other in "happiness" (*evermore*), and acknowledging incompatibility without blame in "Midnight Rain" (*Midnights*), to name a few. Self-blame even lurks in the most victim-appearing tracks, as she admits to instigating things for no reason other than to emotionally stir the pot in "Cold As You" (*Taylor Swift*) and questions whether it was her own honesty, optimism, or expectations motivating the breakups in "Forever & Always" (*Fearless*), "Dear John" (*Speak Now*), and "All Too Well" (*Red*).

Equally, if not more, important is the fact that nowhere in Swift's job description does it require her to copiously assess all sides of a given situation. In autobiographical songwriting, Swift's role has been to narrate the experiences that happen to her from her perspective and lend validity to her and her fans' feelings. The release of her songs is not a cry for sympathy from

For the Critics 129

others, but a proven way for her to relay her inner monologue: "I've never thought about songwriting as a weapon. I've only thought about it as a way to help me get through love and loss and sadness and loneliness and growing up." *Reputation* and *The Tortured Poets Department* were explicitly stated to be lifelines for Swift, who "needed" to write them.[11] At times, her songwriting beautifully illuminates her ebbing and flowing perspective (as with fame outlined in Chapter 1). While sentiment toward the subject of "Forever & Always" started off as accusatory, it transitioned into devastation in "Last Kiss" (*Speak Now*) and became accepted in "Holy Ground" (*Red*). In *folklore*'s "invisible string" (and in real life), she sent a gift to his newborn baby, eclipsing any previous petty grievances or wistful reminiscing. Boldly, songwriting can also be considered an exceptional embodiment of risk-taking—as it can be difficult to foresee possible consequences of putting your personal life up for public consumption—which according to Kenney, is not something victims do.

On the other career-long dig, two frameworks to examine it come to mind. The first is to refute it on the level of the voiced issue. Swift is fascinated by the quiddities that make us human. This includes the quest for romance, whose prominence cannot be attributed to Swift but rather a conglomerate of societal constructs and messages in film, television, and literature. Hence, in that field, Swift does not only write about "exes" as many seem to believe, but also about projected crushes (*Red*'s "Message In A Bottle") and current partners (the first of many examples depending on who is "current" was the debut album's "Our Song," which Swift performed at her ninth grade talent show). As with romance's pedestal, romance belongs not just to her, but to friends and fictional characters she made up or absorbed from media—*Lover*'s "Death By A Thousand Cuts" was dually inspired by watching the movie *Someone Great* and by being a shoulder to cry on for friends' nonstop breakup chatter.[12] Besides romantic love, universal human experiences include dealing with criticism (*1989*'s "Shake It Off") and overcoming adversity (*Fearless*'s "Change"). They include childhood (*TTPD*'s "Robin"), mental health (*folklore*'s "this is me trying"), and mortality (*Lover*'s "Soon You'll Get Better"); indeed, those constitute the beginning, middle, and end stages of life. Perhaps the reason that gems like these are overlooked is that quite a few songs that are framed in the style of romantic subtext aren't about that at all. *Fearless*'s "Breathe (feat. Colbie

Caillat)" has lyrics that seem to reference a breakup, but is actually intended for a close friend and bandmate of Swift's (speculated to be Emily Poe Stumler, Swift's former violinist, who swapped her fiddle for a degree in law and became a prosecuting attorney specializing in cases involving child abuse).[13] Similarly, while *folklore*'s "my tears ricochet" is about the sale of her masters, Swift has likened it to a couple going through divorce.[14] *Taylor Swift*'s "I'm Only Me When I'm With You" describes a small-town boy and girl, but its music video is a montage of Swift goofballing with friends and family, raising the possible interpretation that the pair might be Swift and her younger brother, Austin.

The second framework is to refute it on the level of the significance of the claim. Let's say that all of Swift's songs arise out of her yapping about her exes. If the music is good, whether it's deemed catchy by casual listeners or profound by involved fans, the inspiration shouldn't matter. Prima facie, songs are meant to be perceived as just that (our analysis in Chapter 3 focused solely on textual and sonic elements). To use the "exes" argument as the only backing of an opinion that her music is insufferable not only blatantly ignores the innumerable types of emotions associated with different exes (the one who hurt you on purpose or on accident; the one you hurt on purpose or on accident; right person, wrong time; right time, wrong person; conflicting values; asymmetric commitment; and so on), but it also desecrates the art form. The cherished "Good Riddance (Time of Your Life)" by Green Day (referred to on radio as "Time of Your Life") was written by frontman Billie Joe Armstrong to express his frustration at his ex-girlfriend moving to Ecuador to start a new life without him.[15] Yet, people take the song as a mellifluous marker of the passage of time, playing it at graduations and birthdays, and don't criticize the song for being inspired by an ex. Doing so would have been a version of the *ad hominem* fallacy, where the character of the person rather than the substance of the argument is attacked. Inspiration should add to, not remove from, the depth of a piece of art, and judgments of the art at face value need not be based upon criteria of the artist's muse. Swift's obsession isn't with exes but with the inventive process of iterating on material until it becomes worthy of being called art: "Everybody in these tabloid gossipy blogs, they think they have you pegged, like 'Taylor's boy-crazy'...I'm work-crazy. That's the thing that I'm crazy about, that I don't stop thinking about, you know?"[16]

For the Critics 131

With the song "Mean" from *Speak Now*, which can stand alone as a tale of an underdog and a villain, the inspiration adds value by elucidating the thin line between constructive and deconstructive criticism. Here, Swift was directly addressing a critic, not general allegations, and the response was saluted by fans and chastised by others. In reviewing Swift's performance at the 2010 Grammys, critic Bob Lefsetz commended *Fearless* for living up to the prestige of its Album of the Year award, but his tone then took an abrupt downward turn: "In one fell swoop, Taylor Swift consigned herself to the dustbin of teen phenoms. Who we expect to burn brightly and then fade away...Taylor's too young and dumb to understand the mistake she made... But last night Taylor Swift SHOULD have auto-tuned. To save her career... It's hard to be a singer if you can't sing."[17] Upon hearing "Mean," Lefsetz took to his computer keys more furiously: "[S]he still can't sing and isn't it time to start acting like an adult? To cast off the high school persona and fly as a woman instead of darting around like a little girl?...Taylor got to live out her adolescent fantasy. Can she now be a woman singing about womanly issues?"[18] *Slant Magazine* writer Jonathan Keefe weighed in with a less biased review of *Speak Now*: "Instead of actually doing something to improve on her inability to find or hold pitch consistently, Swift has simply written a song about how it's 'mean' for people to point out that problem. But it stands to reason that someone who chooses a career as a recording artist might be judged for his or her ability to sing well, and the fact that Swift remains a technically poor singer negatively impacts the overall quality of *Speak Now*, and that's neither unfair nor mean to point out."[19]

Keefe's review of *Speak Now* was balanced and constructive. He described Swift's vocal weaknesses in technical, not crude, terms. He also discussed his perceptions of the project's instinctive strengths and noticeable shortcomings and ended on a forward-looking note: "[I]t's an album that finds Swift getting a lot of difficult stuff right, and it makes it clear what she still needs to develop in order to refine her craft even further. That every song on the album sounds like a viable radio single should buy Swift another couple of years to develop an even more mature, less me-first-all-the-time perspective and, hopefully, to work with a vocal coach." As Keefe stated, pitch is a reasonable criterion for evaluating a professional singer. But Lefsetz's review, although it featured the same base criticism, merely locked in on the idea that Swift could not sing. Rather than analyzing her vocal

132   The Glory of Giving Everything

technique using verifiable metrics, he attacked her character, calling her "awful," "dreadful," "young," and "dumb," and asked questions about her fame and future to which he could not provide concrete answers.

Lefsetz also drew unwarranted comparisons between Swift and other celebrity figures: "Joni Mitchell ultimately sang about the human condition, contemplating suicide in 'Song For Sharon,' is Taylor Swift gonna grow or keep on fighting these petty wars?...[J]ust like Obama doesn't waste time fighting the petty ignoramuses, I'm surprised that Taylor Swift would stoop to this level...They're tearing Jennifer Aniston a new a**hole every day online. Does she complain? No, she puts on a smile and ignores the carping." The esteemed Mitchell released "Song for Sharon" at the age of 33, while Swift was 20 when "Mean" came out. (Soon after, Swift touched on suicide in "Forever Winter," written for *Red* and ultimately released on *Red [Taylor's Version]* when Swift was 31.) The respected Obama was the President of the United States, and the adored Aniston is an actress best known for playing Rachel Green on *Friends*; neither are songwriters whose line of work derives from personal matters. During this period, Swift did start to take on "extensive vocal training," but it's clear as to why her response to Lefsetz was an anti-bullying song and her response to Keefe was to simply improve.[20]

Over the years, listeners have praised Swift's expanded vocal range, particularly in the lower register, and heightened control of her singing voice. Taffy Brodesser-Akner, our friend at *The New York Times* who attended the Eras Tour in Santa (Swiftie) Clara, decided that Swift's voice was "so pure and pretty that it makes you wonder why so many of her musical peers and predecessors *work* so hard." Brodesser-Akner continued, "It's not an otherworldly voice, but a specifically worldly one. She sings how you would sing if you were talking and became so overcome with emotion that your voice was lifted and carried by it."[21] Clearly, her tireless efforts have only amplified her expertise of adapting her voice to the story she's conveying—a skill that Keefe acknowledged was present in a sneer on "Better Than Revenge."

Unlike art, business practices are not shielded under the protection of existing in a vacuum separate from the artist. Disapproval of Swift's art can be rendered invalid if it is based solely on the work's place of conception, but disapproval of her entrepreneurial tactics cannot be as easily disentangled from investigations into her integrity. According to naysayers, all Swift cares about is marketing. They don't consider the possibility that what appear to be shrewd ploys are in reality natural extensions of her artistry—marketing would dissipate without a solid product to revolve around or without insatiable consumers to cater to. Creating value through music is Swift's stunning demonstration of the disciplines' fundamental connection. *The Independent* contributor Laura Barton, who was likely well-meaning, would prefer for Swift to do away with the Easter eggs as in her opinion, the "cutesy gimmicks" were no longer necessary for an artist with a career of her stature.[22] If Swift had designed her layered universe for the sole purpose of marketing, she would have ceased building upon it as soon as she were rich and famous enough (say, the *1989* era). The fact that she hasn't done that reveals that she is motivated instead by a desire to get creative with her creative outlet. Still, the unconvinced would decide that Swift's Easter eggs haven't stopped because she feels that she isn't yet rich and famous enough.

Swift, in their eyes, is a greedy businesswoman, or technically speaking, an exploitative capitalist. Three traditional schools of economic thought can aid in processing this claim.[23] The invisible hand theory, put forth by Scottish economist Adam Smith, states that functioning of the free market relies upon self-interest of the actors in the economy. Welfare of producers and consumers is maximized and naturally governed by market forces like competition, choice, and fluid entry and exit points. Swift's business activity is waved off under this theory as she, her employees, and her fans on aggregate seem generally happy with minimal visible (as opposed to "invisible") regulation. British economist John Maynard Keynes, on the contrary, prescribed government intervention as a remedy to what he considered undermaximized resources in the free market. To address market failures and protect the working class, the state should assist with distributing wealth more equitably. Under this theory, Swift's operations line her pockets inequitably, which is suboptimal for the economy. However, Keynes urged governments to step in as the guiding authority. The responsibility is on the government to establish regulative policies, not on the producer to voluntarily curb profits. Thus, even if Swift were purely self-interested, she shouldn't be expected to act differently.

The harshest view of capitalism was outlined by German philosopher Karl Marx, who believed that the system was inherently exploitative. Workers are forced to perform labor in exchange for wages in order to survive, and the fruits of their labor go primarily toward their employers, who own the means of production. Like other commodities, the price of labor is determined by its cost of production. Employees' cost of labor is what it takes for them to be capable of working, which according to Marx, is only enough to cover the minimum necessities of subsistence (think of higher skilled workers earning higher salaries because more education or experience is required to produce that labor). Unlike other commodities, labor has the ability to create value that goes beyond the value required to produce it. The value of the commodities that a worker can produce during an eight-hour shift exceeds the value of the commodities needed to sustain the worker for the eight-hour shift; the difference is called surplus value. Marx argued that the surplus value is scooped up by the producer, or the capitalist, hence exploiting the worker because the worker does not get a share of the results of their labor. In turn, capitalists "need not produce anything themselves but are able to live instead off the productive energies of workers." Swift's treatment of her crew is inconsistent with this theory. Her employees want to work for her. An accountant by day in Nashville, for instance, applied to be a security guard at the Eras Tour in order to be close to the magic.[24] Emily Poe Stumler herself had auditioned to be part of Swift's band, and was given the freedom to pursue a different career path when she chose to.[25] Surplus value was recognized by Swift through bonuses. In shows, Swift has spotlighted the people on and off the stage that made the productions possible, for example naming each of her dancers one by one during the Reputation Stadium Tour. Finally, unlike Marx's capitalist, Swift bears a significant portion of the labor that the value is derived from.

Here breeds another take on Swift's business savvy, that she tightens the reins with a manipulative sense of control. Interestingly, this is a direct contradiction of the previously mentioned criticism of playing the victim. Supported by a research team led by Rahav Gabay at Tel Aviv University, humanistic cognitive scientist Scott Barry Kaufman described the victimhood mentality as the belief that "one's life is entirely under the control of forces outside one's self, such as fate, luck, or the mercy of other people."[26] If Swift were a devious schemer dead set on conquering charts and dollars, she couldn't simultaneously be a victim because victims relinquish control to others (and complain about it). Therefore, it stands to reason that only one can be true, if either. Having established that Swift is not a victim, it can also be established that she is not power-hungry. Swift strives to hit industry metrics because it allows her further opportunities to create. In the speech for her history-making *Midnights* win for Album of the Year, she compared the feeling to that of writing in the studio, directing a music video, or rehearsing for the stage: "For me, the award is the work. All I want to do is keep being able to do this."[27] Certainly, Swift is prudent with this work. In the music video for "End Game," filmed before the song came out, the actors are dancing to a click track to prevent leaks.[28] She has filed trademarks for phrases that aren't directly part of her songs or albums, such as "Female Rage: The Musical"—the colloquial title of *The Tortured Poets Department* set on the Eras Tour—and "A Girl Named Girl"—the novel drafted by a 14-year-old Swift on summer break that, at the time of writing, has never emerged from her parents' house.[29] Like *A Girl Named Girl's* fictional plot, discussion of her strategized plots remain in a close circle, a "small family business" as characterized by the singer.[30] But her protectiveness of her career is to be saluted, not shamed. When asked which song she wished she'd written, she responded with the *Friends* theme song due to the royalties,[31] which some might see as cynical. Another viewpoint, however, is not that she's after money, but that she has earned the means, faith, and creativity to write any song that she desires. She wouldn't need to "wish" she'd write something she hadn't; she could just do it.

Out of the three pillars of the present dialogue—producers, workers, and consumers—consumption patterns might be more composite than Swift's employees or the star herself. Monetary gains from products, such as multiple digital and physical album variants, come from interested consumers. Without steady demand for a product, the price of that product diminishes (think of clearance bargains) or the availability of that product diminishes (think of discontinued items or lines). The underlying doctrine of capitalism is choice. As long as consumers keep choosing to purchase items from Swift, she will keep producing them; if enough consumers opt out, she will adapt by producing fewer items or pricing them lower, but that isn't the case currently. Either way, each individual consumer has free choice over what they buy. Just like how it's up to them to decide whether souvenirs are worth buying during vacations, they can stream Swift's music and refrain from buying her merchandise.

The Glory of Giving Everything

To play devil's advocate, consider an alternate reality where Swift minimizes her collections of media, apparel, and accessories in her store. This would actually restrict choice. In this parallel universe, all consumers are relegated to the same state of being—those who wouldn't have purchased the items to begin with are fine, but those who would have wanted to do not have the option. Back in the real world, those who don't want to purchase the items don't have to, while those who do want to can. Choice applies to the nonmonetary gains that Swift receives as well. In light of accusations that the singer purposefully released variants of her albums to block other artists' new releases, Billboard crunched the numbers and confirmed that *The Tortured Poets Department* would have continued its reign of the charts without the allegedly blocking variants.[32] Even if the variants had been a factor, the reason that fans would have felt inclined to buy them is because of their connection to the music, which is what the charts aim to measure at their core. Like any astute business mogul, Swift meaningfully competes on the market, and other artists have the choice to do the same. If she does it better than other players on the market, it's an invitation for them to up their game, not a sign for Swift to lower hers. Ultimately, competitive pressure leads to better products and more choice, and consumers reap the benefit.

Bigger than the fight on merch prices is the protest of the usage of Swift's private jet heard 'round the world. Climate change, to take a step back, is considered to be a failure of the free market. In economics, a market failure can be caused by an *externality*.[33] Externalities are benefits or costs to a third party not involved in the transaction of a good. The price of a good with an externality reflects the private benefit or cost to the individuals involved in its transaction, but not the complete social benefit or cost to third parties, which can range in scale from your next-door neighbor to society at large. Landscaping your front yard has a positive externality as it increases the freshness of the neighborhood, hence raising property values of nearby homes. Other examples of positive externalities are education and vaccinations. When more people are educated, society as a whole benefits from their contributions, including those who aren't educated themselves. Similarly, when more people are vaccinated, the likelihood of sickness declines not only for them, but for the folks around them. Negative externality examples are smoking, noise, and drunk driving. Those who have suffered from secondhand smoke were the victims of an externality because

For the Critics   137

they were uninvolved in buying the cigarette and exhaling the fumes, but they had to pay a cost as a result of it. The producers of goods with externalities only realize their private benefit or cost. Since they don't internalize the benefit or cost to others, market failures ensue. Negative externalities result in overproduction of a good because its producers do not need to fully pay for it, while positive externalities result in underproduction of a good because its producers are not fully compensated to provide it. To help adjust the market to be socially optimal, a positive externality can be subsidized and a negative externality can be taxed.

Greenhouse gas emissions are a negative externality of regular human activity like electricity and transportation. The environmental cost of these activities is not adequately priced in the market, so people continue to make choices that end up harming the planet, affecting the people of under-resourced countries and future generations. In the scope of their private transactions, the cost of pollution is not taken into account and does not seem immediately detrimental. Theoretically, if the cost were correctly priced, only those who truly need to pollute would do so, where the need to pollute is measured by willingness to pay (recall WTP from Chapter 7). While this would mitigate the market failure of climate change, this would also mean that the wealthiest individuals, whether or not they "need" to do so, would continue to pollute. If Keynes were around today, he would advocate for the government to enact thoughtful policy; governments imposed the cost of externalities on the affected party until the 1990s, when they shifted to imposing the cost on producers.

In line with that, Swift buys carbon credits in an effort to offset the environmental impact of her travel. Carbon credits serve as a tax on her jet's negative externality, and the money is put toward initiatives of sustainability such as planting trees, investing in renewable energy, and protecting ecosystems. Because the amount of carbon offsets needed for compensation is often underestimated, Swift purchased double the estimated amount needed to offset the negative externality of her travel for the Eras Tour before the tour began.[34] Typically, the point of a tax would be to reduce the production of the taxed good, but in Swift's case, she simply pays. Perhaps the ethics of buying the right to pollute is debatable; perhaps, also, the fact that she overpays on a self-imposed tax—no authority figure has mandated her to—is respectable. Swift's WTP for the ability to travel on her jet conveys her need to do so.

138   The Glory of Giving Everything

To dissect that need, we must borrow a page from public policy's most renowned analysis framework, the eightfold path. Developed by political scientist and University of California, Berkeley professor Eugene Bardach, the eightfold path details the steps to critically examine a problem and devise effective solutions: (1) define the problem, (2) assemble the evidence, (3) construct the alternatives, (4) select the criteria, (5) project the outcomes, (6) confront the trade-offs, (7) decide, and (8) tell your story.[35] Instrumental to the present discussion are steps #3 through #5. Alternatives to Swift flying her private jet might look like flying commercial or business class, limiting travel to work-related events, or shortening her tours. Criteria to evaluate the alternatives might be safety, consumer utility, and environmental impact. Projecting the outcomes involves assessing the status quo and the alternatives according to the criteria. Continuing to fly her jet would keep Swift safe (generally good), maintain her consumers' utility (generally good), and expand her carbon footprint (generally not good). Traveling commercial or business class would decrease safety. Swift and her security personnel would be mobbed by crowds of fans and haters at airports, causing a negative externality via foot traffic and infringing on others' peace in a public space. It would neither increase nor decrease immediate consumer utility. In the short run, it might increase consumer utility for those who get a chance to interact with her on the plane. In the long run, it might decrease consumer utility because Swift isn't getting the rest or transportation she needs to perform consistent physically demanding shows or the inspiration she needs to create (recall from Chapter 4 that "Red" was written on a plane). It would positively affect environmental impact. Swift would not be emitting greenhouse gases by traveling on regular planes. Traveling only for concerts would not affect immediate safety. It could possibly increase safety as Swift would step out only in expected places, decreasing the chance of a surprise ambush. It would lower consumer utility because fans enjoy seeing Swift's outings, reviewing her outfits, etc., as evidenced by the boost in NFL viewers. On the surface level, it would positively affect environmental impact, but it's also possible that if Swift isn't traveling, more people in her circle would travel to her—people who may or may not be purchasing carbon credits. Traveling less via planning a shorter tour would have similar effects. There would be little to positive impact on safety. There would be a decrease in consumer utility of fans who would have wanted Swift to

For the Critics 139

perform in their area and/or fans who have fun following the tour online. Finally, there would be a positive effect on environmental impact, although there'd likely be an uptick in fans traveling to meet the limited tour dates, with airlines adding even more flights than they already did for the Eras Tour.[36]

This exercise was not a comprehensive walk-through of every possibility (what if another criterion were equity? Swift's own utility?), but it was intended for us to appreciate the complexity of the issue, no matter the stance on her jet. The policymaker would dive further into the analysis by supporting their projections with evidence, assigning weights to the criteria (is Swift's safety, consumer utility, or environmental impact most important?), and carefully considering trade-offs in figuring out which solution to pursue. The policymaker might decide that the most suitable course of action for Swift is to keep the status quo. Or the policymaker might decide that the problem of private jet usage extends to the elite as a whole, and they should all be subject to stricter provisions. After all, in 2023 (the first year of the Eras Tour), Swift wasn't among the top 10 carbon emission offenders.[37]

For every person who comments that Swift quietly paying for carbon credits is insufficient work, along comes another person who slams Swift's public voice as performative activism. Media critic Myles McNutt discussed the limited extent of Swift's feminism by drawing on her *1989* voice memos, which "represent[ed] an ideal venue for branded manifestations of popular feminism" but "fail[ed] to develop an explicitly gendered critique of the music industry's masculine norms."[38] Accompanying the deluxe version of *1989* were three voice memos designed to give fans a glimpse into the songwriting process from three different angles. "I Know Places," co-written with Ryan Tedder of pop band OneRepublic, began on piano. "I Wish You Would," co-written with our recurring guest star Antonoff, began with a pre-engineered track. "Blank Space," co-written with Max Martin and Shellback, began on guitar. McNutt denoted that in these memos, Swift highlights herself, a female, as the catalyst of each collaboration, but each memo depicts a session with male co-writers. No voice memo was released for "Clean," the song written with (female) Imogen Heap as we recall from Chapter 5.

While McNutt's criticism is defensible, it could also prove useful to speculate as to the reasons behind Swift's decision. Heap's blog about the creation of "Clean" revealed that the track began on guitar, and given the purpose of the memos to demonstrate different origination points of songwriting, Swift would have had to swap out "Blank Space" for "Clean." This would have made all three memos be for deep cuts, as "I Know Places" and "I Wish You Would" weren't singles. The session of "Blank Space" was important not only because it was one of the biggest songs from the album, but because of its noteworthiness to the reversal of Swift's boy-crazy image. Since, as McNutt commented, the memos "foreground[ed] her own authorship," it was conceivable that she felt the need to take ownership musically and lyrically. Swift was situating herself with mainstream makers of pop to tether herself to pop as a genre and prove that her crossover from country was suitable. In fact, perhaps this was the very reason she chose not to include memos of working with women. Fans scour the internet for videos and interviewers clamor for details on Swift's songwriting, and the memos would have been unsatisfactory if Swift were not positioning herself as dominant in the iterative process, something that might not have been true when writing with female collaborators and, even if it were true, would have come off as ungraceful. When Swift became the first woman to win Album of the Year twice with *1989*, she took the stage with solely male collaborators. The discrepancy was identified on social media, and Heap responded that she would have been up there if she weren't in Cape Town working with creativity brand Design Indaba.[39] In feminist irony, Heap's absence from the Album of the Year acceptance was because she was doing important work elsewhere. The men on stage were simply supporting Swift and did not speak, and making her success about them could be considered an anti-feminist statement in and of itself.

Although "Clean" was written about a natural letting go of a former romantic partner, the song's shelf life has gone beyond that.[40] In 2013, radio DJ David Mueller put his hand under Swift's skirt and groped her ass during a photo opportunity. After Swift's team reported the incident to the radio station, Mueller lost his job. He sued her for defamation for $3 million in 2015. Swift countersued for battery and sexual assault for a symbolic $1 (a $1 bill can be seen in the bathtub of the "Look What You Made Me Do" music video). The judge ruled in her favor, likely due to her steadfast testimony that *Slate Magazine* writer Christina Cauterucci called inspiring to young women. On the one-year anniversary of this decision, Swift was

For the Critics 141

performing in Tampa on the Reputation Stadium Tour, where she spoke openly to her fans about her sexual assault trial, expressed sympathy to anyone who hadn't been believed, and attributed the song "Clean" to the reassurance of getting through difficult times. After the trial, Swift gave fellow singer Ke$ha $250,000 to aid with her legal fees in suing her former producer for sexual assault, and pledged to donate to organizations that supported victims of sexual assault. The case was hailed as significant also because it shed light on the issue of under-reporting among victims due to fear of speaking out; Swift initially didn't take public action to avoid being defined by the incident and reliving it through online ridicule.

Swift was named by *TIME* as part of a group of female "silence breakers" in 2017, prompting mixed responses on social media.[41] On one end: "Taylor Swift was SUED by her ASSAULTER for millions because he couldn't get a job due to his actions. Taylor Swift dealt with the victim-blaming, the jokes, and harassment by media, but still chose to countersue. She IS a silence breaker." On the other: "So, how are we calling Taylor Swift 'silence breaker' when the only time she bothered to break her silence is when the sh★t happened to her?" Her advocacy, then, is performative when she cannot relate to the cause (as with the queerbaiting accusations of the "You Need to Calm Down" controversy) and self-serving when she can. In a crossword with no right answer, we must turn to the authenticity that drives her music. Her autobiographical, semi-autobiographical, and fictional tales are woven from a place of genuine interest—in herself and others, in reality and imagination—why can't her vocals outside of the studio be considered in the same way?

Billboard certainly did, as the entertainment magazine honored Swift as their first Woman of the Decade in 2019.[42] In her acceptance speech, Swift reflected on the decade and how she'd become a "mirror for [her] detractors," changing her musical style, work methods, and personal choices to "appease" her critics. In a move that McNutt might have approved, she took a moment to name women who she believed were influential to the industry: Lana Del Rey, Lizzo, Rosalia, Tayla Parx, Hayley Kiyoko, King Princess, Camila Cabello, Halsey, Megan Thee Stallion, Princess Nokia, Nina Nesbitt, Sigrid, Normani, H.E.R., Maggie Rogers, Becky G, Dua Lipa, Ella Mai, and Billie Eilish. The end of her 15-minute speech was met with applause: "[L]ately I've been focusing less on doing what they say I can't do and more on doing whatever the hell I want." For the bulk of her career, Swift's seminal responses to disparagers have helped her navigate, last in, and impact her industry. They have earned her troops of fans and scholars who will take aim at the critics on her behalf, allowing her the creative freedom to now embark on the journeys that she, not her critics, desires.

10

The Evolution
of Miss Americana

Just before marking the end of her (first) career-shaping decade at Billboard's Women in Music by emancipating from the critics, Swift made a statement that would resound for every decade of her career to come: "[N]o matter what else enters the conversation, we will always bring it back to music."[1]

In dynamically defining the evolving role of Miss Americana, music presides. The title of "America's Sweetheart" was first unofficially bestowed onto the endearing, precocious girl as she strummed her way into the American public's hearts. The label was stripped in the 2016 turn of events that has become so entrenched into Swift's lore that it remained a topic in interviews and material for songs years later. Nevertheless, her well-worn "hero's journey" (as identified by Sam Lansky in *TIME*'s 2023 Person of the Year issue) isn't the most interesting part; what stands out is that only after this dethroning did Swift actively work the concept into her life. She was no longer passively the delightful girl whose existence was born out of American borders (a sweetheart belonging to the nation), but she was commanding herself as the bold embodiment of American values (Americana, following the respectful address of Miss, acting as a surname). Testing the waters during her comeback, she viewed herself in the eyes of her partner as his "American queen" in "King of My Heart" on *Reputation*, her first direct lyrical reference to being "American." Granted, this was intended as a cultural distinction, but her relationship with Joe Alwyn wasn't the first time she flirted with the British. There had been Harry Styles, and she felt no need to crown herself as American during that time because that would have only been stating the obvious. When the marker of Americanism was no longer obvious, she was liberated to interpret the symptom on her own terms: "It's so strange trying to be self-aware when you've been cast as this always smiling, always happy 'America's sweetheart' thing and then having that taken away and realizing that it's actually a great thing that it was taken away, because that's extremely limiting."[2] Now, whether or not she was beloved or worthy was not at the discretion of the masses. It was at hers.

Recall her first lyrical political critique on *Lover* (from Chapter 8). "Miss Americana & The Heartbreak Prince" could easily serve as a thesis for her discography. As a product, it is devoted to the central metaphor (a technique detailed in Chapter 3)—the bridge consists of echoes that emulate cheerleader chants—and it is layered with decodable lyrics (a technique detailed in Chapter 4)—the first couple of lines mention that she is "crazier" than she was in a "film scene," a possible reference to Swift penning and performing the song "Crazier" in *Hannah Montana: The Movie* in 2009. As a piece of art, although the track is a decisive entry point into political commentary, it has the essence of a return to form. The introduction of new themes melds with the revitalization of classic themes. The mention of voting is a clear reference to citizens' rights, but it also is a play on high school superlatives (for instance, Most Likely to Succeed). High school and fairytale imagery (the prom dress, the damsels), which were prevalent in her early work, come off here not as overdone but as an introspective review. In line with her later work up until that point, her romantic counterpart is relief from a burdened climate, not the cause of it as one might expect from someone whose superlative is the "Heartbreak Prince." She concludes that she is "Miss Americana" based on her public and private journey thus far, and for the first time, she questions what it means. She also positions herself to rise to the challenge of answering the call. Narratively, the song follows the Swift formula of the championing underdog. She deconstructs the idealism she acknowledges having at the age of 16, documents the intensity of feelings she had while out of the spotlight, and ultimately declares that her cause will win. Here, though, the formula becomes complex because she is

The Evolution of Miss Americana 145

aware that she'll face pushback, likening it to school gossip in the hallways. She chooses to end the song not on her triumph, but on the whispers of adversaries who label her a "bad, bad girl." Titling her 2020 Netflix documentary *Miss Americana* accentuated the persona's complexity. Popular culture critic Wesley Morris of *The New York Times* commented that the documentary "asserts that Swift's creative and personal maturity comes at a cost, and the most exhilarating disclosure is that she finds herself determined to pay it."[3] Swift might have exemplified American values as America's Sweetheart, an approachable apolitical country singer picking up the nickname from silent film star Mary Pickford and household name Julia Roberts.[4] But as Miss Americana, a real-life role she originated, she was compelled to do the work that a twenty-first century American protagonist is expected to undertake. As with "Miss Americana & The Heartbreak Prince," her songs have been an essential foreground to rewriting the script that was prescribed to her by the entertainment industry.

After *Lover*, the next noticeable shift in patriotism occurs in *The Tortured Poets Department*. Prior to this 2024 body of work, Swift had always sewn in American states with tinges of positivity. The very first lyric people heard from her, in debut single "Tim McGraw," compared her blue eyes to the stars in the Georgia sky. This was sweetly uttered by the subject of the song (a boy whose romantic entanglement with Swift ended because he went off to college, not actually Tim McGraw because Swift is "not a stalker"[5]). In *folklore's* "seven," she wistfully remembers a bliss moment in her home state of Pennsylvania. The state of Rhode Island in "the last great american dynasty" (four songs before "seven") frames jovial rebellion. "Carolina," written after reading nature-set murder mystery *Where the Crawdads Sing* by Delia Owens, stunningly personifies the book's North Carolina location. (North) Carolina lays the narrator's unravelable secret and clear conscience to rest. Because the story moved Swift to create (in the middle of the night, of course), she pitched "Carolina" to the producers when she heard it was being made into a movie. Like Seth Meyers from *SNL* with "Monologue Song (La La La)," film director Olivia Newman described "Carolina" as a gift: "When I heard the song, I couldn't believe it was tonally so perfect… Every time the movie ends and that song comes on, it captures the feeling where you need to sit and digest what just happened. The song is the perfect vessel for those feelings…[Swift writing a song] was very serendipitous

The Glory of Giving Everything

because we hadn't shot the movie yet. For it to be such a perfect match was a gift."[6] With *TTPD*, American states malleableized to become a stage for scandal rather than safety, contention rather than comfort. First track and lead single "Fortnight (feat. Post Malone)" instigates the project's dismantling of the American dream: "'Fortnight' exhibits a lot of the common themes that run throughout this album, one of which being fatalism, longing, pining away, lost dreams...I've always imagined that it took place in this American town where the American dream you thought would happen to you didn't. You ended up not with the person that you loved and now you have to just live with that every day, wondering what would have been, maybe seeing them out..." Neighborly pleasantries in the song are a facade for the narrator's insanity. The states that appear on *TTPD*, notably Texas and Florida, are reputationally notorious compared to states like Georgia and Pennsylvania. In "I Can Fix Him (No Really I Can)," the object of affection—someone who must be "fixed"—is said to be on a highway in Texas, a place that warrants his "dangerous" activities of smoking, drinking, and shooting pistols. "Florida!!! (feat. Florence + the Machine)" cites a "sh★tstorm" in Texas in passing and focuses on Florida as the escapist's enabler: "What happens when your life doesn't fit or your choices you've made catch up to you? You're surrounded by these harsh consequences and judgment and circumstances did not lead you to where you thought you would be...is there a place you could go?"[7] Laced with discussions of crime, drugs, and regret, Swift and Florence Welch sing of succumbing to Florida. America was no longer a blanket of pride ("Tim McGraw"), hope ("seven"), identity ("the last great american dynasty"), or solace ("Carolina"), but an absorption of dark fantasies and murky affairs.

On a more granular level, Swift's stories are landscaped in American cities as well as states, most recurrently Los Angeles and New York. The concepts of suburbia and urbanism present themselves in "Suburban Legends," a gem resigned to the vault during the writing of *1989* possibly because its title made little sense on an album that embraced the Big Apple. This paradoxical nature, however, makes it an anchor of the era, as the song deploys a love story to allegorize her departure from her country sound and Nashville living. The romance unfolds in a suburban town, at a school that predated the institution in "Miss Americana & The Heartbreak Prince." Before there were the hallway whisperers that Swift and her paramour were running from,

The Evolution of Miss Americana

147

there were the admiring classmates of "Suburban Legends"—paralleling her relationship with the public post- and pre-*Reputation* (as we know by now, *Reputation* was between *1989* and *Lover*). The twist is that the admiring classmates only exist in Swift's imagination; she breaks her "own heart" for a reason undisclosed in the lyrics, but inferable from real-life actions. Swift "ruined" life as she knew it in favor of pursuing experiences of higher grandeur. Her transition to New York necessitated the end of the fling between the two people who were meant only to survive in suburbia, a simultaneous geographical location and abstract concept affiliated with youth and happy endings. Yet, moving doesn't require forgetting. On the contrary, the two become legends. Legends are typically unauthenticated, but interesting enough to be continuously retold and passed down. Put together, suburban legends—which bring to mind television characters Love Quinn of *You*'s Madre Linda ("exile," "Anti-Hero," and "Guilty as Sin?" play in Seasons 3, 4, and 5, respectively) and Mary Alice Young of *Desperate Housewives*'s Wisteria Lane ("You Belong With Me" is referenced in Season 8)—inflate the simplicity of suburbia with stories that seem too fantastical to be true. Swift's perfect small town romance is crushed under the weight of a big city scale, but the story emerges as their legacy, something larger than just a doomed relationship. At the crossroads between country and pop, holding on and growing up, Swift discovers that past lives don't expire, but they endure in the form of tales, while we embark on new lives with raw intricacy.

Indeed, *1989* saw Swift adopt a new perspective on romance in general: "On this album, I'm writing about more complex relationships...feeling a sense of pride even though it didn't work out, reminiscing on something that ended but you still feel good about it...And I think there's actually sort of a realism...[Wildest Dreams] is actually a really good example of the way I go into relationships now. If I meet someone who I feel I have a connection with, the first thought I have is: 'When this ends, I hope it ends well. I hope you remember me well.'...[I]t's the anomaly if something works out; it's not a given." Contrast this with *Fearless*, her previous Album of the Year, whose prologue implored listeners to "believe in love stories and Prince Charmings and happily ever afters" even when believing proved difficult.[8] Like any real love, her relationship with romance itself is ever-changing. When prefacing "Last Kiss" on the Speak Now World Tour, she was open about her innocent adoration of love: "[W]e need music the most when

148 The Glory of Giving Everything

we're feeling things really intensely, and I think the most intense times in your life are when you're either falling in love or losing it, don't you think? And I think I fall into the category of the hopeless romantics, and you do too, because you're here."[9] She was met with the passionate cheers of a crowd about to shed tears to one of her most heartbreaking confessions. Two tours later, prefacing a mashup of "Enchanted" and "Wildest Dreams" on the 1989 World Tour, she explicated the theme of love within her songs: "I think the most popular thing that has been said that is a tiny bit accurate is…'all she does is write songs about guys'…I would like to amend that…I write songs about things that I find to be romantic and magical…I think that so many things other than boys and breakups are romantic and magical…a city can be romantic, being by yourself and happy can be romantic, friendship is romantic…"[10] The seventh and final single from *1989* was called "New Romantics" and celebrated a version of herself that wasn't hopeless. Two album cycles later, in a video announcement for *Lover*, she explained that the album's name was not a topic but a lens: "This album in tone, it's very romantic and not just simply thematically like it's all love songs or something because I think that the idea of something being romantic, it doesn't have to be a happy song…You can find romance in loneliness or sadness or going through a conflict or dealing with things in your life. It just looks at those things with a very romantic gaze."[11] (Clearly, the battle with Chapter 9's critics of romance writing is one best fought by Swift herself.)

By *Lover*, Swift was under the impression that she had found her "anomaly" of a lasting relationship. When it fragmented, she kindled a flame masquerading as another anomaly, and when that imploded, her take on love became tragically fatalistic. It was love that left her wanting to flee to Florida, that ignited a desire to set her possessions ablaze ("The Black Dog"), that rendered her to believing her existence futile ("Down Bad"). Unlike her early work, where she was often detailing "pain that was caused by someone else and felt by [her]," she divulged on *TTPD*'s epilogue poem that it was not love per se that caused her condition, but her projections of love: "'In summation, it was not a love affair!' I screamed while bringing my fists to my coffee-ringed desk…It was self harm."[12] It's no wonder that Swift's revisit to the picket fence in "Fortnight" saw the town in a completely different light. The suffering protagonist, should she act on her

The Evolution of Miss Americana

149

thoughts, would become a suburban legend unrecognized by the radiant time-frozen lovers of *1989*, but validated by fictional Love Quinn and Mary Alice Young—driven by despair instead of fondness and portrayed as a warning instead of a model, a lesson instead of an aspiration. Swift's reinventions of character and self have always been multidimensional, but "Fortnight" coats familiarity with foreignness at a level no other lead single had yet accomplished.

The addition of *TTPD* to Swift's musical family confounded Swift's religious journey as well. Although the United States is governed by a separation of church and state, the topic of religion frequently pervades American conversations and surveys, where Americans opine on religion as an establishment, various groups within that establishment, or its ideal intersection (or lack of) with politics.[13] The impetus for these debates is in part the Pledge of Allegiance, which states that the country is "under God," and our dollar bills, which state "In God We Trust." Religious identity, though, isn't as clear-cut as claiming membership of a group. While around 75 percent (as of 2023) of all Americans are religiously affiliated, only 32 percent (as of 2023) attend church regularly (compared to 44 percent in 2000 and 49 percent in 1958).[14] In *Miss Americana*, Swift identified herself as a Christian, the dominant religion among Americans (68 percent as of 2023), and mapping her piety illustrates how her singular trajectory is analogous to the uncertainty of a broader population. In her early work, Swift turned to faith in times of gratitude. She asks God to replay a promising first date in prayer that seems to be a nightly routine in "Our Song" (*Taylor Swift*) and praises God's protection over her family in "The Best Day" (*Fearless*). Later, she turned to faith in times of desperation, calling to the Lord and to Jesus on "Is It Over Now?" (*1989*) and "Soon You'll Get Better" (*Lover*), respectively, when tempting fate in the former and pleading with fate in the latter. During this phase, she regarded faith as powerful rather than procedure, and she intertwined it with love by way of being an experience out of her control. A meaningful love, in "Cornelia Street" (*Lover*), is said to become her religion. In "Don't Blame Me" (*Reputation*), she surrenders to the Lord to save her from a lifelong addiction to a lover; in "False God" (*Lover*), she treats intimacy with said lover as a worshiped idol.

Religion retained its power on *TTPD*, but the power was something to resist rather than respect. She began to critique faith as an institution,

150 The Glory of Giving Everything

separating herself as the driving narrator from a "they" that appeared in multiple plotlines. In "But Daddy I Love Him," she shuns the "judgmental creeps" dressed in their "Sunday best" and alleges that their care for her well-being is a mask for disdain. Similarly, "Cassandra" explicitly calls out Christians for showing disingenuity through their actions. "Guilty as Sin?" and "I Can Fix Him (No Really I Can)" pocket faith in untraditional manners. As Swift indulges in an undignified fantasy, she relies on the Biblical reference of rolling the stone away to appraise her guilt. In the Bible, Jesus's resurrection after he was crucified became known by a rolled away stone, revealing an empty tomb.[15] In everyday language, rolling the stone away represents rising above obstacles. In "Guilty as Sin?," Swift reverses the sequence. She envisions that removal of the stone would still lead to her crucifixion by the masses ("they"), and decides that the one thing that is holy—the one thing she can place her trust in—is the feeling of the lover in her fantasy. When the lover becomes real life in "I Can Fix Him (No Really I Can)," Swift goes out of her way to reassure onlookers, who disapprove and feel the need to pray for her salvation, that "only" she can fix him, hence shifting the power once reserved for supernatural entities to herself.

However, the record isn't a simple divorce between Swift and religion. She conjures another Biblical story, the one of Adam and Eve in the idyllic Garden of Eden, in "The Prophecy," by perceiving a curse on her life as similar to the way Eve was bitten. In the first book of the Bible, Eve was deceived by Satan into eating the forbidden fruit from the Tree of Knowledge of Good and Evil. She was joined by Adam, and afterward, the two were suddenly self-conscious, as the fruit had given them newfound knowledge of shame, vulnerability, and mortality. They had unleashed, per the Greek mythological parallel, Pandora's box, and the human race could no longer live in harmonic bliss—men would need to work for a living, women would need to undergo pain during childbirth, and all would eventually face death. Christian followers question whether Adam or Eve should primarily bear the blame for the effects on humankind, but the consensus is that the Scripture faults Adam because Eve was tricked into eating the fruit, while Adam deliberately chose to do so.[16] Still, both were equally punished for their sin. In Swift's rendition, she promotes the theory that Eve's actions were out of her control. She aligns herself with Eve in that her demise was externally cast upon her by an omniscient decider of prophecies

The Evolution of Miss Americana   151

(interestingly, not explicitly God but nonetheless a divine force in the sky). She wonders if her ill-fated prophecy was punishment and spends the song begging for a different ending, indirectly prompting the query of whether Eve deserved the same punishment as Adam.

The religious leaders who were astonished by Swift's apparent blasphemy seem to have missed, or even played into, her point of the danger of religious institutional loyalty blocking true goodness and open-mindedness beyond the church.[17] Swift wasn't discrediting faith, but she was re-establishing her relationship with it by subverting religion as a construct. She was engaging with millenniums-old religious texts the same way she annotated and incorporated literary motifs. Instead of taking all teachings as given, she was lending nuance to them and charting her own interpretations. Her personal reconciliation was representative of the mismatch between the proportion of Americans who are religious and the proportion of those who attend church. Echoing public sentiment, Swift materializes as a nontraditional Christian through her music. *Midnights*, the collection of awake-inducing occurrences that were scattered throughout the course of her life,[18] affirms this. "Karma" emphasizes her belief in the even distribution of everyone receiving what they deserve, conceivably arranged by a higher power. Here, Swift blends her old and new approaches to religion. On one hand, karma is compared to "a god," an improper noun that refers to any spiritual deity rather than Christianity's God. On the other hand, the context of the "god" is positivity. Unlike *1989, Reputation,* and *Lover,* she wasn't using a "god" to seek answers to personal problems or attain understanding of fervent emotions. Instead, she took a backseat and appreciated the power's guiding presence, more in line with the days of *Taylor Swift* and *Fearless.* As *Midnights* entails, "Would've, Could've, Should've" warps the linearity of our timeline. Again, she involves her old and new attitudes, doing so this time with a pivotal incident that starkly divides them. The incident, which is said to happen at the age of 19, is poignantly documented in "Dear John" (*Speak Now*), with no religion infused (and no need for it). Much later, at the age of 32 (pointedly, John Mayer's age when he was linked to 19-year-old Swift[19]), she considers it a "crisis of [her] faith," a swap of righteousness for the taste of a devil in disguise. Only with hindsight does she realize that she was enduringly altered by the incident, even though it is neatly wrapped up in "Dear John" as she gets out just in time. Upon this

152   The Glory of Giving Everything

realization, she asks God for redemption in "Would've, Could've, Should've," but she is painfully aware that she is incapable of reverting to the previous version of herself. While this was a loss in one sense, it was a gain in another; she was positioned to delve into more mature perspectives to shape the discourse of more adult realities.

Such a revisitation of past events through updated lenses demonstrates the fluidity of self-discovery—introspectively and relationally, individually and culturally, personally and professionally. In fact, Swift and American apparel company Abercrombie & Fitch have one prominent thing in common: "The brand is growing up with its customer."[20] Standing for over 130 years, Abercrombie & Fitch first achieved success with its cool-kids-only, lascivious, elitist messaging. But when this aura crept into serious areas of the corporation, including discriminatory hiring practices, the business suffered. Abercrombie & Fitch was proclaimed America's most hated retailer in 2016 (timing that eerily parallels the valley of Swift's career). In its revival, along with making conscious efforts to improve the fit of its clothing and include diverse body types, Abercrombie & Fitch met its customers at their stage of life. Instead of trying to rehash outdated products or scrambling to find an entirely new target, the company's design team researched the lifestyles of its consumer base. In the 1990s and 2000s, its demographic was high schoolers. The brand's revamp appealed to those in their twenties, who were once teenage patrons. In 2023, Abercrombie & Fitch had the highest performing stock on the S&P 500, which is a market-capitalization-weighted index of the 500 top publicly traded companies in the United States,[21] with a 285 percent gain. The marketing team of Abercrombie & Fitch recognizes that buyers now consist of those who remember the brand from earlier days and those who are freshly discovering it, in a fashion not unlike Swift's enterprise.

"I always used this metaphor," Swift told *Vogue* in 2019. "[W]ith every reinvention, I never wanted to tear down my house. 'Cause I *built* this house. This house being, metaphorically, my body of work, my songwriting, my music, my catalog, my library. I just wanted to redecorate. I think a lot of people, with *Reputation*, would have perceived that I had torn down the house. Actually, I just built a bunker around it."[22] (The house is best represented visually by the Lover House, which debuted in the "Lover" music video less than a month after this interview and served as a backdrop during

The Evolution of Miss Americana   153

the Eras Tour.) It was a more eloquent version of the "I will never change, but I'll never stay the same either" from her Myspace bio and our Chapter 1. As only the songwriter can do, characterizing her work as a house is the perfect figurative description. Swift, as the homeowner, enjoys both opening the space up for guests and retreating from the outside world into the living space—akin to crafting songs both for career fulfillment and for personal catharsis. Some will only ever walk by, admiring or judging the exterior from a distance. Some, squarely in the middle of the high-friction acquisition system from Chapter 5, venture inside and get cozy on the furniture. The most dedicated of all are recurring callers, who know the floor plan by heart—the themes of her music and mannerisms of her personality—but notice the ways in which the rooms are repurposed with each visit, from the minuscule detail to the all-encompassing shift. To make the redecorations shine, she solicits other experts—architects and interior designers in our house metaphor, or co-writers and producers, some of whom were mentioned in Chapter 6, in our literal translation.

Every reinvention of her music is an iterative process between the artist and her listeners to ascribe meaning to their realities and reveries. Verbally, the closest thing we have to a constructed lexicon of the emotional caverns of ourselves and others is the *Dictionary of Obscure Sorrows* by John Koenig.[23] Published in 2021, the dictionary is a collection of coined terms that address the "huge blind spot in the language of emotion" and "shine a light on the fundamental strangeness of being a human being." Swift's work can be viewed as a companion handbook. The desire to have been left in the unknown in "Would've, Could've, Should've" channels *irrition*, the "regret at having cracked the code of something, which leaves you wishing you could forget the pattern"; the pondering of the significance of a glance in "I Look in People's Windows" channels *soufrise*, the "maddening thrill of an ambiguous flirtation…leaving you guessing what's going on inside their chest"; the plan to swap frenzy for stillness in "the lakes" channels *trumpspringa*, the "longing to wander off your career track in pursuit of a simple life…which is just the kind of hypnotic diversion that allows your thoughts to make a break for it and wander back to their cubicles in the city." That second part of the definition of trumpspringa rightfully predicts Swift's inevitable return to the spotlight, or the tendency of ordinary people to not stray from their paths despite momentary lapses. The songs that evolve into healing journeys

154 The Glory of Giving Everything

and take on lives of their own as a byproduct of ongoing conversation within Swift's universe—like the fan-led redefining of "All Too Well" discussed in Chapter 7—could be described as *harke*, a "painful memory that you look back upon with unexpected fondness…a tough experience that has since been overridden by the pride of having endured it, the camaraderie of those you shared it with, or the satisfaction of having a good story to tell." The mere existence of Swift's discography, all glorious decorative phases of it, weave two concepts that function in tandem with each other: *onism*, the frustration of being stuck in just one body that inhabits only one place at a time, and *sonder*, the realization that each random passersby is living a life as vivid and complex as your own.[24] Coping with such existentialism, in turn, can be done by "extrapolating outward from the world you know"—forming mental pictures of the unexplored via secondhand accounts that can spur from singular jumping off points. For Swift, this manifests in the saturated ideas she derives from the tiniest of lightbulbs, in songs like the ones in Chapter 2 that are only adjacently inspired by her life. Swifties, who stake claims in specific songs or eras, conversely cognize the songs and eras that are less directly pertinent to their lives, and use those extraneous components to glean insight into the "vivid and complex" narrative lives outside of themselves.

To be Miss Americana is to navigate a multitude of roles with grit and grace. If there were an election for the position, Swift's gentle advocacy efforts and encouragement of democracy, fierce examples of individualism and pursuing passion, and lucrative impact on local markets and global economies would sharpen her candidacy. The win would be secured by the quilt of music—the heart that pulses through the meticulous branding and the carved niches; drives the relationships with fans, friends, and foes; and excavates universal truths from intensely personal experiences and profoundly collective events. But there was no official pageant of beauty or intellect for the crown of Miss Americana. From "Tim McGraw" to "Fortnight," Swift has subconsciously and consciously refined the duties of Miss Americana, developing a rank that is uniquely hers. Consistent with the Taylor Swift business model, she will continue to do so for every lead single to come, in every department she chairs: that of tortured poets, activist stances, and marketing whizzes.

Epilogue

My favorite part of any gathering is the goodbye. This preference is conceivably difficult to defend. The economist would compute my personal utility function with heavier weight on remembered, rather than anticipatory or experienced, utility. The *Dictionary of Obscure Sorrows* would turn to the Latin origins of the word *sadness*. Sharing the root of *satis* with *satisfaction*, sadness was not intended to be a simplistic lack of pleasure. *It* was intended to be a satiating state of mind that opened one to pure, aware absorption of joy, beauty, hope, and grief.

For me, the goodbye is the perfect collision of nostalgia and expectation. Simultaneously fleeting and fulfilling, the goodbye is a standstill point between interactions passed that, despite photographs and journaling, you can never quite relive, and interactions to come that, despite plans and intentions, you can never quite arrive at. It's the moment where time slows in a rare attempt to catch the light of brief, actionable moments (the exuberance of the party, for instance) but often instead sheds light on lasting, impalpable sentiments (the gratitude of the friendship, for instance). It's the poignant exchange of words that, even if it wasn't enough inherently, it suddenly was, by nature of its very utterance at that very instance. I'm of the opinion that when executed well, a farewell does well for the soul. In my eyes, *The Glory of Giving Everything* is more than a book; it's a celebration of generosity, brilliance, and humanity. It's only fitting that it receives a goodbye. To embark on a one-sided goodbye is to bid adieu to two intangibles at once: the version of myself that was learning to compose chapters

156 Epilogue

out of ruminations, and you as the reader, for whom this conclusion exists only because I, in my romantic propensity of preservation, imagine that you care about it.

Lately, I've spent time contemplating the natural and acquired ways in which I synthesize information. Much of the book's core stemmed from an autoethnographic place, and in drafting my work, my ongoing time in the fandom propelled me—the sheer delight of feeling a song come alive after a pivotal experience, the validating relief of watching an interview clip of Taylor Swift verbalizing my own philosophy, the magnetic wonder of mapping out observations from live performances. Similarly, these recollections were the starting line for the "Artistry, Policy, & Entrepreneurship: Taylor's Version" lesson plan. Content informed by knowledge as a Swiftie, however, wasn't the only component of an engaging curriculum. In teaching the course, I needed to translate the specifics of Taylor's career into generalized patterns of thinking, strategy, and impact. I needed to sketch creative spaces, in and out of class time, for students coming from all kinds of backgrounds and getting ready for all kinds of futures to apply those patterns. I launched the course during my first year in the workforce, and balancing the two milestones made my life an interesting seesaw between expertise and novelty. The analytical coherence found in the book, through written logic and visual exhibits, was undoubtedly sharpened by exposure to the industry of economic consulting.

On one hand, I felt as though I'd always been subconsciously preparing for this project, a homecoming in some way. On the other hand, I felt as though I were diving into something completely fresh. While I was leveraging concepts from my course and techniques from my job, writing a book was different from anything I'd undertaken prior, and wondrously so. Lectures tend to be holistic learning environments, where examples are livened by displaying videos, collaging pictures, and bouncing off of the energy of inquisition and commentary. The written word is more of a singular medium. It brims with more possibilities, as it isn't constricted by time and attention, and it necessitates more rigor to expound on examples comprehensively. As I hope Taylor would appreciate, studying her intricacies lends itself to a deeper understanding of intersectional disciplines and people. In the classroom—colloquial yet insightful—I've enjoyed coming across students' individual stories and learning methods.

Epilogue　　　　157

With the book—studious yet gratifying—I've enjoyed unearthing more facets of myself and my writing style.

I've learned that the more I care about a subject, the more chaotic my outline is. In my lifetime, I've framed many neat outlines for school papers or work memos, but the only organized portion of my outline for this book is the sequential list of chapter titles. Looking at it now, it reeks of disarray. The bullet points are peppered with information that I feel was bold for me to assume I would understand at a later date: album names with no context, article titles with no links, and the standout note of "that one slide," and astonishingly, I still know exactly which class material it refers to. I think that more often than not, roadmaps are extremely helpful, but there are some extraordinary moments in which a passion can transcend an outline, and I've been fortunate to have one or two of those. I've learned the extent of the lengths I will go to in order to avoid using the same word multiple times. In essays for schools, whether they were argumentative or self-reflective, I avidly perused thesauruses to produce alternates for words I'd already used, and I typically succeeded in having no more than a couple instances of common synonyms of words like "explained" in any given assignment. Now, as I quickly discovered, this was not an easy task to achieve when creating a full-length, 10-chapter body of work. At least I was trying— whenever I was bursting to get an idea on the page but couldn't settle on the right adjective or verb or noun to complete the thought, I would put brackets around a placeholder word and revisit it. In the reverse direction, when I had fragments but not the fully formed idea, I would separately start a mini paragraph to hyperfocus on it, and re-insert it into the text when I felt pleased with it. I've learned that voice, whether it emanates from you deliberately or subtly, is a key driver of writing. I was co-writing a chapter for an edited collection right around the time I was writing Chapters 3 and 4 of this book, and it surprised me how even though the overarching project topics were similar, my voice needed to markedly shift between the two endeavors. It made me wonder whether Taylor undergoes a similar operation when writing across genres or with collaborators versus alone. Lastly, I've learned that concluding sentences of paragraphs can be great first sentences of next paragraphs in disguise, just waiting to be expanded upon.

Throughout the process of this book, I of course consumed Taylor's music. There were unwitting listens of old favorite songs and intent listens

158 Epilogue

of new favorite songs. There was, once or twice, the sacred Swiftie zenith of being out and about and sensing a lyric wash over me to narrate the real-time unfolding of my life. From all of these, I mined eureka takeaways from treasured melodies. Curiously, though, I didn't listen to these songs at all during the actual writing sessions. Like Taylor, I'm an album person, and I describe my music taste as "popular artists' unpopular songs." Some of the female-made records that kept me typing were (in alphabetical order by artist's first/stage name): *sweetener*, Ariana Grande; *Love Sux*, Avril Lavigne; *Brat and it's the same but there's three more songs so it's not*, Charli xcx; *Along the Way*, Colbie Caillat; *The Secret of Us (Deluxe)*, Gracie Abrams; *Vertigo*, Griff; *Something To Tell You*, HAIM; *BADLANDS (Deluxe Edition)*, Halsey (well, every album of Halsey's); *Golden Hour*, Kacey Musgraves; *chemistry (Deluxe)*, Kelly Clarkson; *Born to Die*, Lana Del Rey; *You Heard Right*, Lexie Hayden; *Melodrama*, Lorde; *Silver Landings*, Mandy Moore; *Endless Summer Vacation*, Miley Cyrus; *Short n' Sweet*, Sabrina Carpenter (*fruitcake*—EP around the holidays); and *Simple Like 17*, Sadie Jean.

The one time I did have Taylor's voice in my vicinity was while working on Chapter 2. It was Miami Night 1 of the Eras Tour, and although I was seldom able to tune in to the livestreams, I felt compelled to do so for the opening night of the final leg of the tour. As I wrote about her entry into country music, Taylor strummed her guitar in a never-before-seen surprise song dress, and when I heard the first lines of "Tim McGraw," a never-before-felt gasp escaped me. Not only was it my most precious song (in a streak of fun, I once rewrote the whole thing with the hook "When you think Taylor Swift, I hope you think of me"), but also the timing was acute—she and I were thinking of her first move in the music scene at the exact same time on opposite coasts. I was so engrossed in the performance that I forgot she was doing mashups for every acoustic section. When she infused the second song, "Timeless," I must have shrieked loud enough to meld with the cheers all the way over in Miami. Before "Timeless" was summoned from the vault of *Speak Now*, the competition for my favorite Taylor Swift song of all time was fierce, and several floated in and out of rotation. But like the true love described in the song, I knew instantly upon encountering it that this was the one. Soaking in "Timeless" for the first time on a swing bench overlooking the Zambezi River, my eyes welled, which was

Epilogue 159

uncharacteristic of me. (I listened to "Timeless" a week after its release, as I had just finished a bike expedition whose start date coincided with the drop of *Speak Now (Taylor's Version)*. Even before the record's release was announced, I named my bike Sparks, partly inspired by *Speak Now*'s second track and mostly in line with my collection of S-named bikes: Sapphire Blue, Storm, and Sabotage.) Back in California, writing Chapter 2, the "Tim McGraw x Timeless" mashup felt serendipitous.

Indeed, Swifties' most fascinating tales to relay are those of synchronicities. Carl Jung, who denoted the archetypes of Chapter 5, introduced synchronicities into the psychological discourse as events that appear to be meaningfully connected without a clear causal relationship (like the story above). Another one for me, which goes back some years, was discovering that my Jungian archetype was the Lover, just before the title of *Lover* was revealed. Most recently, there was an agreement among Swifties that on the Eras Tour, Taylor didn't play the surprise song you wanted, but the surprise song you needed. In the crowd at Amsterdam Night 2, I held my breath as she promised us a song she'd never played live before. After she performed "imgonnagetyouback" on guitar (mashed up with "Dress"), she said that she thought we'd like it because of the bike lyrics. I marveled at how she picked the night I was there, out of the three nights in the bicycle city of Amsterdam, to conjure the cyclist in me. In relation to this book, my favorite happy accident is how Chapter 5 lined up to be about the fans. I had initially planned for that portion to be in a different chapter, but when I finished Chapter 4, realized the imperative update to flow. In my mind, the way that Chapter 5 emerged as the longest chapter and crown jewel of the project splendidly mirrors the way that the notion of Track Fives as the emotional centerpiece of Taylor's albums emerged from the fans themselves.

The making of each chapter, not only Chapter 5, was special to me. I surmise that the chapters blend together for the reader, who can seamlessly transition from one to the next without pausing to think of idiosyncrasies, unlike with songs on an album whose features protrude to the listener. But on the backend, to me, each chapter was distinctly textured—the examples I was dying to use, the perspectives I was encumbered to convey with conviction, the new things I gleefully stumbled upon in research. Some conceptual threads were the text format of my favorite devised in-class

160 Epilogue

workshops; some exploratory chunks were the formal version of my memorable animated discussions with friends. On that note, the hardcover gracefully encapsulated elements of my two favorite eras, the deep purple emblematic of *Speak Now* and the awards show look during the span of *The Tortured Poets Department*; the title, adapted from "Clara Bow" of *The Tortured Poets Department*, and the playful "Next Chapter" insert after Chapter 1, taken from "The Story of Us" of *Speak Now*, cemented my favorites. I never knew that writing about somebody else could be so personal.

Perhaps that's the reason for this drawn-out goodbye, the bittersweet (for me) bookend to the end of my first book. Teaching is something that I've learned to love through a subject that I adored. But writing is something that, as a student and an adult, I've simply loved. If writing is a tenderly upkept open house for Taylor, it's an exclusive sanctuary for me that I can enter, design, and renovate anytime. Up until this point, my best prose and poems only lurked in the archives of my diary, like a secret hobby that I've treated with the comfort of having something all to yourself. Occasionally, they've snuck out into the living world in the form of gifts or assignments. I considered minoring in creative writing at the encouragement of my English instructor freshman year of college and after a self-written audition monologue earned compliments from my director sophomore year of college. I opted for public policy instead. In some meandering, fateful manner, it has landed me here, on the cusp of the most important occasion of my words greeting the world. Every late night, which began after I sent off my last corporate email of the day and ended when I'd deemed my progress substantial, was worthwhile. Every weekend spent in the glow of my laptop, concocting intriguing methods of effective communication and sprinkling musicality into nonfiction, was rewarding. Here, at the end of the party, I'm experiencing that standstill moment. I've parsed the emotions and approaches involved in executing this project, and now my dream is that it means something different to you than it does to me—an enhanced appreciation of existing phenomena or an amplified motivation to push your own boundaries with the innovative fusion of your own passions. I don't know what will happen when this goes to print and becomes tangible and develops stakes, but I do know that if you have a chance to say something, whisper into a soul, or scream into the void, you should take it. Perhaps that's the reason for this drawn-out goodbye.

Epilogue

I started this journey off with numerology, so I think it'd be apt to close with it. My publication date is scheduled for the 16th. The 16th is at the middle point between Taylor's birth date (13th)—also my mother's birth date—and mine (19th). The Eras Tour concerts that I had the fortune of attending were the 19th and 39th cities on the tour. The latter number is representative of the birth year, 1939, of my late maternal grandmother, who bequeathed wisdom in the form of exceptionally perceptive observations on art and culture. Tying these with a bow is my ISBN-10, whose numerical string begins with "139." Its last digits are "44," reminding me of the parallel timeline in "Timeless" that takes place in 1944—a song inspired by Taylor's grandparents.

The End

Endnotes

Prologue

1. Molly Seghi, "The Taylor Swift Society celebrated "1989 (Taylor's Version)" release," *The Independent Florida Alligator*, October 29, 2023; "The Eras Tour Intro (It's Been a Long Time Coming)," *Genius*, accessed October 6, 2024.
2. "Why 13 is taylor's lucky number," posted December 2, 2021, by repumore, YouTube, 40 sec; Michaela Zee, "Taylor Swift's 'Tortured Poets Department' Reclaims No. 1 Spot on Albums Chart," *Variety*, August 4, 2024.

Chapter 1

1. Eliana Dockterman, "Taylor Swift Tops iTunes Canada Chart With a Song That Was 8 Seconds of Static," *Time*, October 22, 2014.
2. Taylor Swift, "If I didn't write, I wouldn't sing," posted October 29, 2014, by CBS Mornings, YouTube, 1 min 3 sec.
3. Taylor Swift, "Taylor Swift talks to Fearne Cotton about 1989," posted November 14, 2014, by BBC RADIO, YouTube, 20 min 21 sec.
4. Rachel Treisman, "Costco hot dogs have cost $1.50 since the 1980s. Here's why prices aren't changing," *NPR*, June 4, 2024.
5. Brooke Steinberg, "Here's how much you spend per minute while shopping at Costco," *New York Post*, September 16, 2024.

163

Endnotes

6. Janelle Bitker, "Boichik Bagels ready to open in Berkeley with New York-style bagels," *San Francisco Chronicle*, November 8, 2019.

7. Patience Haggin, "Tesla Dives into Advertising After Years of Resistance," *The Wall Street Journal*, March 29, 2024; Elon Musk, Tesla, accessed October 13, 2024.

8. Hannah Dailey, "Taylor Swift's 'Tortured Poets' Breaks Spotify Record for Most Pre-Saved Album Countdown," *billboard*, April 18, 2024.

9. Gregory Raiz, "Why The Quality of Successful Products Declines Over Time (And How To Keep This In Check)," *Forbes*, May 22, 2017.

10. Phil Gallo, "Taylor Swift Q&A: The Risks of 'Red' and The Joys of Being 22," *billboard*, October 19, 2012.

11. Jason Lipshutz, "Taylor Swift Reveals 'Never Ever' Inspiration," *billboard*, September 24, 2012.

12. Hoda Kotb, "On tour with Taylor Swift," *NBC News*, May 31, 2009; Taylor Swift, "Taylor Swift - I'd Lie (ACOUSTIC LIVE!)," posted October 14, 2009, by Billboard, YouTube, 3 min 48 sec.

13. "Taylor Swift (album)," Taylor Swift Wiki, Fandom, Last Updated January 12, 2025.

14. "Teardrops On My Guitar (Alternate Demo)," Genius, accessed October 13, 2024. Reportedly, Drew's life choices did not pan out. *See* Dee Lockett, "Drew Hardwick, Subject of Taylor Swift's 'Teardrops on My Guitar,' Arrested for Child Abuse," *Vulture*, December 29, 2015

15. "Dear John" doubly refers to a letter intended to terminate a relationship. *See* "Dear John Definition & Meaning," Merriam-Webster, Last Updated January 10, 2025.

16. "Taylor talking about 22, birthdays, and more for Glamour," TikTok, May 10, 2023.

17. Sylvie Droit-Volet and Sandrine Gil, "The time–emotion paradox," *Philosophical Transactions of The Royal Society B* 364: 1943-1953 ("[A]lthough humans are able to accurately estimate time as if they possess a specific mechanism that allows them to measure time (i.e. an internal clock), their representations of time are easily distorted by the context. Indeed, our sense of time depends on intrinsic context, such as the emotional state..."); Annett Schirmer, "How emotions change time," *Frontiers in Integrative Neuroscience*, October 4, 2011, Volume 5–2011 ("Emotional stimuli with a larger share in one[']s sentience are then perceived as

Endnotes 165

longer than neutral stimuli with a smaller share."); Tavi Gevinson, "Taylor Swift Has No Regrets," *ELLE*, May 7, 2015 ("A heartbroken person is unlike any other person. Their time moves at a completely different pace than ours. It's this mental, physical, emotional ache and feeling so conflicted.").

18. Taylor Swift, "For Taylor Swift, Pop Is Personal," *ELLE*, February 27, 2019.

19. Ben Sisario, "Sales of Taylor Swift's '1989' Intensify Streaming Debate," *The New York Times*, November 5, 2014.

20. *Taylor Swift: Reputation Stadium Tour*, directed by Paul Dugdale (Arlington, TX: Den of Thieves, SR Films, Taylor Swift Productions, 2018), Streaming.

21. Taylor Swift, "For Taylor Swift, Pop Is Personal," *ELLE*, February 27, 2019.

22. Ashley Lasimone, "Taylor Swift on 'Cruel Summer' Becoming a Single Four Years After Its Release: 'No One Understands How This Is Happening'," *billboard*, June 17, 2023; Nate Hertweck, "Taylor Swift Plots 2020 World Tour With U.S. Dates For Lover Fest East & West," *GRAMMY*, September 17, 2019.

23. *Taylor Swift folklore the long pond studio sessions*, directed by Taylor Swift (Long Pond Studios Hudson Valley, NY: Taylor Swift, Robert Allen, Bart Peters, 2020), Streaming.

24. Caitlin O'Kane, "Taylor Swift announces surprise album, recorded "in isolation"," *CBS News*, July 23, 2020.

25. Patagonia, "Don't Buy This Jacket, Black Friday and the New York Times," *Patagonia*, November 25, 2011; "Unconventional Patagonia Marketing Solutions," Algofy, accessed October 13, 2024; Uri Neren, "Patagonia's Provocative Black Friday Campaign," *Harvard Business Review*, November 23, 2012; Trevor Nace, "After 44 Years Patagonia Released Its First Commercial & It's Not About Clothing," *Forbes*, July 24, 2018.

26. Jem Aswad, "Taylor Swift to Release New Album, 'Evermore,' Tonight," *Variety*, December 10, 2020.

27. Mac Bell, "Boscov's celebrates 110th anniversary; offering $20,000 in giveaways," *abc27 WHTM*, October 4, 2024.

28. Bill O'Boyle, "Boscov's looks ahead to 50th store, continued success," *Times Leader*, April 7, 2023.

Endnotes

29. *Taylor Swift folklore the long pond studio sessions*, directed by Taylor Swift (Long Pond Studios Hudson Valley, NY: Taylor Swift, Robert Allen, Bart Peters, 2020), Streaming.

30. "Taylor Swift's Songwriting Process on 'evermore' | Apple Music," posted December 15, 2020, by Apple Music, YouTube, 56 min 7 sec.

31. *Taylor Swift folklore the long pond studio sessions*, directed by Taylor Swift (Long Pond Studios Hudson Valley, NY: Taylor Swift, Robert Allen, Bart Peters, 2020), Streaming.

32. "Taylor Swift - 2012 MTV First - Interview with Sway," posted September 21, 2024, by B-side Archive (Obscure Music & Lost Media), YouTube, 29 min 46 sec.

33. "Taylor Swift's mom explains the making of song Love Story 😂," TikTok, July 13, 2023; Taylor Swift, "10 Questions for Taylor Swift," *Time*, April 23, 2009.

34. Lauren Rearick, "Taylor Swift Dressed as "The Little Mermaid" For New Year's Eve," *Teen Vogue*, January 1, 2019.

35. "Taylor Swift - A Place In This World (Live From Soho)," posted May 17, 2012, by WLYW13, YouTube, 3 min 28 sec; *taylor swift folklore the long pond studio sessions*, directed by Taylor Swift (Long Pond Studios Hudson Valley, NY: Taylor Swift, Robert Allen, Bart Peters, 2020), Streaming; "Taylor Swift reveals meaning of Fortnight, Clara Bow and more THE TORTURED POETS DEPARTMENT tracks," posted April 23, 2024, by Miss Americana and You Guys, YouTube, 6 min 17 sec; "Taylor Swift talks about The Lucky One," posted "n.d.", by taylorvideos, Dailymotion, 1 min 2 sec.

36. "Taylor Swift | Artist," GRAMMY, accessed October 13, 2024.

37. Raisa Bruner, "How *1989* Changed Taylor Swift's Career Forever," *Time*, October 26, 2023.

38. Chris Willman, "Taylor Swift: No Longer 'Polite at All Costs'," *Variety*, January 21, 2020.

39. "Taylor Swift My Life," Internet Archive Wayback Machine, accessed October 13, 2024.

Chapter 2

1. "Niche Definition & Meaning," Merriam-Webster, Last Updated January 10, 2025; "NICHE Definition & Meaning," Dictionary.com, accessed October 27, 2024.

Endnotes

2. "10 Facts About Taylor Swift," Penguin Random House, accessed October 27, 2024; "Taylor Swift Journey To Fearless Texas The Full DVD," posted April 5, 2018, by Taylor Music, YouTube, 2:10:51; "Taylor Swift - Speak Now Tour (Full Concert HD)," posted December 8, 2022, by Swift Leaks Backup, YouTube, 2:09:26.

3. "Shop By Pet," exoticnutrition.com, accessed October 27, 2024.

4. "WHO WE ARE," We are Lush, accessed October 27, 2024.

5. "ABOUT US," Lefty's San Francisco: The Left Hand Store, accessed October 27, 2024; "Left-Handers Day: Amazing facts about lefties," *BBC*, August 13, 2024.

6. "Exotic Nutrition," walmart.com, accessed October 27, 2024; "Exotic Nutrition," chewy.com, accessed October 27, 2024; "Lush is investing £7.6M in growing retail spaces," We are Lush, accessed October 27, 2024; Aryn Braun, "American lefties have never had it so good," *The Economist*, November 22, 2018; Victoria Vallecorse, "It's a left-handers paradise at Lefty's Pier 39," *ABC7 News*, February 8, 2023.

7. John Preston, "Taylor Swift: the 19-year-old country music star conquering America - and now Britain," *The Telegraph*, April 26, 2009.

8. Chris Willman, "Getting to know Taylor Swift," *Entertainment Weekly*, July 25, 2007; "ABOUT US," CRS, accessed October 27, 2024.

9. "Taylor Swift Journey To Fearless Texas The Full DVD," posted April 5, 2018, by Taylor Music, YouTube, 2:10:51; Jack Irvin, "Taylor Swift CD of Original Music and Country Covers Recorded at Age 11 Sold for Over $12,000 at Auction," *People*, June 19, 2024.

10. "Taylor Swift Journey To Fearless Texas The Full DVD," posted April 5, 2018, by Taylor Music, YouTube, 2:10:51; Chris Willman, "Getting to know Taylor Swift," *Entertainment Weekly*, July 25, 2007; Hoda Kotb, "On tour with Taylor Swift," *NBC News*, May 31, 2009; "Labels & Content Divisions," Sony Music, accessed October 27, 2024.

11. John Preston, "Taylor Swift: the 19-year-old country music star conquering America - and now Britain," *The Telegraph*, April 26, 2009.

12. "Taylor Swift Journey To Fearless Texas The Full DVD," posted April 5, 2018, by Taylor Music, YouTube, 2:10:51; Chris Willman, "Getting to know Taylor Swift," *Entertainment Weekly*, July 25, 2007.

13. "Taylor Swift Journey To Fearless Texas The Full DVD," posted April 5, 2018, by Taylor Music, YouTube, 2:10:51.

Endnotes

14. Chris Willman, "Getting to know Taylor Swift," *Entertainment Weekly*, July 25, 2007; Taylor Swift, "10 Questions for Taylor Swift," *Time*, April 23, 2009; Tom Roland, "Love Story: The Impact of Taylor Swift's First Decade in Music," *billboard pro*, July 7, 2016.

15. @TheChainsmokers, "Awesome article @taylorswift13 https://elle.com/uk/life-and-culture/a26546099/taylor-swift-pop-music/ about song writing and thanks for mentioning one of our," X (formerly known as Twitter), March 2, 2019.

16. "Taylor Swift - Live at the 2019 American Music Awards," posted November 26, 2019, by Taylor Swift, YouTube, 11 min 39 sec; Nina Braca, "Taylor Swift Announces Camila Cabello & Charli XCX as Reputation Tour Opening Acts," *billboard*, March 01, 2018; "Taylor Swift: 'Lover', Politics, & Friendship with Selena Gomez | Apple Music," posted October 30, 2019, by Apple Music, YouTube, 8 min 57 secW.

17. Steven Hyden, "Taylor Swift, indie-rock star? Long, long ago, this might have felt strange" *The New York Times*, March 10, 2021.

18. Chris Willman, "Getting to know Taylor Swift," *Entertainment Weekly*, July 25, 2007.

19. John Preston, "Taylor Swift: the 19-year-old country music star conquering America - and now Britain," *The Telegraph*, April 26, 2009; Hoda Kotb, "On tour with Taylor Swift," *NBC News*, May 31, 2009.

20. "2009 CMT Music Awards: Winners," Internet Archive Wayback Machine, accessed October 27, 2024.

21. "Taylor Swift ft. T-Pain - Thug Story (Official Video) [4K Remastered]," posted February 21, 2024, by MASTER RJ, YouTube, 1 min 25 sec; r/TaylorSwift, "Let's Discuss 'Thug Story'," Reddit, n.d.

22. Jonathan Van Meter, "Taylor Swift: The Single Life," *Vogue*, January 16, 2012.

23. JJ Staff, "Taylor Swift Fans Point Out the Significance of 'Enchanted' Being the Only 'Speak Now' Song on the Eras Tour," *Just Jared*, March 28, 2023.

24. Jason Lipshutz, "Taylor Swift Reveals 'Never Ever' Inspiration," *billboard*, September 24, 2012.

25. "Taylor Swift reveals meaning of Fortnight, Clara Bow and more THE TORTURED POETS DEPARTMENT tracks ♡," posted April 23, 2024, by Miss Americana and You Guys, YouTube, 6 min 17 sec.

Endnotes 169

26. "MTV Video Music Awards (VMA) (2009)," IMDb, accessed October 27, 2024.

27. Heran Mamo, Anna Chan, & Hannah Dailey, "A Timeline of Ye & Taylor Swift's Relationship," *billboard*, August 5, 2024.

28. Chris Willman, "Taylor Swift and Kanye West's 2016 Phone Call Leaks: Read the Full Transcript," *Variety*, March 21, 2020.

29. "Taylor Swift: Nils Sjoberg ... You're Dead to Me," *TMZ*, July 18, 2016; Melody Chiu, "Taylor Swift Wrote Ex Calvin Harris and Rihanna's Hit 'This Is What You Came For,' Her Rep Confirms," *People*, July 13, 2016; Gil Kaufman, "Calvin Harris Says It's 'Hurtful' That Taylor Swift's Team Is 'Trying to Make Me Look Bad'," *billboard*, July 13, 2016; Tatiana Cirisano, "Calvin Harris Explains Why He 'Snapped' on Twitter After Taylor Swift Breakup," *billboard*, June 30, 2017.

30. Alexandra Holterman, "The History of Taylor Swift & the Snake," *billboard*, August 21, 2017.

31. "Taylor Swift Web Photo Gallery," Taylor Swift Web, accessed October 27, 2024.

32. Kathryn Lindsay, "Update: Taylor Swift Has Posted The (Hopefully) Last Piece Of Her Instagram Puzzle," *Refinery29*, August 23, 2017; Nate Hertweck, "Taylor Swift Announces New Album, 'Reputation'," *GRAMMY*, August 23, 2017.

33. Tatiana Cirisano, "Taylor Swift Tops PSY's 24-Hour YouTube Record With 'Look What You Made Me Do'," *billboard pro*, August 29, 2017.

34. Alice M. Tybout and Michelle Roehm, "Let the Response Fit the Scandal," *Harvard Business Review*, December 2009; "Alice M. Tybout," Kellogg School of Management, Northwestern University, accessed October 27, 2024; Mike Ferlazzo, "Bucknell Names Michelle Roehm Next Dean of the Freeman College of Management," *Bucknell University News*, February 8, 2024.

35. "Taylor Invited The Reporters in The Rep Intro," TikTok, January 6, 2025; "Karyn," Taylor Swift Wiki, Fandom, accessed October 27, 2024.

36. Denise Warner, "Taylor Swift Kicks Off 'Reputation' Tour by Calling Out Bullies," *The Hollywood Reporter*, May 9, 2018; Brittany Hodak, "Taylor Swift Breaks U.S. Record With 'Reputation' Stadium Tour," *Forbes*, November 30, 2018; Eric Frankenberg, "Taylor Swift Closes Reputation Stadium Tour with $345 Million," *billboard*, December 6, 2018.

Endnotes

37. *Taylor Swift: Miss Americana*, directed by Lana Wilson (Nashville, TN and New York, NY: Tremolo Productions, 2020), Streaming; Nate Hertweck, "What's The Difference? GRAMMY Record Of The Year Vs. Song Of The Year," *GRAMMY*, December 26, 2017; Ana Monroy Yglesias, "Ariana Grande Wins Best Pop Vocal Album For 'Sweetener' | 2019 GRAMMYs," *GRAMMY*, February 10, 2019.

38. "[FULL • 4K] Taylor Swift • The 1989 World Tour Live (Remastered)," posted May 28, 2022, by EAS Music Channel, YouTube, 2:11:45.

39. Rebecca Macatee, "Taylor Swift Cried and 'Ate a Lot' of In-N-Out Burger When Red Didn't Win a Grammy for Album of the Year," *E! News*, October 9, 2015.

40. *Taylor Swift folklore the long pond studio sessions*, directed by Taylor Swift (Long Pond Studios Hudson Valley, NY: Taylor Swift, Robert Allen, Bart Peters, 2020), Streaming.

41. Jessica Nicholson, "Taylor Swift Accepts Songwriter-Artist of the Decade Honor at Nashville Songwriter Awards: Read Her Full Speech," *billboard*, September 21, 2022.

42. David Kindy, "The Accidental Invention of Play-Doh," *Smithsonian Magazine*, November 12, 2019.

43. Julie Littman, "Why Chipotlanes are Chipotle's future," *Restaurant Dive*, November 21, 2022.

44. Kara K. Nesvig, "Taylor Swift Admitted That Her Public Call-Out of Joe Jonas on "Ellen" After Their Breakup Was "Too Much"," *Teen Vogue*, May 15, 2019; Randy Lewis, "She's writing her future," *Los Angeles Times*, October 26, 2008.

45. Anna Lewis, "The lengths Kate Winslet went to get her Titanic role will blow your mind," *Cosmopolitan*, June 8, 2016; Rachel Chang, "Kate Winslet and Leonardo DiCaprio's A-List Competition for 'Titanic'," *Biography*, April 7, 2020.

46. "Titanic," Oscars, Academy of Motion Picture Arts and Sciences, accessed October 27, 2024.

47. Silvio Pietroluongo, "DeRulo Tops Hot 100, But Swift Swoops In With Record-Breaking Debut Sum," *billboard*, November 5, 2009; Gary Trust, "Taylor Swift Claims Record Top 14 Spots on Billboard Hot 100, Led by 'Fortnight' With Post Malone," *billboard*, April 29, 2024.

48. "Taylor Swift | Biography, Music & News," billboard, accessed October 27, 2024; Jonathan Cohen, "T.I. Returns To No. 1 On The Hot

Endnotes

171

100," *billboard*, October 23, 2008; Jonathan Cohen, "T.I. Replaces Himself Again Atop Hot 100," *billboard*, November 6, 2008; Jonathan Cohen, "Taylor Swift Notches Six Hot 100 Debuts," *billboard*, November 20, 2008; "Hey Stephen," Ultimate Pop Culture Wiki, Fandom, accessed October 27, 2024; "Breathe," Taylor Swift Wiki, Fandom, accessed October 27, 2024; Jonathan Cohen, "Pink Notches First Solo Hot 100 No. 1," *billboard*, September 18, 2008; Jonathan Cohen, "T.I. Leads Hot 100; Kanye, Taylor Debut High," *billboard*, November 13, 2008; "Fifteen," Taylor Swift Wiki, Fandom, accessed October 27, 2024; "Two Is Better Than One," Taylor Swift Wiki, Fandom, accessed October 27, 2024.

49. "Two Is Better Than One (feat. Taylor Swift)", Taylor Swift Switzerland, accessed October 27, 2024.

50. Alex Hopper, "Behind the Meaning of Taylor Swift's 'Speak Now'," *American Songwriter*, July 4, 2023.

51. Tanner Stransky, "Taylor Swift tells EW about new album 'Speak Now': 'I've covered every emotion that I've felt in the last two years.'" *Entertainment Weekly*, December 20, 2019; "Speak Now [Liner Notes]," Genius, accessed October 27, 2024.

52. Allison Sadlier, "This is the age most people start thinking about their dream wedding," *New York Post*, June 17, 2019; "Median age at first marriage: 1890 to present", United States Census Bureau, accessed October 27, 2024.

53. "Speak Now (Taylor's Version) [Prologue]," Genius, Last Updated July 7, 2023.

54. Rachel Sonis, "Taylor Swift's 'All You Had To Do Was Stay' Is Criminally Underrated," *Time*, October 26, 2023; "iHeart Secret Sessions special - excerpt of Taylor talking", TBN, Last Updated November 11, 2017.

55. Randy Lewis, "She's writing her future," *Los Angeles Times*, October 26, 2008.

56. Megan Maloy, "YA Friday: Fearless (Taylor's Version)," *San Jose Public Library Blogs*, June 30, 2023; The Boot Staff, "Taylor Swift, 'You Belong With Me' — Story Behind the Song," *The Boot*, November 21, 2014.

57. "Tied Together With A Smile by Taylor Swift," Songfacts, accessed October 27, 2024; "Mary's Song (Oh My My) by Taylor Swift," Songfacts, accessed October 27, 2024.

58. Tanner Stransky, "Taylor Swift tells EW about new album 'Speak Now': 'I've covered every emotion that I've felt in the last two years.'," *Entertainment Weekly*, December 20, 2019.

Chapter 3

1. Lauren Huff, "Seth Meyers says he was blown away by Taylor Swift writing 'the perfect SNL monologue'," *Entertainment Weekly*, October 31, 2023.
2. "Shelf life Definition & Meaning," Merriam-Webster, Last Updated January 9, 2025.
3. "How long can you keep dairy products like yogurt, milk, and cheese in the refrigerator?," AskUSDA, Last Updated May 17, 2024; "Shelf Life of Non-food Items," Simply Prepared with CFD, accessed November 7, 2024.
4. "CONA Full Record," The J. Paul Getty Trust, accessed November 7, 2024; Bridget Katz, "The 'Mona Lisa' May Leave the Louvre for the First Time in 44 Years," *Smithsonian Magazine*, March 9, 2018, https://www.smithsonianmag.com/smart-news/mona-lisa-may-leave-louvre-first-time-44-years-180968425.
5. Carly Silva, "Eiffel Tower Turns Into an 'Epic' Taylor Swift Tribute Ahead of Paris Eras Tour," *Y! Entertainment*, May 7, 2024; Carly Silva, "Big Ben Morphs Into Must-See Taylor Swift Tribute Ahead of London Eras Tour Dates," *Parade*, June 6, 2024; Keith Spera, "Dome's friendship bracelet is unique to the New Orleans Eras Tour. Here's how it came to life," *nola*, October 24, 2024; Drew Weisholtz, "Travis Kelce tried to give Taylor Swift his phone number at her concert. His plan failed," *Today*, July 26, 2023; I confirm the seeping of bracelet culture into other fandoms from personal and anecdotal experience. Fall Out Boy is one of Swift's greatest songwriting inspirations, and Charli xcx opened for Swift on the Reputation Stadium Tour. *See* Brian Hatt, "Taylor Swift: The Rolling Stone Interview," *Rolling Stone*, September 18, 2019, https://www.rollingstone.com/music/music-features/taylor-swift-rolling-stone-interview-880794/; Nina Braca, "Taylor Swift Announces Camila Cabello & Charli XCX as Reputation Tour Opening Acts," *billboard*, March 01, 2018, https://www.billboard.com/music/pop/camila-cabello-charli-xcx-taylor-swift-reputation-tour-opening-acts-8223861/.

Endnotes 173

6. Jake Viswanath, "Buying Taylor Swift Tickets Sparked 'The Great War' & She's Not Happy About It," *Bustle*, November 18, 2022.

7. Will Kenton, "The Law of Diminishing Marginal Utility: How It Works, With Examples," *Investopedia*, May 4, 2024; Andrew Bloomenthal, "Marginal Utilities: Definition, Types, Examples, and History," *Investopedia*, June 26, 2024; E. T. Berkman, L.E. Kahn, & J.L. Livingston, "Diminishing Marginal Utility," *Self-Regulation and Ego Control*, pages 255-279, 2016.

8. G.J., "The utility of bad art," *The Economist*, August 7, 2013 ("The more we experience good art the more we learn to like it, whereas bad art has diminishing marginal utility.").

9. Nicole Mastrogiannis, "Taylor Swift Shares Intimate Details of 'Lover' Songs During Secret Session," *iHeart*, August 23, 2019.

10. "[Remastered 4K] Out Of The Woods - Taylor Swift - Grammys Museum 2015 - EAS Channel," posted February 19, 2023, by EAS Music Channel, YouTube, 5 min 34 sec. https://www.youtube.com/watch?v=pRWr7t3TjAs; Fine Line Tattoos Melbourne, "TAYLOR SWIFT FLASH EVENT - FLASH SHEET," posted July 13, 2023, Instagram.

11. "Taylor Swift - The making of Breathe Part 2," posted July 5, 2010, by 013Fearless, YouTube, 6 min 8 sec.

12. Elias Leight, "Here's Why Shorter Songs Are Surging (And Why Some Welcome It)," *billboard pro*, November 18, 2022.

13. *Taylor Swift folklore the long pond studio sessions*, directed by Taylor Swift (Long Pond Studios Hudson Valley, NY: Taylor Swift, Robert Allen, Bart Peters, 2020), Streaming.

14. "Don't Blame Me," Z Taylor Swift Switzerland, accessed November 7, 2024.

15. As labeled, the albums considered in this exhibit are the fullest digital versions released during those eras and do not include music released outside of the named albums at any point or vault tracks. Note that *Lover* and *Midnights (The Til Dawn Edition)* do not include "All Of The Girls You Loved Before" and "You're Losing Me," respectively. Note that *Fearless (Platinum Edition)* does not include "Untouchable" because it is a cover song. Note that not every structure is present on every album. The structures and categorization are based on my own interpretation of the songs, and what I feel is the most methodical way to sift through them. I consider outros to be melodically and lyrically distinct from the rest of the song, and hence do not consider repetitions of choruses

174 Endnotes

or pre-choruses as outros. I do not consider instances where the first and second verse are melodically distinct, as with "Question...?," to be a separate structure. I acknowledge that some categorization is ambiguous and hence subjective. For instance, I understand that instrumental breaks can be considered bridges, but I consider bridges to be lyrical for this purpose. I recommend applying this framework to non-Swift songs as a fun exercise. For instance, "You and Me" by Lifehouse is a Circular song.

16. Some of the countless examples include the last chorus in "Should've Said No" at the Academy of Country Music Awards, "we need love" in "New Romantics" on the 1989 World Tour, the bridge in "I Did Something Bad" on the Reputation Stadium Tour, and "take her home" in "the 1" on the Eras Tour. At times, Swift uses live performances to direct listeners to potentially overlooked parts of the studio recordings. On the 1989 World Tour, for instance, she asked the audience to vocalize for "Out of the Woods," and only after this performance did I notice her backup singers do it on the studio recording.

17. *See, e.g.,* Samantha Cooney et al., "Taylor Swift's Best Bridges, Ranked," *Time,* April 16, 2024.

18. "Taylor Swift's Songwriting Process on 'evermore'," posted December 15, 2020, by Apple Music, YouTube, 56 min 7 sec.

19. "Maroon Definition & Meaning," Merriam-Webster, Last Updated January 14, 2025; "Taylor Swift - Maroon (Official Lyric Video)," posted October 21, 2022, by Taylor Swift, YouTube, 3 min 42 sec.

20. "Taylor Swift talks about the significance of the red scarf as a metaphor," posted n.d by @box__office, YouTube, 38 sec.

21. "[FULL • 4K] Taylor Swift • The 1989 World Tour Live (Remastered)," posted May 28, 2022, by EAS Music Channel, YouTube, 2:11:45.

22. "Figurative Language - Definition, Types, and Examples," Corporate Finance Institute, accessed November 7, 2024; "Alliteration Definition & Meaning," Merriam-Webster, Last Updated December 10, 2024; "Zeugma Definition & Meaning," Merriam-Webster, accessed November 7, 2024; "Allusion - Definition and Examples," LitCharts, accessed November 7, 2024.

23. Capital FM, "Taylor Swift's Poem She Wrote At 10 Years Old Is Proof Her Writing Has Always Been Magical," *Capital,* December 8, 2022;

Endnotes 175

PIONEER PRESS, "Taylor Swift tells kids: Read for a better life," *Twin Cities Pioneer Press*, November 12, 2015.

24. "Taylor Swift sings the National Anthem in Phoenix (2006)," posted October 1, 2023, by NASCAR, YouTube, 1 min 44 sec; "Taylor Swift sings the National Anthem before 2008 World Series Game 3!," posted June 23, 2015, by MLB, YouTube, 2 min 22 sec.

Chapter 4

1. Sinéad O'Sullivan, "Why Normal Music Reviews No Longer Make Sense for Taylor Swift," *The New Yorker*, April 30, 2024; "Robert A. Iger", The Walt Disney Company, accessed November 15, 2024; Sam Lansky, "Taylor Swift 2023 TIME Person of the Year," *Time*, December 6, 2023.

2. Marisa LaScala, "41 Disney Movie Easter Eggs That Only Die-Hard Fans Can Spot," *Good Housekeeping*, March 3, 2020.

3. "Taylor Swift - Why She Disappeared [Poem]," Genius, Last Updated November 10, 2017.

4. Callie Ahlgrim, "The ultimate guide to every song on 'Red (Taylor's Version)'," *Business Insider*, November 13, 2021; "Taylor Swift's 'Red' Prologues: Original Vs. Taylor's Version (Full Text)," Swifty Sung Stories, accessed November 15, 2024.

5. "Alchemy Definition & Meaning," Merriam-Webster, Last Updated January 25, 2025.

6. "Taylor Swift - Fortnight (feat. Post Malone) (Behind the Scenes)," posted June 21, 2024, by Taylor Swift, YouTube, 3 min 39 sec.; Kelsie Gibson, "Clara Bow's Family Share Their Thoughts on Taylor Swift's Song Named for the Star: 'Hauntingly Beautiful' (Exclusive)," *People*, April 19, 2024.

7. Taylor Soper, "How this agency helped Microsoft create the viral 'Children of the 90s' IE ad," *GeekWire*, April 26, 2013; "'Child of the '90s' Video for Microsoft's Internet Explorer," Column Five, accessed November 15, 2024.

8. Angel Cohn, "Suit Up for How I Met Your Mother Scoops," *Television Without Pity*, October 3, 2008; Amy K Brown and Ryan Heffernan, "The 25 Best 'How I Met Your Mother' Episodes, Ranked According to IMDb," *Collider*, January 6, 2025; One fan favorite Easter egg of *How*

I Met Your Mother is the subtle reveal of Tracy's name in the first season through a joking aside, much before the official reveal in the series finale.

9. "@taylorswift is a Mastermind at hiding easter eggs in her music," posted May 26, 2023, by fallontonight, Instagram.

10. Dr Henry Irving, "Keep Calm and Carry On – The Compromise Behind the Slogan," *History of Government*, June 27, 2014.

11. Joel Calfee and Chelsey Sanchez, "A Comprehensive Guide to Every Matty Healy Reference on The Tortured Poets Department," *Harper's Bazaar*, April 19, 2024.

12. "Bloke Definition & Meaning," Merriam-Webster, Last Updated January 4, 2025.

13. Robert Chan, "'How I Met Your Mother' Creators Reveal Most Coveted Show Props and Who's Taking Home MacLaren's Bar," *Yahoo TV*, September 16, 2014.

14. Rania Aniftos and Anna Chan, "Here's Every Time Taylor Swift Has Appeared on 'Saturday Night Live'," *billboard*, October 17, 2023; "How I Met Your Mother Monologue - Saturday Night Live," posted October 22, 2013, by Saturday Night Live, YouTube, 5 min 12 sec; "Save Broadway - SNL," posted October 22, 2013, by Saturday Night Live, YouTube, 6 min 22 sec.

15. Jessica Nicholson, "Taylor Swift Accepts Songwriter-Artist of the Decade Honor at Nashville Songwriter Awards: Read Her Full Speech," *billboard*, September 21, 2022; *See also* Apple Music playlists entitled "Taylor Swift's Quill Pen Songs," "Taylor Swift's Fountain Pen Songs," and "Taylor Swift's Glitter Gel Pen Songs."

16. Sara Donnellan, "An Unofficial Ranking of Taylor Swift's Emotionally Devastating Track 5 Songs," *Us Weekly*, April 23, 2024.

17. Li Cohen and Victoria Albert, "Critics seek clarity after Trader Joe's says it will keep "Trader Ming's" and "Trader José" products, denies they're racist," *CBS News*, July 3, 2020; Joey Skladany, "The 30 most iconic Trader Joe's foods of all time," *Today*, April 4, 2023.

18. "Los Angeles Artist creates tons of Trader Joe's Murals," L Star Murals, accessed November 15, 2024; Jessica Kaplan, "Trader Joe's Has a Secret Scavenger Hunt for Kids—This Is How It Works," *Taste of Home*, December 18, 2023.

Endnotes 177

19. Nick Owchar, "The Artful Writing of Trader Joe's Fearless Flyer (I'm not kidding)," *Impressive Content*, January 9, 2023.
20. Makenna Leiby, "'iPad Kids' and the future of early childhood development," *The Spartan Shield*, March 1, 2022.
21. Josh Howarth, "iPhone vs Android User Stats (2024 Data)," *Exploding Topics*, June 14, 2024.
22. Steven Hyden, "Ask A Music Critic: When (If Ever) Will Taylor Swift's Popularity Fade?," *UPROXX*, July 26, 2023.
23. Nicole Mastrogiannis, "Taylor Swift Shares Intimate Details of 'Lover' Songs During Secret Session," *iHeart*, August 23, 2019; Halie LeSavage, "Taylor Swift Revealed the One "Lover" Lyric That Was Almost So Different," *Glamour*, December 24, 2019.

Chapter 5

1. Lauren Huff, "Taylor Swift says new Midnights track 'Anti-Hero' is 'a guided tour' of her insecurities," *Entertainment Weekly*, October 3, 2022.
2. BilingualBeatdown, "Is Taylor 5'11?," Reddit, n.d.
3. "Taylor Swift Accepts The Song Of The Year Award At The 2023 iHeart-Radio Music Awards," posted March 27, 2023, by iHeartRadio, YouTube, 2 min 12 sec.
4. "Taylor Swift Wanted People to Dance to At Least 1 of Her Songs," posted May 22, 2023, by @Sweet_Hammy, YouTube, 25 sec.
5. Tanner Stransky, "Taylor Swift tells EW about new album 'Speak Now': 'I've covered every emotion that I've felt in the last two years.'" *Entertainment Weekly*, December 20, 2019.
6. *See* Apple Music playlists entitled "I Love You, It's Ruining My Life Songs," "You Don't Get to Tell Me About Sad Songs," "Am I Allowed to Cry? Songs," "Old Habits Die Screaming Songs," and "I Can Do It with a Broken Heart Songs."
7. "Taylor Swift - Fortnight (feat. Post Malone) (Behind the Scenes)," posted June 21, 2024, by Taylor Swift, YouTube, 3 min 39 sec; @taylornation13, "Minutes from last week's #TSTTPD meeting" X (formerly known as Twitter), February 22, 2024.
8. "Beauty Insider," Sephora, accessed December 2, 2024; "Analyzing Sephora Rewards Program: Sephora Beauty Insider," BON Loyalty,

February 28, 2024; Amit Sharma, "How These 3 Brands Are Taking Loyalty Beyond Points," *Adweek*, April 25, 2018.

9. Jenn McMillen, "7 Consumer Loyalty Trends That Will Shape Retail in 2023," *Forbes*, January 9, 2023 ("Consumers spend an average of $132 a month with retailers that have earned their fandom, compared with just $71 a month among non-fans… ").

10. Andrew Unterberger, "Five Reasons Why Taylor Swift Was Able to Make Chart History With Her 'Midnights' Debut Week," *billboard*, October 31, 2022; Rex Woodbury, "What Taylor Swift Can Teach Us About Business," *Digital Native*, March 16, 2023.

11. likeadevils, "Speak Now Timeline," Tumblr, May 6, 2023.

12. Bryanna Cappadona, "Explaining Taylor Swift's Easter eggs and the website error that hinted at her new album," *Yahoo! News*, March 4, 2024; Sweeney Preston, "A Bunch Of Taylor Swift's Inner Circle Has Changed Their Insta DP's & Fans Think They Know Why," *PEDESTRIAN.TV*, January 21, 2024; Michaela Zee, "Taylor Swift Reveals 'Backup Plan' for 'Tortured Poets Department' Announcement if She Didn't Win at Grammys," *Variety*, February 7, 2024.

13. "Taylor Swift New Album 1989 Was Inspired By Late '80s Pop | GRAMMYs," posted October 14, 2014, by Recording Academy/GRAMMY, YouTube, 2 min 19 sec.

14. Phil Gallo, "Taylor Swift Q&A: The Risks of 'Red' and The Joys of Being 22," *billboard*, October 19, 2012.

15. Thao-Vy Duong, "'Folklore' and the Impact of Taylor Swift's Musical Storytelling During the Pandemic," *The Bottom Line UCSB*, October 17, 2020; Kate Reggev, "What Exactly Is Cottagecore and How Did It Get So Popular?," *Clever*, October 21, 2020; Anita Rao Kashi, "'Cottagecore' and the rise of the modern rural fantasy," *BBC*, December 8, 2020; Nicole, "The Comforts and Criticisms of Cottagecore," *Farrago*, accessed December 2, 2024; Marcia Layton Turner, "Gen Z Is Driving Demand For Cottagecore Goods," *Forbes*, February 27, 2021.

16. Jonathan Van Meter, "Taylor Swift: The Single Life," *Vogue*, January 16, 2012.

17. Taylor Swift, "30 Things I Learned Before Turning 30," *ELLE*, March 6, 2019.

Endnotes

179

18. Isabel Mohan, "Why Taylor Swift's Old Albums Are Back on the Charts: 'Folklore' and 'Evermore' Climb for Fall," *Us Weekly*, October 15, 2024.

19. Samantha Grindell, "Taylor Swift switching her nail color in between Eras Tour weekends proves she has more hours in a day than everyone else," *Yahoo! News*, May 16, 2023.

20. "Taylor Swift Now Ep. 4 - Speak Now Album Photo Shoot," posted December 21, 2016, by Sabrina Lopes, YouTube, 20 min 33 sec.

21. "The Changing Generational Value," Imagine, John Hopkins University, Published on November 17, 2022; Jason Brow, "Taylor Swift Made 'Eras' Dictionary.com's Vibe of the Year for 2023," *Us Weekly*, December 19, 2023.

22. Angelique Jackson, "Anna Kendrick Says Directing 'Woman of the Hour' Required More Vulnerability Than Releasing Her Memoir: 'I'm Revealing Something About Myself in Every Frame'," *Variety*, October 22, 2024.

23. killjoy-glitchrat, "Taylor Swift albums as ~*vibes*~ (I'd love to hear other opinions)," Reddit, n.d.; Starstreak24, "Personality of each album?," Reddit, n.d.

24. Joe Garcia, "Listening to Taylor Swift in Prison," *The New Yorker*, September 2, 2023.

25. "M&M's Characters," M&M's, accessed December 2, 2024; Tracy Saelinger, "M&M's revives iconic Christmas commercial: Find out what happened to Santa," *Today*, December 1, 2017.

26. "What Are the 12 Jungian Archetypes?," Centre of Excellence, October 15, 2023; "There are as many archetypes as there are typical…," LIBQUOTES, accessed December 2, 2024.

27. "Mosaic Steps on 16th Avenue in San Francisco," California Through My Lens, accessed December 2, 2024.

28. Maria Tatar, "The Cambridge Companion to Fairy Tales," *Cambridge University Press*, accessed December 2, 2024.

29. Margaret Rossman, "Taylor Swift, remediating the self, and nostalgic girlhood in tween music fandom." *Transformative Works and Cultures*, Vol. 38 (2022).

30. Isaac Muk, "One in every 25 vinyl albums sold in USA in 2022 was by Taylor Swift," *mixmag*, January 13, 2023.

Endnotes

31. Roisin O'Connor, "Half of all new guitar players are women, finds study," *The Independent*, October 18, 2018.

32. "Taylor Swift Journey To Fearless Texas The Full DVD," posted April 5, 2018, by Taylor Music, YouTube, 2:10:51; Jenna Mullins, "45 Things You Didn't Know About Taylor Swift Songs," *E! News*, November 13, 2014; orlybb, "Imogen Heap blogs about writing with Taylor Swift," *LiveJournal: OH NO THEY DIDN'T!*, October 30, 2014.

33. Sarah Al-Arshani, "Taylor Swift fans insist bride keep autographed guitar, donate for wedding," *USA Today*, March 10, 2024.

34. Taylor Swift. *The Official Taylor Swift | The Eras Tour Book*. United States: Taylor Swift Publications, 2024.

35. "Taylor Swift is against dynamic pricing of Eras Tour tickets, rather, she made a bold choice; here's what that is," *The Economic Times*, November 1, 2024.

36. Mahita Gajanan, "Taylor Swift Crashes Fan Wedding for Surprise Performance," *Vanity Fair*, June 5, 2016.

37. "13 Hour Meet & Greet," Taylor Swift Switzerland, June 13, 2010; "Taylor Swift Now - Ep1: 13 Hour Meet & Greet (Part 1)," posted February 20, 2017, by Taylor Swift Station, YouTube, 9 min 35 sec.; "Taylor Swift Now - Ep1: 13 Hour Meet & Greet (Part 2)," posted March 1, 2017, by Taylor Swift Station, YouTube, 6 min 20 sec.

38. Nicole Mastrogiannis, "Taylor Swift Shares Intimate Details of 'Lover' Songs During Secret Session," *iHeart*, August 23, 2019; NPR Staff, "'Anything That Connects': A Conversation With Taylor Swift," *NPR*, October 31, 2014; Randy Lewis, "How does Taylor Swift connect with fans? 'Secret sessions' and media blitzes," *Los Angeles Times*, October 28, 2014.

39. Maddie Lymburner, "How Maddie Lymburner became YouTube's premier pandemic fitness guru," *Toronto Life*, May 28, 2020.

40. Giusy Bounfantino, "New Research Shows Consumers More Interested in Brands' Values than Ever," *Consumer Goods Technology*, April 27, 2022.

41. Gil Kaufman, "Taylor Swift Challenges Fans to Expose Their Insecurities For YouTube Shorts #TSAntiHeroChallenge," *billboard*, October 21, 2022; "It's me, Benjamin 🐱 joining the #TSAntiHeroChallenge," posted November 11, 2022, by Taylor Swift, YouTube, 15 sec; The

Endnotes 181

YouTube Music Team, "Taylor Swift's 'Fortnight' era is upon us," *YouTube Official Blog*, April 20, 2024.

42. Hannah Dailey, "Taylor Swift Says She's 'So Moved' by Single Mother's 'Vulnerable' TikTok About Daughter," *billboard*, December 22, 2023.

43. justinbieber, "Taylor swift what up," Tumblr, June 30, 2019.

44. Cecilia Giles, "Look What You Made Them Do: The Impact of Taylor Swift's Re-recording Project on Record Labels," *University of Cincinnati Law Review*, Vol. 92 (2024); Brendan Morrow, "The most notable records broken by Taylor Swift," *The Week*, accessed December 2, 2024.

45. Karli Bendlin, "Taylor Swift's Eras Tour: A Timeline of the Ticketmaster Fiasco," *People*, March 29, 2023; David Mccabe and Ben Sisario, *The New York Times*, January 24, 2023.

46. Chase Binnie, "REI CO OP Revolutionized Outdoor Retail," *RetailWire*, July 10, 2023.

47. "The Cheese Board: A Worker-Owned Collective Since 1971," The Cheese Board Collective, accessed December 2, 2024.

48. Bob Haegele, "Stakeholders vs. shareholders: What's the difference?," *Bankrate*, January 8, 2024.

49. NPR Staff, "'Anything That Connects': A Conversation With Taylor Swift," *NPR*, October 31, 2014.

50. Marielle Mohs, "Taylor Swift sings surprise song at Minneapolis show after fan's post honoring late brother goes viral," *CBS News*, June 25, 2023.

51. NPR Staff, "'Anything That Connects': A Conversation With Taylor Swift," *NPR*, October 31, 2014.

52. "Taylor Swift's 10-Minute Version of All Too Well Almost Wasn't Recorded (Extended) | Tonight Show," posted November 11, 2021, by The Tonight Show Starring Jimmy Fallon, YouTube, 9 min 38 sec.; Angie Martoccio, "Bye Bye, 'American Pie': Taylor Swift's 10-Minute 'All Too Well' Becomes Longest #1 Hit," *Rolling Stone*, November 22, 2021.

53. "Lana Del Rey on collaborating with Taylor Swift 🫶," posted April 11, 2024, by @Rayanxiix, YouTube, 18 sec.

54. I maintain that the saddest lyric of Swift's discography is "flowers pile up in the worst way." *See* Jamie Cesanek, "Taylor Swift's Song 'Ronan' Tells Story of 4-Year-Old Boy Who Died From Cancer and More,"

182   Endnotes

CURE, November 19, 2021; Cassie Carpenter, "Taylor Swift breaks down as she debuts song Ronan about young cancer victim at charity event," *Daily Mail,* April 10, 2015; @rockstarronan, "REMOVE THIS PHOTO. THIS IS AFTER SHE PERFORMED A SONG ABOUT MY DEAD CHILD" X (formerly known as Twitter), September 15, 2024; @rockstarronan, "For those of you saying, "How would anyone know where that photo was from?" One quick Google image search would tell you where this photo is from" X (formerly known as Twitter), September 15, 2024; @rockstarronan, "It's been deleted. Thank all of you so much. I love you. 🖤," X (formerly known as Twitter), September 15, 2024.

55. "and now she makes millions so happy 🎶," posted May 30, 2024, by @louisettexyz, YouTube, 49 sec.

56. Taylor Swift, "For Taylor Swift, the Future of Music Is a Love Story," *The Wall Street Journal,* July 7, 2014.

57. Matt Stopera, "Taylor Swift's Deleted Myspace Comments And Pictures May Actually Make You Like Her," *BuzzFeed,* April 26, 2019; Chibears85, "Taylor Swift's MySpace Bio in 2008," Reddit, n.d.; "Taylor Swift My Life," Internet Archive Wayback Machine, accessed December 2, 2024.

58. Madeline Boardman, "Taylor Swift Wears Hilarious "No It's Becky" Shirt Referencing Meme: Pic," *Us Weekly,* September 25, 2014.

59. Austin Scaggs, "Taylor Swift on Her Confessional New Album," *Rolling Stone,* November 10, 2010.

60. "@taylorswift is a Mastermind at hiding easter eggs in her music," posted May 26, 2023, by fallontonight, Instagram; "Hidden messages in song lyrics," Taylor Swift Wiki, Fandom, accessed December 2, 2024.

Chapter 6

1. Lauren Huff, "Taylor Swift explains the story behind 'murder mystery song' 'No Body, No Crime'," *Entertainment Weekly,* May 11, 2022.

2. Samantha Olson, "It's Time to Deep Dive Into Taylor Swift and Haim's Decade-Long Friendship," *Cosmopolitan,* September 16, 2024.

3. Chris Murphy, "Taylor Swift and Haim Join Forces Once Again on 'Gasoline' Remix," *Vulture,* February 18, 2021; Sophie Thompson,

Endnotes

"Haim write song about how hungover they're about to be while on their way to Oscars," *Indy100*, March 28, 2022; Glenn Garner, "Laura Dern Recognized by a Taylor Swift Fan During a 'Jurassic Park' Tour After 'Bejeweled' Video," *People*, January 8, 2023; @olivegarden, "If @taylorswift13 & @HAIMtheband don't sing No Body, No Crime this weekend, we'll be wiping our tears away with our Never-Ending Breadsticks. 😢," X (formerly known as Twitter), July 21, 2023.

4. Barbara Smith, "Taylor Swift's massive fanbase sets Disney Plus up for an easy win with its new 'folklore' concert album," *Business Insider*, November 25, 2020; I was among the fans who subscribed to Disney+ upon the release of *folklore: the long pond studio sessions*, and I confirm the reverse effect of current Disney+ subscribers being drawn to Taylor Swift with *folklore: the long pond studio sessions* from anecdotal experience.

5. Daniel Frankel, "Disney Plus Mobile Downloads Spike 72% Amid 'Hamilton' Premiere," *Next TV*, July 6, 2020.

6. Dessi Gomez, "Taylor Swift Takes Over Disney+ Home Page With Eras Layout," *The Wrap*, March 14, 2024.

7. Todd Spangler, "'Taylor Swift: The Eras Tour' Breaks Disney+ Record as No. 1 Most-Streamed Music Film," *Variety*, March 19, 2024.

8. Erin Johnson, "Taylor Swift: The Eras Tour's Disney+ Record Makes This Release From 4 Years Ago More Impressive," *Screen Rant*, March 26, 2024; Brandon Katz, "Disney's $75M 'Hamilton' Acquisition Is About a Lot More Than One Movie," *Observer*, February 11, 2020.

9. Alyssa Bailey, "Inside Taylor Swift's Tortured Poets Spotify Pop-Up Library," *ELLE*, April 16, 2024; Alyssa Norwin, "Taylor Swift's 'TTPD' Library Pop-Up in L.A. Has Easter Eggs About Ex Joe Alwyn and More," *Life & Style*, April 17, 2024; "It's a 2am surprise," posted April 18, 2024, by taylorswift, Instagram.

10. Tiago Bianchi, "Global market share of leading desktop search engines 2015-20245," *Statista*, January 23, 2025.

11. Meghan Roos, "It Didn't Take Taylor Swift Fans Long to Unlock Vault Track Titles," *Newsweek*, September 20, 2023.

12. Bernadette Giacomazzo, "Target Revealed the First-Week Taylor Swift Book Numbers, and They're Quite Impressive," *RetailWire*, December 9, 2024; Natalie Allison, "Taylor Swift shows up to a Nashville Target to buy her album and fans freak out," *USA Today*, November 16, 2017;

"The Official 'Taylor Swift | The Eras Tour Book' — Available Exclusively at Target — Sells Nearly 1 Million Copies in First Week," Target Corporation Press Release, December 6, 2024.

13. "Taylor Lautner Teaches Jimmy to Tornado Kick and Talks Starring in Taylor Swift's Music Video," posted October 31, 2023, by The Tonight Show Starring Jimmy Fallon, YouTube, 10 min 1 sec.

14. "TAYLOR SWIFT - MAKING OF "TEARDROPS ON MY GUITAR" VIDEO," posted on May 17, 2007, by AveryIslandTV, YouTube, 4 min 5 sec.

15. "Taylor Swift & Martin McDonagh | Directors on Directors," posted on December 12, 2022, by Variety, YouTube, 46 min 9 sec.; Gil Kaufman, "Sadie Sink Relied On 'Years of Research As a Swiftie' To Tap Into Character's Pain in Taylor Swift's 'All Too Well' Short Film," *billboard*, August 8, 2024.

16. Kelsie Gibson, "Taylor Swift and Jack Antonoff's Friendship Timeline," *People*, April 19, 2024; Ethan Millman, "Jack Antonoff Credits Taylor Swift for Launching Production Career," *Rolling Stone*, December 5, 2024; Jon Pareles, "How Aaron Dessner Found His Voice (With an Assist From Taylor Swift)," *The New York Times*, August 19, 2021.

17. "Taylor Swift Journey To Fearless Texas The Full DVD," posted April 5, 2018, by Taylor Music, YouTube, 2:10:51; Rachel DeSantis, "Taylor Swift's Cowriter Aaron Dessner Recalls Her 'Cooking Everyone Breakfast and Dinner' at Her Home (Exclusive)," *People*, December 5, 2023; Alyssa Lapid, "TikTok Is Just Realizing Taylor Swift's "Untouchable" Is A Cover Of A Rock Song," *Bustle*, January 12, 2023; Nathan Barlowe, "Nathan Barlowe of Luna Halo talks about Taylor Swift and 'Untouchable'," *The Tennessean*, November 24, 2009; "Kelly Clarkson Defends Encouraging Taylor Swift to Rerecord Her Masters," posted September 9, 2019, by The Tonight Show Starring Jimmy Fallon, YouTube, 4 min 42 sec.; Rania Aniftos, "Kelly Clarkson Says Taylor Swift Sends Her Flowers After Every Re-Recording Release," *billboard*, November 9, 2023; Vinita J, "How Did Taylor Swift And Charlie Puth Become Friends? Complete Timeline Of Their Collabs," *Pinkvilla*, May 7, 2024; Whitney Danhauer, "Charlie Puth Seemingly Hints That Taylor Swift Gave Him a 'Sign' to Release His Upcoming Song," *Y! Entertainment*, May 4, 2024; Ilana Kaplan, "Charlie Puth Thanks Taylor Swift for

Endnotes 185

Encouraging Him to Release 'Hero': 'Never Put Out a Song Like This Before'," *People*, May 21, 2024; Ashley Iasimone, "Taylor Swift Sends 'Babe' Co-Writer Pat Monahan Flowers, Making Him a 'Cool' Dad," *billboard*, April 28, 2018.

18. "Dr. Seuss Storytime," 510 Families, accessed December 23, 2024.

19. "e.l.f. Cosmetics Announces 'Get Ready With Music, The Album,' a Soundtrack of Self-Expression," e.l.f. Beauty, Inc. Investors Press Releases, September 4, 2024; Peter Adams, "E.l.f. Cosmetics bows entertainment brand with original album release," *Marketing Dive*, September 4, 2024; Edwin Roman, "E.l.f. Beauty is 'rapidly moving up the market share ranks'," *Yahoo! Finance*, January 13, 2024.

20. "GoPro and Red Bull Form Exclusive Global Partnership," GoPro News, May 24, 2016.

21. Kayla Harrington, "Taylor Swift explains why she flanked studios with Eras Tour movie," *Dexerto*, December 6, 2023; Shannon Power, "How Taylor Swift's Dad Created the Game-Changing Eras Concert Film," *Newsweek*, September 1, 2023.

22. Sophie Vershbow, "Taylor Swift Is Coming for Book Publishing," *Esquire*, November 18, 2024.

23. "Taylor Swift - Once Upon a Prom," posted November 15, 2012, by XK Cheung, YouTube, 41 min 36 sec.; Ashley Iasimone, "Taylor Swift Dedicates 'Fifteen' to 'Beautiful, Redheaded High School Best Friend' Abigail in Nashville: See Her Reaction," *billboard*, May 7, 2023; Sam Lansky, "Taylor Swift 2023 TIME Person of the Year," *TIME*, December 6, 2023; John Moore, "Taylor Swift fans are losing their minds over Coloradan Mandy Moore's choreography," *The Denver Gazette*, July 12, 2023.

24. "Taylor Swift Interviewed By Ryan Adams !!," posted January 31, 2018, by sozy j, YouTube, 3 min 49 sec.

25. Neil Shah, "Taylor Swift's Eras Tour Changed Everything," *The Wall Street Journal*, December 4, 2024.

26. Rob LeDonne, "The Rise and Rise of Gracie Abrams," *Vogue*, June 21, 2024; "That's so true 💚 || #edit #shorts #fyp #taylorswift #erastour #gracieabrams," posted November 7, 2024, by LavenderTays.13[TS], YouTube, 19 sec.; Gil Kaufman, "Gracie Abrams Says Final Eras Tour Show Like Last Day of School: 'Everyone Was Walking Around With Their [Eras] Books'," *billboard*, December 17, 2024; While Swift and

186   Endnotes

Abrams agree on the goal of output velocity, Swift might not share Abrams's point of view of less pressure: "An interesting dynamic happens between you and your previous work…Everything you do is a standing ovation on your first record if you're having that breakthrough record. And then you put out your second body of work, and then you realize that everything you're putting out now is being compared to what they liked about your first record. But then you put out the third one, and then it's compared to the first two, then you put out the fourth one, then it's compared to the first three, and it goes on and on and on." *See* "Taylor Swift: 'Lover', Politics, & Friendship with Selena Gomez," posted October 30, 2019, by Apple Music, YouTube, 8 min. 57 sec.

27. Gary Trust, "'Sweet' Success: Hozier Hits No. 1 on Billboard Hot 100 for First Time," *billboard*, April 22, 2024; George Griffiths, "Sabrina Carpenter gets major caffeine hit! Espresso is her first UK Number 1 single," *Official Charts*, May 2, 2024; Thania Garcia, "Summer of Sabrina Carpenter: Hitting No. 1 on the Charts, Getting Advice From Best Friend Taylor Swift and What Barry Keoghan Really Thinks About Her Lyrics," *Variety*, August 6, 2024.

Chapter 7

1. Murray Stassen, "Taylor Swift's music is streamed more in the US than the entire Jazz and Classical genres," *Music Business Worldwide*, January 15, 2024.

2. Eric Todisco, "Move over, Rihanna: Taylor Swift is now the richest female musician with $1.6 billion net worth — but by how much?," *New York Post*, October 7, 2024; Jessica Sager, "He's Got 99 Problems, but His Wealth Ain't One! Jay-Z's Massive Net Worth in 2025," *Parade*, January 1, 2025; Mehera Bonner, "Just Calculated Taylor Swift's Net Worth and Now I'm Crying," *Cosmopolitan*, October 9, 2024; Anna Kaplan, "When did Taylor Swift become a billionaire?," *Today*, April 3, 2024; Megan Cerullo, "Taylor Swift becomes a billionaire with new re-recording of '1989' album," *CBS News*, October 27, 2023; Net worth is calculated as the value of assets minus the value of liabilities, and is not simply the amount of liquid cash one has on hand. *See* Akhilesh Ganti, "Net Worth: What It Is and How to Calculate It," *Investopedia*, June 20, 2024.

Endnotes   187

3. Zack O'Malley Greenburg, "Artist, Icon, Billionaire: How Jay-Z Created His $1 Billion Fortune," *Forbes*, June 3, 2019.

4. Jasmine Browley, "How Rihanna Went From Nearly Bankrupt To Billionaire," *ESSENCE*, October 31, 2022; Amanda Lundgren, "What Is Rihanna's Net Worth? Asking Cuz I Like Pain," *Cosmopolitan*, May 3, 2024; Jonathan Feniak, Esq MBA, "Everything Owned by LVMH," LLC Attorney, accessed January 2, 2025; "Rihanna's family office and how she manages her wealth," Simple, Updated on January 16, 2024; Roshida Khanom, "Fenty Beauty: Targeting women of all colours," *Mintel*, October 2, 2017.

5. Olivier Gillotin, "Wonderstruck Taylor Swift for women," Fragrantica, accessed January 2, 2025; "Incredible Things Taylor Swift for women," Fragrantica, accessed January 2, 2025.

6. Nicole Mastrogiannis, "Taylor Swift Shares Intimate Details of 'Lover' Songs During Secret Session," *iHeart*, August 23, 2019.

7. Julie Dietz, "Customers Buy Experiences, Not Products," *Higher Logic*, February 28, 2024.

8. Sam Lansky, "Taylor Swift 2023 TIME Person of the Year," *Time*, December 6, 2023; Stefanie Dazio, "Plan to attack Taylor Swift's Vienna shows intended to kill thousands, CIA official claims," *PBS News*, August 29, 2024; Taylor Swift. *The Official Taylor Swift | The Eras Tour Book*. United States: Taylor Swift Publications, 2024.

9. "Red Tour," Taylor Swift Wiki, Fandom, accessed January 2, 2025; "The 1989 World Tour," Taylor Swift Wiki, Fandom, accessed January 2, 2025; "Reputation Stadium Tour," Taylor Swift Wiki, Fandom, accessed January 2, 2025; My Reputation Stadium Tour surprise song was "The Best Day."

10. "Speak Now World Tour Arm Lyrics," Taylor Swift Switzerland, accessed January 2, 2025; "The Speak Now Tour: Arm Lyrics," The Swift Agency, accessed January 2, 2025; Rebecca Aizin, "Selena Gomez Is Worth Over $1 Billion! Here's How the Singer Built Her Wealth," *People*, October 1, 2024, https://people.com/selena-gomez-net-worth-movies-business-8710343.

11. "[FULL • 4K] Taylor Swift • The 1989 World Tour Live (Remastered) • EAS Channel," posted May 28, 2022, by EAS Music Channel, YouTube, 2:11:45; Elias Leight, "Taylor Swift Talks Female Role Models, Aging

188   Endnotes

Gracefully & Her (Eventual) Grandkids in 'Time'," *billboard*, November 13, 2014; Jessica Derschowitz, "Taylor Swift 1989 tour: Kobe Bryant surprises singer with Staples Center banner," *Entertainment Weekly*, August 22, 2015; Chuck Schilken, "A perfect night? Kobe Bryant's daughter gets Taylor Swift's '22' hat during L.A. concert," *Los Angeles Times*, August 4, 2023.

12. Katie Louise Smith, "All of Taylor Swift's cardigans released so far including new Lover version," Capital UK, January 23, 2025, https://www.capitalfm.com/news/music/taylor-swift-cardigans-merch/; Hannah Dailey, "Taylor Swift Declares 'No One's Prouder to Be a Millennial' on Her 34th Birthday," *billboard*, December 132, 2023; "Today's Experience Economy: Audiences pay to be wowed and inspired," *Cosm*, January 1, 2021; Dan Goldman, Sophie Marchessou, and Warren Teschner (McKinsey & Company), "Cashing in on the US experience economy," Private Equity and Principal Investors Practice, December 2017; Meaghan Yuen, "3 ways Gen Z is leading social media usage," *eMarketer*, September 19, 2024.

13. "Utility Theory - an overview," ScienceDirect, accessed January 2, 2025; "Von Neumann-Morganstern Expected Utility Theory," EconPort, accessed January 2, 2025; Neil Thakral, Brown University and Linh T. Tô, Boston University, "Anticipation and Consumption," December 2020; Daniel Kahneman, Princeton University, "Experienced Utility and Objective Happiness: A Moment-Based Approach," in *Choices, Values and Frames*, ed. D. Kahneman and A. Tversky, pp. 673–692, New York: Cambridge University Press and the Russell Sage Foundation, 2000.

14. Amit Kumar, Matthew A. Killingsworth, and Thomas Gilovich, "Spending on doing promotes more moment-to-moment happiness than spending on having," *Journal of Experimental Social Psychology*, 88, 103971, 2020; "Spending on Experiences Versus Possessions Advances More Immediate Happiness," *UT News*, March 9, 2020.

15. Taffy Brodesser-Akner, "My Delirious Trip to the Heart of Swiftiedom," *The New York Times Magazine*, October 12, 2023.

16. Jonny Thomson, "How to measure happiness: hedonia vs. eudaimonia," *Big Think*, February 27, 2022

17. "Generating $5 billion, the Taylor Swift The Eras Tour has an Economic Impact Greater than 50 Countries," *GlobeNewswire*, June 8, 2023, https://

Endnotes

189

www.globenewswire.com/en/news-release/2023/06/08/2684710/0/en/Generating-5-billion-the-Taylor-Swift-The-Eras-Tour-has-an-Economic-Impact-Greater-than-50-Countries.html ("The average concert goer spent about $720 more than their budget for a total average of $1,327.74, including expenses such as tickets, outfits/costumes, merchandise, food & drink, and travel...Despite paying more than budgeted, the Eras Tour achieved a Net Promoter Score of 68, putting it on par with the top 3 admired brands such as Costco, USAA, and Southwest Airlines [it would be tied with Apple and the Ritz Carlton for fourth]...More than 70 percent said going to this event was worth it and a whopping 91 percent said they are likely to attend another concert—and would pay up to $1,311.35 to go again."); Sam Lansky, "Taylor Swift 2023 TIME Person of the Year," *Time*, December 6, 2023.

18. Neil Shah, "50,000 Screaming Fans Is Nothing in the Mega Concert Era," *The Wall Street Journal*, October 22, 2024.

19. Taylor Swift. The Official Taylor Swift | The Eras Tour Book. United States: Taylor Swift Publications, 2024; "Taylor Swift - Begin again Paris version," posted May 17, 2024, by Tengfei Ma, YouTube, 5 min 13 sec.; Bryan West, "Every way dancer Kameron Saunders has said 'like ever' on Taylor Swift's Eras Tour," *USA Today*, December 10, 2024.

20. Kathryn Milewski, "Taylor Swift Announces 'Speak Now (Taylor's Version)' & Performs With Phoebe Bridgers During Nashville Concert," *Live365*, May 8, 2023; Daniela Avila and Rachel DeSantis, "Florence Welch Joins Taylor Swift Onstage in London to Sing 'Florida!!!' in Song's Eras Tour Debut," *People*, August 20, 2024; "Full Video of Taylor Swift recreating the getaway car bridge with Jack Antonoff at the eras tour," posted August 21, 2024, by Swiftly Explained, YouTube, 48 sec.

21. Ximena Garcia-Rada, Michael I. Norton, and Rebecca K. Ratner, "Research: Consumers Choose Shared Experiences Over Quality Ones," *Harvard Business Review*, September 21, 2023.

22. Tom Huddleston Jr., "Bill Gates: This childhood habit helped me end up a billionaire—it was 'crucial to my success later on'," *CNBC*, December 4, 2024.

23. Taylor Swift: Reputation Stadium Tour, directed by Paul Dugdale (Arlington, TX: Den of Thieves, SR Films, Taylor Swift Productions, 2018), Streaming; Rob Sheffield, "Why 'All Too Well' Is Taylor Swift's

190 Endnotes

Greatest Song," *Rolling Stone*, October 22, 2024; Nina Braca, "Taylor Swift's 'All Too Well': How the 'Red' Fan Favorite Became One of Her Biggest & Most Important Songs," *billboard*, November 10, 2021; Taylor Swift | The Eras Tour (Taylor's Version), directed by Sam Wrench (Los Angeles, CA: Taylor Swift Touring, 2024), Streaming; Steven Hyden, "Ask A Music Critic: When (If Ever) Will Taylor Swift's Popularity Fade?," *UPROXX*, July 26, 2023.

24. "Taylor Swift, imperfect capitalist?," *The Economist*, December 6, 2024 ("[F]ans are even more eager to see the show than they were in 2023; secondary-market tickets for the last stop in America (Indianapolis) cost $1,273 more than for her first stop (Glendale). By comparison, the median resale ticket for Beyonce's first American show in 2023 cost $182; by the final show, it had fallen to $109. And the median resale ticket price for the closing night of Sir Elton John's recent farewell tour—one of the longest-running and the third highest-grossing tour in the world—was $187, one seventh of the price of tickets for Ms Swift.").

25. "Williams Sonoma In-Store Events," Williams Sonoma, accessed January 2, 2025; Zach Williams, "How to Attract the DIY Consumer Like Williams-Sonoma," *The DIY Consumer*, accessed January 2, 2025; Laura Alber, "The CEO of Williams-Sonoma on Blending Instinct with Analysis," *Harvard Business Review*, September 2014; "Williams-Sonoma, Inc. announces first quarter 2024 results," Investor Information, Williams-Sonoma, Inc May 22, 2024.

26. Chris Willman, "Taylor Swift Has Fans Losing It With the Revealing Lyrics of New Song 'You're Losing Me'," *Variety*, May 26, 2023; Megan Cerullo, "Taylor Swift's Eras Tour book hits Target stores today. Here's what to know," *CBS News*, November 29, 2024; Ishita Verma, "Taylor Swift Acoustic Piano Collection is Selling Out Fast," *Y! Entertainment*, November 21, 2024; Charles Passy, "Here's how many billions of dollars Taylor Swift fans spent on her 'Eras Tour'," *MarketWatch*, December 9, 2024.

27. Adam Hayes, "What Is the Law of Demand in Economics, and How Does It Work?," *Investopedia*, June 24, 2024; Leslie Kramer, "How Does the Law of Supply and Demand Affect Prices?," *Investopedia*, November 15, 2024.

Endnotes 191

28. Meg Dowdy, "Remember When Taylor Swift Played a $20 Concert for a Tiny Alabama High School?," *MSN*, accessed January 2, 2025.

29. Ashley King, "Taylor Swift Has Released 34 Different Versions of 'The Tortured Poets Department' Across Vinyl, CDs, Cassettes," Digital Music News, June 23, 2024; "The Tortured Poets Department Vinyl + Bonus Track 'The Manuscript'," Taylor Swift Official Online Store, accessed January 2, 2025; "Taylor Swift - The Tortured Poets Department: The Anthology (Target Exclusive)," Target, accessed January 2, 2025; Lindsay Lowe and Anna Kaplan, "Taylor Swift 'The Eras Tour' concert film: Everything you need to know," *Today*, October 12, 2023; "The Official Taylor Swift | The Eras Tour Book (Target Exclusive)," Target, accessed January 2, 2025; "Taylor Swift | The Eras Tour Self-Titled Album T-Shirt," Taylor Swift Official Online Store, accessed January 2, 2025.

30. Larisha Paul, "This Swiftie Went to 20 Eras Tours. It Only Cost Her $5,000," *Rolling Stone*, September 1, 2023.

31. Ben Sisario, "Taylor Swift's Eras Tour Grand Total: A Record $2 Billion," *The New York Times*, December 9, 2024; "Taylor Swift's 'Eras Tour' Smashes All-Time Touring Record, Surpasses $2 Billion," *Pollstar*, December 9, 2024; Pollstar Staff, "Pollstar 2024 Year End Analysis: Industry Remains Strong & Steady, Taylor Swift & Coldplay Set All-Time Touring Records," *Pollstar*, December 13, 2024; Emma Fox, "$11,000 to see Taylor Swift? How concert tickets got so expensive," *Los Angeles Times*, August 21, 2023; "Taylor Swift, imperfect capitalist?," *The Economist*, December 6, 2024.

32. James Mackintosh, "How Taylor Swift Fans Broke Economics," *The Wall Street Journal*, August 21, 2024; Daniel Kahneman, Jack L. Knetsch, and Richard H. Thaler, "Anomalies: The Endowment Effect, Loss Aversion, and Status Quo Bias," *The Journal of Economic Perspectives*, 5(1), pp. 193–206, 1991; Daniel Kahneman and Amos Tversky, "Prospect Theory: An Analysis of Decision under Risk," *Econometrica*, 47(2), pp. 263–292, 1979; Andrew Caplin, "The Effect of Default Options on Retirement Savings," *The Bulletin on Aging and Health*, October 18, 2011.

33. Joseph Pisani, "$1,500 Bedazzled Jacket, $350 Dress: Fans Shell Out to Look Like Taylor Swift," *The Wall Street Journal*, March 31, 2023; Adel Toay and Mia Hunt, "'I'm the problem, it's me': Taylor Swift fans, TikTok cause Seattle bead store to sell out of merchandise," *KING 5*,

192   Endnotes

July 14, 2023; Bryan West, "Taylor Swift fans book last-minute travel to Miami for Eras Tour," *USA Today*, October 14, 2024; Hannah Dailey, "Taylor Swift Reflects on Drawing Hilltop Crowd of '50,000 People' Outside Her Munich Eras Tour Show," *billboard*, July 31, 2024; Anna Kaplan, "'Taylor-gating': Why some Taylor Swift fans gather in parking lots to watch her concerts," *Today*, May 19, 2023.

34. Tourism Consulting Team, Tourism Economics, "The Concerts and Live Entertainment Industry: A Significant Economic Engine," *Oxford Economics*, July 26, 2021; Rob Wile, "Federal Reserve credits Taylor Swift with boosting hotel revenues through her blockbuster Eras Tour," *NBC News*, July 13, 2023; Auzinea Bacon, "The end of an era: How Taylor Swift boosted the US economy," *CNN*, December 8, 2024; Ben Sisario, "Taylor Swift's Eras Tour Grand Total: A Record $2 Billion," *The New York Times*, December 9, 2024.

35. Theo Burman, "Taylor Swift Eras Tour: Map Shows Which Countries Got Biggest Economic Boost," *Newsweek*, December 10, 2024.

36. Since our in-house calculation, based on the multiplier effect from out-of-town concertgoers, is in line with *Newsweek*'s reported statistic, it appears that the majority of Eras Tour attendees did indeed travel to see the concert. Our in-house calculation, which focuses on expenses related to tourism, approaches *GlobeNewswire*'s reported average spending from earlier in the chapter, which included expenses specific to the Eras Tour, such as outfits.

37. Caitlin Parr, "Taylor Swift foodbank donation feeds more than 900," *BBC News*, September 30, 2024.

38. Parija Bhatnagar, "Taylor Swift gives 'life-changing' $100,000 bonuses to Eras Tour truck drivers," *CNN*, August 3, 2023; Taylor Fishman, "Taylor Swift gives $197 million in bonuses to Eras Tour crew after record-breaking success," *CBS Austin*, December 10, 2024.

39. Ranjay Gulati, Sarah Huffman, and Gary L. Neilson, "The Barista Principle — Starbucks and the Rise of Relational Capital" *strategy + business a pwc publication*, July 17, 2002.

40. "Mastermind," Swift Alert, accessed January 2, 2025; "All-Access," Swift Alert, accessed January 2, 2025. The user statistics were revealed as part of a Spotify-Wrapped-esque recap of the game entitled "The Manuscript." "The Manuscript" also gave individual statistics to each player

Endnotes 193

of their performance over the course of the game. Apparently, my most frequently guessed guitar surprise song was "Mary's Song (Oh My My My)," which never materialized as she played it on piano in Amsterdam Night 3.

41. Daniel Griffiths, "'A standout year for female artists': But Taylor Swift didn't bag Spotify Wrapped's most streamed song of 2024," *MusicRadar*, December 4, 2024.

42. Anna Chan, "Taylor Swift Drops 'You're Losing Me' on Streaming to Celebrate Being Spotify's Most Streamed Artist," *billboard*, November 29, 2023.

Chapter 8

1. Todd Spangler, "Peloton Stock Drops After 'And Just Like That' Character's Shocking Post-Workout Death," *Variety*, December 10, 2021; Ramishah Maruf, "Peloton has a response for the 'Sex and the City' reboot shocker involving Mr. Big," *abc7 EYEWITNESS NEWS*, December 13, 2021; Isabella Grullón Paz, "The Big Question: Could Peloton Sue Over Its 'And Just Like That' Appearance?," *The New York Times*, December 12, 2021.

2. "#CrockPotIsInnocent,", The Shorty Awards, accessed January 7, 2025; Max Ehrenfreund, "The unfulfilled promise of the Crock-Pot, an unlikely symbol of women's equality," *The Washington Post*, January 23, 2015.

3. Nikki DeMentri, "By the numbers: Taylor Swift's impact on NFL, from viewership to jersey sales," *CBS News*, February 12, 2024; Randall Williams, Julie Fine, and Jason Kelly, "Taylor Swift Spurred 30% Boost in Chiefs' Fan Base, CEO Says," *BNN Bloomberg*, August 14, 2024; Bruce Gil, "How much money Taylor Swift is worth to the Kansas City Chiefs before the Super Bowl," *Quartz*, January 30, 2024; "Heinz Ketchup & Seemingly Ranch," *Contagious*, October 4, 2023; Cassey, "My wildest dream just came true and I'm DYING," *Blogilates*, April 20, 2024; Alexandra Holterman, "The History of Taylor Swift & the Snake," *billboard*, August 21, 2017; Danielle Gay, "Instagram will now let everyone use the comment filters celebrities have had access to," *Vogue*, September 13, 2016.

194 Endnotes

4. Taylor Swift: Miss Americana, directed by Lana Wilson (Nashville, TN and New York, NY: Tremolo Productions, 2020), Streaming; taylorswift, "I'm writing this post about the upcoming midterm elections on November 6th, in which I'll be voting in the state of Tennessee" Instagram, October 7, 2018; Kelly Garrity, "What it's like to be endorsed by Taylor Swift," *Politico*, February 1, 2024; Gil Kaufman, "Was There a Taylor Swift Bump in the Midterm Elections? Vote.org Says Yes," *billboard*, November 8, 2018.

5. @taylorswift13, "I spoke to @vmagazine about why I'll be voting for Joe Biden for president" X (formerly known as Twitter), October 7, 2020; Stefan Becket and Gillian Morley, "Taylor Swift drove 405,999 visitors to vote.gov in 24 hours after Kamala Harris endorsement," *CBS News*, September 12, 2024.

6. "Will Taylor Swift's endorsement of Kamala Harris matter?," *The Economist*, September 12, 2024; "2024 Presidential Race: Can't Get Much Closer, Quinnipiac University National Poll Finds; 64% Want To See The Two Candidates Debate Again," Quinnipiac University, September 24, 2024, https://poll.qu.edu/poll-release?releaseid=3908.

7. Jedidajah Otte, "'She could absolutely change my mind': readers on Taylor Swift's political influence," *The Guardian*, February 6, 2024; "Swifties 4 Kamala," Swifties4Change, Swifties for Kamala, accessed January 7, 2025; Ella Robinson, "Meet the Taylor Swift fans who have raised $235,000 for the Harris campaign," *The Wash*, November 4, 2024; Todd Spangler, "Taylor Swift Has Gained More Than 1.8 Million Spotify Followers Since She Endorsed Kamala Harris for President," *Variety*, October 3, 2024; Rhona Tarrant, "Trump shares fake 'Swifties for Trump' images," *CBS News*, August 26, 2024.

8. Mallika Mitra, "Taylor Swift's new song 'You need to calm down' drives donations to LGBTQ advocacy group, but not without critics," *CNBC*, June 25, 2019; Mia Osmonbekov, "President Joe Biden failed to enact the Equality Act," Politifact, November 27, 2024; Few-Clothes7435, "The You Need to Calm Down Appreciation Post," Reddit, n.d.

9. Madison Feller, "When Laith Ashley Got Cast in Taylor Swift's 'Lavender Haze' Music Video, He Thought It Was a Prank," *ELLE*, January 27, 2023.

Endnotes

10. Abby Aguirre, "Taylor Swift on Sexism, Scrutiny, and Standing Up for Herself," *Vogue*, August 8, 2019.

11. Alison B. Hammond, et al. "From Taylor Swift to MLK: Understanding Adolescents' Famous Character Role Models." *Journal of Moral Education* 53 (1), pp. 157–175, 2022.

12. Brian A Primack et al. "Exposure to Cannabis in Popular Music and Cannabis Use among Adolescents." *Addiction* (Abingdon, England) 105(3), pp. 515–523, 2011.

13. Jeff Opperman, "Taylor Swift Is Singing Us Back to Nature," *The New York Times*, March 12, 2021 ("Songs like this—in which nature is a place to bond, seek solace or just hang out—may be even more needed than songs that preach about saving it."); Jeff Opperman, "Quantifying the Nature of Taylor Swift," *Medium*, March 12, 2021.

14. "Taylor Swift: 'Lover', Politics, & Friendship with Selena Gomez," posted October 30, 2019, by Apple Music, YouTube, 8 min 57 sec.

15. Marni Rose McFall, "'I Hate It Here': Taylor Swift Spotify Streams Surge Following Trump Win," *Newsweek*, November 14, 2024.

16. Sophie Caldwell, "Taylor Swift donates to food banks on 'Eras Tour' route: 'When Taylor donates, people follow'," *Today*, August 16, 2023.

17. Hannah Dailey and Rania Aniftos, "A Timeline of Taylor Swift's Generosity," *billboard*, January 17, 2025; Travis Beckman, "HMC Wins Taylor Swift Concert," *Harvey Mudd College News*, October 4, 2012.

18. Patrick Guerriero and Susan Wolf Ditkoff. "When Philanthropy Meets Advocacy." *Stanford Social Innovation Review* 16(3), pp. 49–54, 2018.

19. Amanda Breen, "Shark Tank's Most Successful Brand of All Time Wasn't Even Supposed to Be a Business at First. Here's How It Became One With $1 Billion in Lifetime Revenue" *Entrepreneur*, October 30, 2023; "Giving Back," Bombas, accessed January 7, 2025; Jane Thier, "How the Bombas founders navigated tumultuous early careers to create the best-selling Shark Tank product in history," *Fortune*, December 22, 2024.

20. "Adidas and Billie Jean King Collaborate to Drive Change for Girls in Sport," Adidas News, August 26, 2018; "Adidas Unveils Special Edition Billie Jean King Speedfactory Footwear," Adidas News, August 24, 2018; "Billie Jean King," National Women's History Museum, Published June 2021; "Battle of the Sexes Tennis Match," Billie Jean

196 Endnotes

King, accessed January 7, 2025; "adidas Breaking Barriers," Common Goal, accessed January 7, 2025; "Diversity, Equity, and Inclusion," adidas Annual Report 2022, accessed January 7, 2025; "History," adidas Group, accessed January 7, 2025.

21. Peter Helman, "Read Taylor Swift's Open Letter To Apple Music," *Stereogum*, June 21, 2015; Jacqueline Andriakos, "Apple Responds to Taylor Swift's Open Letter, Says It Will Pay Artists During Apple Music Free Trial Period: 'We Hear You'," *People*, June 22, 2015; Katie Shonk, "Streaming Toward Win-Win Negotiation: Spotify Upgrades Its Negotiating Strategy," *Daily Blog, Program on Negotiation at Harvard Law School*, December 16, 2024; Constance Grady, "Taylor Swift puts all her music back on streaming, continues to be a PR genius," *Vox*, June 9, 2017; Luke Morgan Britton, "Spotify boss explains how he convinced Taylor Swift to return to the streaming service," *NME*, April 3, 2018.

22. Elias Leight, "Taylor Swift Talks Female Role Models, Aging Gracefully & Her (Eventual) Grandkids in 'Time'," *billboard*, November 13, 2014; Neil Shah, "Taylor Swift's Eras Tour Changed Everything," *The Wall Street Journal*, December 4, 2024.

23. Pioneer Press, "Taylor Swift tells kids: Read for a better life," *Twin Cities Pioneer Press*, November 12, 2015; Taylor Swift, "For Taylor Swift, the Future of Music Is a Love Story," *The Wall Street Journal*, July 7, 2014.

Chapter 9

1. Nancy Luna, "McDonald's testing 'evolved paper straw' after U.K. backlash," *Nation's Restaurant News*, November 15, 2019; Olivia Arnold, "4 Companies Leveraging Customer Feedback To Enhance Their Product Experience," *Built In NYC*, April 6, 2023; "How Did Samsung Overcome the Galaxy Note 7 Crisis?," Pepper Content, April 5, 2023.

2. Exciting_Feedback_47, "Taylor's dancing has improved a whole lot for Eras," Reddit, n.d.; Sam Lansky, "Taylor Swift 2023 TIME Person of the Year," *Time*, December 6, 2023; therustler9, "Taylor's dancing has improved a whole lot for Eras," Reddit, n.d.; John Moore, "Taylor Swift fans are losing their minds over Coloradan Mandy Moore's choreography," *The Denver Gazette*, July 12, 2023; Brian Seibert, "How to

Endnotes

Command a Stage Without Great Dance Moves (Taylor's Version)," *The New York Times*, August 9, 2023.

3. Madison Mainwaring, "Britney Separs Has Always Fought Back. By Dancing," *The New York Times*, January 10, 2022; While top reasons for stanning Swift vary, dancing is typically not among them. *See, e.g.,* Bryan Parys, "Why Taylor Swift Is So Popular (Berklee's Version)," *Berklee News*, accessed January 16, 2025; "Top 10 Reasons to Love Taylor Swift," The Top Tens, accessed January 16, 2025.

4. "Taylor performs "Blank Space" at The GRAMMY Museum," posted January 7, 2016, by Taylor Swift, YouTube, 5 min 56 sec.

5. @seb9394, "I wish Taylor Swift would write a song called 'Maybe I'm the problem'" X (formerly known as Twitter), January 14, 2013.

6. Sam Lansky, "Taylor Swift 2023 TIME Person of the Year," *Time*, December 6, 2023.

7. Maura Zurick, "Taylor Swift Responds to Witchcraft Taunts With Extraordinary Video," *Newsweek*, November 13, 2023; Swifties started using the quote as well. *See, e.g.,* JessiSwiftTok, "She's never beating the sorcery allegations and I love that journey for her. 💚," TikTok, October 21, 2024.

8. Neringa Utaraitė and Franka Dervishi, "KFC Proposal Shaming Gone Wrong! (Update on the KFC Couple)," *Bored Panda*, December 4, 2023; Aisha Salaudeen, "He was mocked for proposing in KFC, but the internet found them and gave them their dream wedding," *CNN*, January 2, 2020.

9. "Taylor Swift Accepts Woman of the Decade Award | Women In Music,", posted December 12, 2019, by Billboard, YouTube, 15 min 16 sec.

10. Rodger Dean Duncan, "Do You Want To Be Victim Or Victor? It's Your Choice," *Forbes*, January 20, 2021; justinbieber, "Taylor swift what up," Tumblr, June 30, 2019.

11. Nancy Jo Sales, "Taylor Swift's Telltale Heart," *Vanity Fair*, March 15, 2013; "Taylor Swift: 'Lover', Politics, & Friendship with Selena Gomez," posted October 30, 2019, by Apple Music, YouTube, 8 min 57 sec.; "Taylor Swift announces TTPD (The Bolter edition) at The Eras Tour - Melbourne N1," posted February 16, 2024, by midnight rain, YouTube, 1 min 57 sec.

Endnotes

12. billboard, "This is the song I wrote for my ninth grade talent show." 🖤," posted March 25, 2023, Instagram. In a "meta" moment, the director of *Someone Great*, Jennifer Kaytin Robinson, actually credited *1989* as the catalyst for the movie. *See* Mary J. DiMeglio, "Taylor Swift Calls Rom-Com Inspiration Behind 'Lover' Song the 'Most Meta Thing That's Ever Happened to Me'," *billboard*, August 23, 2019; "Taylor Swift: NPR Music Tiny Desk Concert," posted October 28, 2019, by NPR Music, YouTube, 28 min 58 sec.

13. "Taylor Swift - The making of Breathe Part 2" posted July 5, 2010, by 013Fearless, YouTube, 6 min 8 sec.; Chris Sutter, "Southern Indiana prosecuting attorney remembers her days on stage as Taylor Swift's fiddle player," *WDRB Louisville*, June 7, 2023.

14. *Taylor Swift folklore the long pond studio sessions*, directed by Taylor Swift (Long Pond Studios Hudson Valley, NY: Taylor Swift, Robert Allen, Bart Peters, 2020), Streaming.

15. "Good Riddance (Time of Your Life)," Green Day Wiki, Fandom, accessed January 16, 2025.

16. "Ad Hominem," Department of Philosophy, Texas State University, accessed January 16, 2025; Nancy Jo Sales, "Taylor Swift's Telltale Heart," *Vanity Fair*, March 15, 2013.

17. bob, "Grammys," *The Lefsetz Letter*, February 1, 2010.

18. bob, "That Taylor Swift Song. . .," *The Lefsetz Letter*, October 19, 2010.

19. Jonathan Keefe, "Review: Taylor Swift, Speak Now," *Slant*, October 25, 2010.

20. "Speak Now" Prologues: Comparing Original vs. Taylor's Version (Full Text)," Swiftly Sung Stories, accessed January 16, 2025; Keefe commended this improvement. *See* Jonathan Keefe, "Review: With *Speak Now (Taylor's Version)*, Taylor Swift Continues to Fine-Tune Her Voice," *Slant*, July 8, 2023, https://www.slantmagazine.com/music/taylor-swift-speak-now-taylors-version-album-review/.

21. Taffy Brodesser-Akner, "My Delirious Trip to the Heart of Swiftiedom," *The New York Times Magazine*, October 12, 2023.

22. Laura Barton, "Taylor Swift is a serious artist so it's time to give up on the cutesy gimmicks," *The Independent*, September 30, 2023.

23. Sarwat Jahan and Ahmed Saber Mahmud, "What Is Capitalism?," *Finance & Development*, Vol. 52, No. 2, June 2015; Kelli Chavez, "Public-Private

Endnotes

199

Partnerships from a Neoclassical and Keynesian Political Economy Perspective," Advocates' Forum, Crown Family School, University of Chicago, June 1, 2017; Matt Zwolinski, Benjamin Ferguson, and Alan Wertheimer, "Exploitation," *The Stanford Encyclopedia of Philosophy*, October 3, 2022.

24. Aaron Cantrell, "Nashville fan becomes a security guard to get into Taylor Swift's The Eras Tour," *NewsChannel 5 Nashville*, May 18, 2023.

25. Chris Sutter, "Southern Indiana prosecuting attorney remembers her days on stage as Taylor Swift's fiddle player," *WDRB Louisville*, June 7, 2023.

26. Scott Barry Kaufman, "Unraveling the Mindset of Victimhood," *Scientific American*, June 29, 2020.

27. "TAYLOR SWIFT Wins Album Of The Year For 'MIDNIGHTS' | 2024 GRAMMYs Acceptance Speech," posted February 4, 2024, by Recording Academy / GRAMMYs, YouTube, 3 min 20 sec.

28. "End Game - Behind The Scenes," posted February 9, 2018, by Taylor Swift, YouTube, 5 min 1 sec.

29. Minyvonne Burke and Elizabeth Maline, "Taylor Swift trademarks 'Female Rage: The Musical'," *NBC News*, May 14, 2024; "A Girl Named Girl," Taylor Swift Switzerland, accessed January 16, 2025.

30. Alice Fulwood, "How to get rich (Taylor's version)," *The Economist*, July 24, 2024 ("Taylor Inc remains a family business. Swift and her family are in charge of her tours, fan clubs, and rights management. In 2006, before Swift had even released her first album, her family established a company called Firefly Entertainment to oversee her affairs. Today this handles her personal services: hiring drivers, dealing with estate agents and managing her private jet."); Sam Lansky, "Taylor Swift 2023 TIME Person of the Year," *Time*, December 6, 2023.

31. "73 Questions With Taylor Swift | Vogue," posted April 19, 2016, by Vogue, YouTube, 9 min 41 sec.

32. "Billboard Confirms Taylor Swift's New Variants Aren't Blocking Other Artists From #1 Spot on Album Chart," *Just Jared*, August 19, 2024.

33. "Why do economists describe climate change as a market failure?," The Grantham Research Institute on Climate Change and the Environment, The London School of Economics and Political Science, March

21, 2014; Will Kenton, "Externality: What It Means in Economics, With Positive and Negative Examples," *Investopedia*, June 18, 2024.

34. Lola Mendez, "Taylor Swift claims she offsets her travel carbon footprint - how does that work?," *BBC*, February 13, 2024.

35. Ian Clark, "Bardach's Eightfold Path to More Effective Problem Solving," Atlas of Public Management, Last Modified September 12, 2017.

36. "Taylor Swift's Tour Drives Surge in Air Travel Demand," *ABC Mundial*, September 24, 2024.

37. Patricia Green, "What Celebrities Utilize Private Jets The Most For Travel?," *Simple Flying*, December 15, 2024.

38. Myles McNutt, "From "Mine" to "Ours": Gendered Hierarchies of Authorship and the Limits of Taylor Swift's Paratextual Feminism," *Communication, Culture and Critique*, Volume 13, Issue 1, pp. 72-91, March 2020; orlybb, "Imogen Heap blogs about writing with Taylor Swift," *LiveJournal: OH NO THEY DIDN'T!*, October 30, 2014.

39. @janetmock, "The first woman to win Album of the Year twice but no women producers standing behind you. #Grammys," X (formerly known as Twitter), February 15, 2016.

40. Allison Takeda, "Taylor Swift Tells the Story Behind "Clean," Says She Learned About Love From Lena Dunham," *Us Weekly*, May 7, 2015; "Taylor Swift awarded $1 in groping trial," *CBS News*, August 14, 2017; "Taylor Swift sexual assault case: Why is it significant?," *BBC*, August 15, 2017; Taylor Swift: *Miss Americana*, directed by Lana Wilson (Nashville, TN and New York, NY: Tremolo Productions, 2020), Streaming.

41. Constance Grady, "Is Taylor Swift a 'Silence Breaker'? The case for and against her place on Time's cover.", *Vox*, December 6, 2017.

42. "Taylor Swift Accepts Woman of the Decade Award | Women In Music,", posted December 12, 2019, by Billboard, YouTube, 15 min 16 sec.

Chapter 10

1. "Taylor Swift Accepts Woman of the Decade Award | Women In Music,", posted December 12, 2019, by Billboard, YouTube, 15 min 16 sec.

2. Abby Aguirre, "Taylor Swift on Sexism, Scrutiny, and Standing Up for Herself," *Vogue*, August 8, 2019; During this interview, a "7" balloon

happened to float by, with the writer remarking that it was "high in the sky," an unintentional foreshadowing of the lyrics to "seven" on future album *folklore*.

3. Wesley Morris, "'Taylor Swift: Miss Americana' Review: A Star, Surprisingly Alone," *The New York Times*, January 30, 2020.

4. Shaunacy Ferro, "9 People Who Have Been Called America's Sweetheart," *Mental Floss*, October 18, 2018.

5. "Tim McGraw by Taylor Swift," Songfacts, accessed January 27, 2025; "Taylor Swift - Tim McGraw (ACOUSTIC LIVE!),", posted October 19, 2009, by Billboard, YouTube, 4 min 31 sec.

6. Hannah Dailey, "Taylor Swift Explains the Story Behind Her New Song 'Carolina' – And Why It's Taken So Long to Come Out," *billboard*, June 24, 2022; John Orquiola, "Olivia Newman Interview: Where The Crawdads Sing," *Screen Rant*, May 17, 2022.

7. "Taylor Swift reveals meaning of Fortnight, Clara Bow and more THE TORTURED POETS DEPARTMENT tracks ♡," posted April 23, 2024, by Miss Americana and You Guys, YouTube, 6 min 17 sec.

8. "'Anything That Connects': A Conversation With Taylor Swift," *NPR*, October 31, 2014; "Taylor Swift - Fearless [Liner Notes]," Genius, Last Updated November 11, 2008.

9. "Taylor Swift - Speak Now Tour (Full Concert HD)," posted December 8, 2022, by Swift Leaks Backup, YouTube, 2:09:26.

10. The quoted introduction to "Enchanted x Wildest Dreams" on the 1989 World Tour in the text is strung together from a few performances. *See* "1989 Tour - Intro to Wildest Dreams/Enchanted," posted August 3, 2015, by Kayla Marie, YouTube, 2 min 18 sec.; "1989 World Tour - Enchanted/Wildest Dreams intro," posted June 24, 2015, by Manu Berk, YouTube, 48 sec.; "Enchanted WildestDreams w Intro PA 6 12 15," posted August 14, 2018, by ShineyPennyM ★, YouTube, 7 min 29 sec.; "1989," Taylor Swift Wiki, Fandom, accessed January 27, 2025.

11. "Taylor Swift - all of the album announcements (Red-Tortured Poets Department)," posted February 5, 2024, by evrim, YouTube, 8 min 1 sec.

12. "'Anything That Connects': A Conversation With Taylor Swift," *NPR*, October 31, 2014; "'In Summation': TTPD's Epilogue Poem, Explained Line By Line," Swiftly Sung Stories, accessed January 27, 2025.

202 Endnotes

13. "First Amendment and Religion," United States Courts, accessed January 27, 2025; "The Pledge of Allegiance," USHistory.org, accessed January 27, 2025.

14. "How Religious Are Americans?," *Gallup*, March 29, 2024.

15. Jenna Brooke Carlson, "Why Is 'The Stone Was Rolled Away' so Essential to Christianity?," *Bible Study Tools*, May 19, 2022.

16. "Adam and Eve," Story, Meaning, & Facts, Britannica, Last Updated December 17, 2024; Dr. Georgia Purdom, "Who Gets the Blame for Original Sin—Adam or Eve?," *Answers In Genesis*, May 29, 2012; "Who was responsible for the first sin – Adam or Eve?," Christian Questions, accessed January 27, 2025; "Why is Adam blamed for the fall of humanity when Eve sinned first?," Got Questions, accessed January 27, 2025.

17. Nicole VanDyke, "Taylor Swift's new album draws criticism from Christian leaders who say it mocks God, Christians," *The Christian Post*, April 26, 2024.

18. taylorswift, "Midnights, the stories of 13 sleepless nights scattered throughout my life, will be out October 21. Meet me at midnight," Instagram, August 28, 2022.

19. Sophie Dodd, "Taylor Swift and John Mayer's Relationship: A Look Back," *People*, July 6, 2023.

20. Elizabeth Segran, "How Abercrombie went from America's most hated retailer to a Gen Z favorite," *Fast Company*, January 22, 2024; Kat Weller, "The Generation That Grew Up With Taylor Swift," *Odyssey*, November 9, 2015; "To anyone who has been a fan of Taylor since earlier eras, what made you stay?," Reddit, n.d.

21. Will Kenton, "S&P 500 Index: What It's for and Why It's Important in Investing," *Investopedia*, June 12, 2024.

22. Abby Aguirre, "Taylor Swift on Sexism, Scrutiny, and Standing Up for Herself," *Vogue*, August 8, 2019.

23. "About the Book," The Dictionary of Obscure Sorrows, accessed January 27, 2025; "Words," The Dictionary of Obscure Sorrows, accessed January 27, 2025.

24. "Onism," The Dictionary of Obscure Sorrows, accessed January 27, 2025; "Sonder," The Dictionary of Obscure Sorrows, accessed January 27, 2025.

Acknowledgments

I'd like to express my gratitude to John Wiley & Sons, Inc., for its confidence in enlisting me to write this one-of-a-kind book.

My sincere appreciation goes to Prof. Ori Brafman of UC Berkeley's Haas Business School. Drawing from his expertise in leadership, he provided enriching feedback to the Taylor Swift course in support of its launch.

I am thankful to Prof. Amy Slater of UC Berkeley's Goldman School of Public Policy. Her background as a general counsel offered an informative perspective when the course evolved to include elements of law and policy.

Index

1989 (Swift album)
  advocacy, 8, 122–123
  Album of the Year, 7–8, 140, 147
  secret messages (change), 82
  Secret Sessions, 75, 79
  song structure, 38
  lead single, 57–58
  LGBTQIA+ advocacy, 118
  lyrics, case study, 16
  origin story, 21
  romance, perspective, 147–148
  voice memos, 139–140

A

Abercrombie & Fitch, Swift
  (association), 152
Abrams, Gracie, 50, 93–94, 123
Adaptable authenticity, 1–2,
  impact (Swift), 7–8
Adidas, product (re-creation), 122
Advocacy, philanthropy
  (contrast), 121
African Parks Foundation of
  America, Swift donation, 120
Allen, Marcie, 123
Alliteration, usage, 42, 49
Allusions, usage, 43–44

Alwyn, Joe, 53, 66–67, 143–144
Anderson, Abigail (song mention),
  3, 92
Anticipatory utility, 100
Antonoff, Jack, 40, 84, 89, 102, 139
Archetypes, 69–70, 76–77
Aristotle, human happiness, 100–101
Armstrong, Billie Joe, 130
Attention spans, 37
Authentic appreciation, positive
  feedback loop, 89–90

B

Bardach, Eugene, 138
Bead World, 108–109
Behavioral economics,
  impact, 106–107
Bernoulli, Daniel, 99
Beth's Furry Friends, Swift
  donations, 120–121
Big Machine Records, 13, 77
Billionaire, 95–96
Bluebird Cafe, 13
Boichik Bagels, debut, 2
Bombas, community problem
  involvement, 121
Borchetta, Scott, 13, 23, 77–78, 90

206   Index

Borderless online communities
(promotion), social media
(leveraging), 76–77
Boscov, giveaway strategy, 5–6
Bow, Clara, 7, 50, 160
Boy-crazy image, reversal, 130, 140
Brand
consistency, 3
curation (dichotomy), 8, 22
success, 2, 7–8
Braun, Scooter, 77–78
Brodesser-Akner, Taffy, 100, 101, 132
Bryant, Kobe/Bianka, 98–99
Buyer-seller relationship, 122

C
Cabello, Camila, 14, 141
Caillat, Colbie, 36–37, 129–130
Capitalism
views, 133–134
doctrine, 135
Carbon credits, Swift
purchases, 137–139
Carpenter, Sabrina, 93–94, 123
Carter, Shawn (Jay-Z)
ventures, 95–96
wealth, 95
Chainsmokers, The, 14
Cheese Board Collective, The
(worker ownership), 79
Chegg (learning platform), Swift
(partnership), 120
Chipotle, Chipotlanes
(introduction), 22
Choice
application, 136
capitalism doctrine, 135
Chorus lyrics/melodies, alteration,
38–39
Circular (song structure), 34e,
35–36, 39e

Clarkson, Kelly, 13, 17, 90
Collective unconscious, archetypal
figures, 69–70
Competitive edge, fostering, 30
Constructive criticism,
impact, 125–126
Consumers
active roles, 61–62, 81–82
Content engagement, increase, 50–51
Continuity, 50–51
Costco, prices (control), 2, 73
Cottagecore, popularity, 64–65
Country/pop, crossroads, 4–5, 21, 147
Criticism
types, 125–126
Crock-Pot, impact, 114
Cue, Eddy, 123

D
Deconstructive criticism, 126
Defamation, lawsuit, 140
Del Rey, Lana. *See* Grant
Demand relationship, 104–105
Demographic, expansion, 12–13
Dessner, Aaron, 6, 89
Dictionary of Obscure Sorrows
(Koenig), 153
Disney, growth, 47–48
Disney+/Swift, alliance, 84–86
Double meanings, 41–42
Downward sloping demand
curve, 105

E
Easter eggs, 48, 59, 82, 133
Eightfold path, 138–139
Ek, Daniel, 123
Emotions, 4
association, 55–56, 130
currency, 71
range, 26–27

Red, 49, 65
reflection, 74–77
songwriting, 34
Empathy, impact, 5–6, 35
Employee retirement plans, defaults (role), 107
Endowment effect, 106–107
Entertainment
purchasable forms, 106
research, 108
evermore (Swift album)
cottagecore, 65
lead single, 50
mainstream, 14
nature, 119
rollout, 5–6
song structure, 38
Exotic Nutrition, niche (example), 12
Experienced utility, 99–100
Explicit topics, appearance, 16–17
Extended Pop Formula (song structure), 34–35, 34e, 39e
types, 34–35
Externality
impact, 136
issues, examination, 136–139
types, 136–137

F
Fairy tales, tropes (mutability), 70, 84
Fanjoy, Trey, 88
Fans
active roles, 61, 77, 81–82
budget sensitivity, 110
consumer/stakeholder role, 57, 61, 77, 80
experience, importance, 78–79
relationship, building, 74–75
Fearless (Swift album)
Album of the Year, 7–8, 131, 147

country, 14
intuition, 23
Platinum Edition, 23–25, 90
romance, perspective, 147–148
songs
chart ranking, 23–25, 24e
reimagining, 23
"Female Rage: The Musical," 135
Fenty, Robyn (Rihanna), 18
LVMH, partnership, 96
wealth, 95–96
Finlay, Marjorie (song mention), 3
folklore (Swift album)
Album of the Year, 7–8, 22
cardigan (merchandise), 99
cottagecore, 64–65
documentary concert, 84–85
mainstream, 14
nature, 119
rollout, 5–6
lyrics, case study, 16–17
love triangle, 37, 44, 49
Food Lifeline, Swift awareness (increase), 120
Frangipane, Ashley (Halsey), 14, 141
Free market
failure, 136
resources, maximization, 133
Friendship bracelets, 31, 41, 59, 92, 102, 116

G
Galaxy Note 7, recalls/preventative measures, 125–126
Garcia, Joe (fan, case study), 67
Gay & Lesbian Alliance Against Defamation (GLAAD), 118
Generation Z (Gen Z)
cottagecore, 64–65
spending habits, 99
"Golden" love, 49–50, 52

208 Index

Google/Swift, partnership, 86–87
GoPro, RedBull (relationship), 91
Grant, Elizabeth (Lana Del Rey),
80, 141
Greenhouse gas emissions, 137

H
HAIM, collaboration, 83–84
Haim, Este, 83
Halsey. *See* Frangipane
Hamilton (streaming), 85–86
Happiness/satisfaction/value,
utility, 99–100
measure, 31–32
Harke, 154
Harkness, Rebekah (song mention),
3, 7, 40
Harris, Calvin. *See* Wiles
Harvey Mudd College, Swift
investments, 120
Hedonia, 100–101
Heinz, limited edition condiment
(development), 114
Hiddleston, Tom, 18
Hilton, Tyler, 88–89
Hopeless romantics, category, 148
How I Met Your Mother (TV
series), 51–53
Human condition, 4, 132
Human experiences, 129–130
Human happiness, conceptions
(Aristotle), 100–101
Hurricanes, Swift donations, 121
Hyperbole, usage, 16–17, 42–43, 48

I
Iger, Bob, 47–48
Image, 14–17, 140
Incredible Things (Swift
fragrance), 96–97
"in my...era" trend, viral explosion, 66

Inspiration
impact, 25–26, 130
open-mindedness, 26–27
Irrition, 153
Intangible capital, 110
Intangible elements, usage, 65–66
Interpretations, writing/rewriting, 56
Introspection, stories (relationship),
6–7

J
Jay-Z. *See* Carter
Jonas, Joe, 22–23, 29
Jung, Carl (archetypes), 69–70

K
Kahneman, Daniel, 106–107
Kardashian, Kim, 17–18, 19, 77
Keefe, Jonathan, 131–132
Kelce, Travis, 31, 53, 114
Kennedy, Robert F. (song mention), 3
Ke$ha, Swift monetary aid, 141
Keynes, John Maynard, 133, 137
King, Joey, 88
Knetsch, Jack, 106

L
Labor
price (determination), production
cost (impact), 134
wages, exchange, 133–134
Lautner, Taylor, 29, 88
Lefsetz, Bob (music review), 131–132
Liles, Stephen Barker (song
mention), 3
Live Nation, 79–80
Loss aversion, 107
Lover (Swift album), 5
house, 152–153
"golden" love, 49, 148
lead single, 50

LGBTQIA+ advocacy, 118
packaging, 66–67
politics, 66, 119, 144
promotion, 5, 14, 54, 70–71, 97
romance, perspective, 147–148
Sagittarius, symbol, 11
working title, 53
Lyricism,
glitter gel pen, 54
fountain pen, 54
quill pen, 53–54
Lyrics, layers (meaning), 42,
    56, 120, 144

M
MadFit, success, 75–76
Marginal utility, 31
    diminishing, 31–32, 33
    increasing, 32, 33, 41
Market
    competition, 136
        niche, 11–12, 14
        secondary, 103, 106–107
        share, 86–87, 95
Martin, Max, 3, 26, 139
Marx, Karl, 133–134
Mastermind, 110
Mayer, John, 62, 63e, 69–70, 151–152
    song mention, 3
McCartney, Stella (Swift
    collaboration), 97
McDonald's, sustainability
    (actions), 125
McManus, Loren, 107
McNutt, Myles, 139, 141
Menzel, Idina, 98
Metaphor, usage, 41, 42–43, 44–45,
    49–50, 119, 144, 152–153
Midnights (Swift album)
    Album of the Year, 7–8, 135
    Billboard, 62

continuity, 48–49, 53, 64
Eras Tour, 8, 31
lead single, 57, 58–59,
    76–77, 127
LGBTQIA+ advocacy, 118
promotion, 71–72, 104
punctuation placement,
    41–42
religion, 151
Millais, John Everett, 41
Millennials
    continuity, 50–51
    spending habits, 99
    Swift, Taylor 65, 99
Miss Americana (documentary), 18,
    119–120, 145, 149
M&Ms, spokescandies (creation/
    popularity), 68–69
Monahan, Pat, 90
Moore, Mandy, 93
Morgenstern, Oskar, 99
Mueller, David, 140
Multiplier effect, 109e
    employee benefits, 109–110
    exemplification, economic growth
        (relationship), 109
"My Boy Only Breaks His Favorite
    Toys" (recording lyric
    variation), 44, 45e, 49

N
Narrative, shaping/control
culture, 19, 102
music, 33
Neumann, John von, 99
New work, old work (contrast), 103
NFL (ticket sales increase), Swift
    (impact), 114–115
Niche, definition, 11
Nonmonetary gains, choice
    (application), 136

210 Index

O

Onism, 154
Opperman, Jeff, 119
Outreach, maximization, 86

P

Partnerships, 84–88
Patagonia, "Don't Buy This Jacket"
    Black Friday ad, 5
Peloton, repercussions, 113–114
Personas, control, 19–20, 145
Personification, usage, 42
Philanthropy, advocacy (contrast), 121
Play-Doh, product (use, change), 22
Political endorsements, 115–118
POPFLEX, sales, 114–115
Pop Formula (song structure), 33–34,
    34e, 38, 39e
Pop songs, Swift citations, 14
Production cost, impact, 105, 134
Productivity, interpersonality
    (impact), 90–91
Psychic constitution, experiences, 69
Punctuation placement, 41–42
Purchasable items, Swift association
types, 97
Puth, Charlie, 45, 90

Q

Quantity, quality (tradeoff), 62–67
Queerbaiting accusations, 118, 141
Queer icons, representation, 118

R

Random Access Memories
    (Daft Punk), 21
Red (Swift album)
    comfort zone, exit, 64
    co-writing sessions, 3
    emotions, 49, 65
    Grammys, impact, 21, 70
    lyrics, case study, 15–16, 20

RedBull, GoPro (relationship), 91
REI customers, stakeholder role, 79
Reinvention, 5, 16, 40, 57–58, 64–65,
    148–149, 152–153
Relational capital, 110
Relevance
    importance, 11
    motivation, 22
Religion, 38, 149–152
Remembered utility, 100
Reputation (Swift album)
    Americanness, reference, 143–144
    comeback, 17–21, 152
    cryptography, 82
    lead single, 19–20, 82
    LGBTQIA+ advocacy, 118
    lifeline, 129
    lyrics, case study, 17, 20
    nominations, 21
    packaging, 66–67
    snake, 19, 21, 50
Re-recordings, 16, 77–78,
    90, 100, 128
Rihanna. *See* Fenty
Roehm, Michelle, 20
Role model, 15, 21, 59, 123
Romance, perspective
    (change), 147–148

S

Samuelson, William, 107
Scale, sense (importance), 43
Schultz, Howard, 110
Schuster, Karl Johan (Shellback),
    3, 139
Secondary market
    consumer-initiated price-setting,
    106
    data, exclusion, 106
    patterns, influence, 106–107
    trend, Eras Tour, 103
Serial dater criticism, 126–127

Index

Sex and the City (TV series), 113–114
Shared experiences, 102
Sheeran, Ed, 57–58, 88, 119
Shelf life
definition, 30
application, 30–31, 47
Shellback. *See* Schuster
Silence breakers, 141
Simile, usage, 42–43
Social benefit/cost, 136–137
Social media
community, 74–75, 76–78, 79–82, 93, 102–103, 110, 127–128
culture, 87, 91, 99, 140, 141
politics, 115, 116
promotion (album), 5, 18–19, 61, 64
community, 74–75, 76–78, 79–82, 93
Sonder, 154
Songs
cannabis reference, impact, 118–119
confessional, 4–5
fame, 7
mashups, 40, 72, 90, 94, 101, 148
nature references, 119–120
products, 30
secret messages, 82
sentiments, 4
Songwriting
autobiographical songwriting, 128–129
bridge, 34–35, 37, 40–41, 44, 46, 93, 144
chords, 72–73
origination points, demonstration, 139–140
philosophy, Swift adherence, 4–5
process, 4, 44–45, 49, 62, 72–73, 93–94
structures, 33–38, 34e, 39e

Soufrise, 153
Speak Now (Swift album)
creation, 58, 62
setlist (Eras Tour), 66
inception, 25, 65
LGBTQIA+ advocacy, 118
lyrics, case study, 16, 20
photoshoot, 65
re-recording, 88
singing quality, criticism, 131–132
song structure, 38
Spears, Britney, 98, 126
Spending habits, knowledge, 103–104
Spotify
exhibit, importance, 86–87
Swift music catalog, withholding, 123
Spotify Wrapped, 87, 111
Stakeholders, role, 57, 77–78
Static, release (success), 1
Status quo bias, concept, 107
Stories, introspection (relationship), 6–7
Storytelling
elevation, 37
versatility (Swift longevity), 2
vulnerability (Swift trademark), 2
Streaming platforms, usage, 103
Stripped (song structure), 34e, 37, 39e
Stumler, Emily Poe, 134
Stump, Patrick, 100
Styles, Harry, 144
Subconscious, impact, 26
Suburbia, concepts, 146–147
Surplus value, 134
Surprise (song structure), 34e, 36–37, 39e
Swift Alert (app), 110
Swifties, 59–60
active roles, 61–62, 81–82
consumer role, 61, 99
experiences, 73

212 Index

Swifties (*continued*)
  patterns (noneconomic), 72,
    110–111, 117, 154
  resources, usage, 62
  track 5, 55
  stakeholder role, 77
Swifties for Kamala
  grassroots organization, 117
  trans representation, 118
Swift, Taylor
  albums
    elevation, 65
    personification, 102
    artistry (extension), 133
  career
    brand (curation), 8
    evolution, 21–22
    examination, frameworks, 129
    fame, 7
    impact, 93–94, 122–123
    in house, 92, 135
    long run, 73, 81
    path, 12
    politics (entry), 115
    quality, commitment, 64–67
    release plans (tailoring), 80
    responsibility, 15
    variety, 27
  corporate language,
    disassociation, 8
  countersuit, 140–141
  COVID-19 pandemic, impact, 5
  creative outlet, 133
  donations, 120–121
  experiences
    accumulation, 15
    narrating, 128–129
  fan base, demographics, 116
  feminism, manifestations, 139
  generic pop writing, abandonment,
    4–5

imagination, 8, 26–27, 141, 147
inspiration, impact, 25–27
leading by example, 118–119
lead singles, purpose, 57–58
main character, 77
market competition, 136
movie, AMC/Cinemark
  Theaters, 91–92
musical releases, timeline, 63e
Nils Sjöberg, 18
next album, plotting, 62, 64
obsession (with), 14
outreach, maximization, 86
paparazzi photos, frequency, 19e
parasocial fixation, 70
patterns (noneconomic), 72, 111
personal statement, impact, 78–79
public, distancing, 17–18, 71
RCA Records development
  deal/exit, 13
rebellion, form, 3
reputation, dismantling, 17–18,
  44, 143–144
SNL monologue, skill set, 29–30
tour
  1989 World Tour, 18, 40, 43, 66, 74,
    83, 98, 148
  Eras Tour, 8, 31, 40, 58–59, 61, 64,
    65–66, 73, 74–75, 78–80, 84,
    85–86, 89, 91–92, 93–94, 95,
    100–104, 106–110, 119, 120,
    126, 134, 137
  Fearless Tour, 15, 62, 72, 74, 75
  Red Tour, 74, 98
  Reputation Stadium Tour, 4, 14,
    20–21, 40, 49, 74, 98, 107–108,
    134, 140–141
  Speak Now World Tour, 40, 74, 90,
    98, 147–148
value, cementing, 75–76
wealth, breakdown, 96e

Index

Swiftverse (Swift universe), 47–48
  accessibility, 60
  customs, 53–54

T

Tangible elements, usage, 65–66
Target/Swift, relationship,
  87–88, 91–92
Taylor Nation, 102, 110
Taylor Swift (debut) (Swift album),
Eras Tour (exclusion), 86, 106
  promotion, 14–15, 89, 105
  secret messages (origination), 82
  sales, 13
  singles, variety, 3, 26–27, 129, 143
  subject naming, 3
Taylor Swift Experience, 97
  epitomization, 101–102
  goods, association, 107–108
  money, expenditures, 104–105
  participation, 102–103
  Taylor Swift Good, connection, 99
Taylor Swift factor, 72–73
Taylor Swift Good, 97
  money, experience, 104–105
  Taylor Swift Experience,
    connection, 99
Taylor Swift Publications, 92
Tedder, Ryan, 139
Teenage boldness, Swift definition, 15
Tesla
  practicality/accessibility (absence),
    claims (combatting), 3
  Taylor, divergence, 2–3
Thaler, Richard, 106
*The Official Taylor Swift | The Eras
  Tour Book*, 87–88, 104
The Tortured Poets Department (TTPD)
  (Swift album)
  criticism, 48–49
  setlist (Eras Tour), 103

hyperbolic lyrics, display, 17
insanity, dramatism, fatalism,
  themes, 17, 61, 146
lifeline, 129
patriotism, 145–146
Phantom Clear vinyl, 87
religion, 149–151
rollout, 60, 64–65, 78, 82, 86
romance, perspective, 147–148
variants, 136
This Is Us (TV series), 114
Three Square Food Bank, Swift
  awareness (increase), 120
Ticketmaster, ticket sale cancellation/
  presale failure, 78–79
Track 5, 55
Trader Joe's, labels (impact), 54–55
Trumpspringa, 153
Tversky, Amos, 107
Tybout, Alice, 20

U

Universe, customers (keeping), 54–56
Universe, musical 47, 52–53, 56, 59,
  60–61, 94, 97, 133, 154
Urbanism, concepts, 146–147
Urie, Brendon, 50
Utility
  happiness/satisfaction/value
    measure, 31–32
  theory, origins, 99–100
  types, 100
    quantitative testament, 103

V

Valon, customer complaints/
  feedback, 125
Vernon, Justin, 54, 89
Very Important Beauty Insider (VIB),
  Sephora selling technique, 61
Victimhood, 128–129, 134–135

Index

Visibility efforts, 22
Voter turnout, Swift (impact), 115

W

Wages/labor, exchange, 133–134
Welch, Florence, 101, 146
West, Kanye, 17–18, 19, 21, 29, 70, 77
Where the Crawdads Sing
(Owens), 145
Wiles, Adam (Calvin Harris), 18
Wild Card (song structure), 34e,
37–38, 39e
Williams, Hayley, 25
Williams-Sonoma, in-store/virtual
events, 104
Willingness to pay (WTP),
104–108, 137

preferences, impact, 105–106
shopper, example (consideration),
105–106
Winslet, Kate, 23
Woman of the Decade (Billboard
honor), 141–142, 143
Women, romance/business
(success), 127
Wonderstruck (Swift fragrance),
96–97
Works of art, marginal utility, 33
World, mapping, 31, 50

Z

Zeckhauser, Richard, 107
Zero-sum game, 84
Zeugma, usage, 42